FLY FISHING FOR TROUT

FLY FISHING FOR TROUT

with Peter Lapsley

STANLEY PAUL
LONDON

For Douglas

'. . . he that hopes to be a good angler must not only bring an inquiring, searching, observing wit, but he must bring a large measure of hope and patience, and a love and propensity to the art itself; but having once got and practised it, then doubt not but angling will prove so pleasant that it will prove to be like virtue, a reward to itself.'

Izaak Walton *The Compleat Angler*

Stanley Paul & Co. Ltd

An imprint of Random House UK Ltd
20 Vauxhall Bridge Road, London SW1V 2SA

Random House Australia (Pty) Ltd
20 Alfred Street, Milsons Point, Sydney, NSW 2061, Australia

Random House New Zealand Ltd
18 Poland Road, Glenfield, Auckland, New Zealand

Random House South Africa (Pty) Ltd
PO Box 337, Bergvlei 2012, South Africa

First published 1992

Set in Century Old Style by SX Composing Ltd., Rayleigh, Essex

Printed and bound by Clays Ltd, St Ives PLC

A catalogue record for this book is available upon request from the British Library

ISBN 0 09 174824 0

Most of the photographs were kindly supplied by the author. The author and publishers would also like to thank the following for allowing the reproduction of copyright photographs: Gordon Carlisle, David Grewcock and Topham Picture Library.

Contents

Acknowledgements

Many people have helped, wittingly or unwittingly, with the making of this book.

Among the 'witting' are Nick Cook, outstanding fly fisher and proprietor of Cooks of Datchet, the surest source of all that is good in flies, fly tying materials and fly fishing tackle, who provided the flies photographed for the colour plates; Peter Dazeley who took those photographs; Rodney Paull and David Woodroffe who burnt much midnight oil to produce the line drawings that illuminate the text; David Goodchild, editor of *Salmon, Trout and Sea-Trout*, and Mark Bowler, editor of *Fly-Fishing and Fly-Tying*, who allowed me to use extracts from two articles first published in their magazines; Roddy Bloomfield, Marion Paull and especially Louise Speller of Stanley Paul, who put so much thought and effort into the book's production; and, last but not least, my wife Liza, who took the photograph for the cover, who has been so enthusiastically supportive, who complained not at all while I was closeted in my study for hours and weekends on end, and who provided much constructive criticism as the manuscript progressed.

Among the 'unwitting' are the many friends with whom I have fished and whose brains I have picked over so many years. I am especially indebted to John Goddard for his expert advice on fly fishing in general and on entomology in particular; to Donald Downs and Charles Jardine, two of the finest casters in the country; to Ron Clark, Neil Patterson and Sidney Vines for all they have taught me about chalk streams and chalk stream trout, and to Roy Darlington who manages so excellently the water upon which I am privileged to be able to put that teaching into practice; to Bruce Sandison and Peter O'Reilly, respectively the two greatest gurus on Scottish lochs and Irish loughs; to Mick Bewick, John Hatherell, Henry Lowe and Peter Firth for sharing with me their vast knowledge of reservoir fly fishing; to Stewart Canham and Bill Sibbons, extractors extraordinaire of large trout from small stillwaters; to Conrad Voss Bark and David Profumo for their advice and encouragement over many years; and to Fred Buller, Brian Clarke, Roy Eaton and the late Dick Walker, who taught me so much of what little I know about fishing and fishing writing.

To these, and to all my fishing friends, I offer my warmest thanks.

Introduction

Some fly fishers seem to have an almost uncontrollable urge to write about their sport. While drought and abstraction reduce streams and rivers to trickles and parch the beds of lakes and reservoirs, the flood of fishing books on to the market continues unabated. Authors have been driven to excuse their efforts and reviewers to question the need for many of them. So, why add yet another tome to an already inundated market?

My reasons are two-fold. Firstly, I think there has been a tendency in recent years for fishing writers to wear their 'expertise' on their sleeves and to write for their peers, for more or less competent fellow anglers, rather than to address the questions most often asked by those less experienced than themselves. The people most likely to seek help and advice are those newly come to the sport, those who have fished only one or two types of water and who wish to try others, and those who are able to fish only occasionally.

Therefore, I have tried to identify and to answer the questions asked most often by these groups of people. My objective has been to take the newcomer – either to the sport as a whole or to a particular type of water or style of fishing – from the simplest principles right through to the point at which he or she may expect to be able to catch trout reasonably consistently at all stages in the season and under most conditions. In taking this course, I hope that I may also have provided a coherent and reasonably comprehensive work from which the more experienced fly fisher may be able to fill in such gaps as there may be in his or her knowledge.

Secondly, I have become concerned by the tendency for fly fishers to judge the success of a day wholly or largely by numbers of trout caught – a tendency exacerbated by some fishing magazines, which fill their pages with stories and pictures of huge catches of ever larger fish, and evidenced by some people's preoccupation with competitive fly fishing.

Of course we go fishing to catch fish. There is little or nothing to be said for paying for a day's fishing simply so that we may be by the water and commune with nature. If that is all we want from our sport, there is no shortage of places in which we can do it for free. But I do believe that there really is much more to fishing than just catching fish, that it provides us with opportunities to relax in pleasant and peaceful surroundings, to watch the wealth of wildlife in, on and around the water, and to increase our understanding of the world about us, and that we deny ourselves much of the pleasure to be had from fishing if we fail to make the most of these opportunities.

For this reason, and while it is not for me or anyone else to tell people what they should do in order to enjoy their sport, I have tried in this book to draw a picture of fly fishing as a whole, rather than simply as a means of catching trout.

Two other aspects of the work seem important to me, too. Fly fishing – and especially stillwater fly fishing – is a dynamic and rapidly developing pursuit. The enormous growth in the sport's popularity over the past twenty or thirty years has brought new minds to bear on it and has produced a wealth of new ideas. Some of the innovations have taken the sport forward; braided butts for leaders, the development of ranges of emerger and dry fly patterns for use on stillwaters and the development of new tactics for the use of sinking lines in various densities for loch-style reservoir fishing are examples. Others have been 'flashes in the pan' – clever in theory but less than consistently effective in practice.

In trying to produce a book that is both up to date and sound, I have had to steer a course between the tried and trusted on the one hand and experimental gimmickry on the other. If I have erred, it has probably been towards conservatism, and I think that is as it should be.

I have extended this approach to the flies I have recommended, too, but for a different reason. Most modern writers on fly fishing seek to persuade their readers to take up fly dressing or assume their readers already tie their own flies. This gives those writers the opportunity to promote ranges of innovative and esoteric patterns often unavailable from tackle shops, on the basis that if their readers cannot buy them they can always tie them.

While fly dressing is an intriguing pastime in its own right and can add enormously to the fun of fishing, I do not think it reasonable to presume that every fly fisher has both the time and the inclination to dress his or her own flies. Therefore, in deciding which flies to suggest, I have limited myself to those that are generally available from tackle shops and mail order houses.

Finally, I should reiterate that we go fishing in order to have fun. I count myself very lucky to have been able to start fishing at an early age; I have been enjoying the fun of it for over forty years and intend to continue to find fun in it for many years to come. If this book increases your enjoyment of the sport it will be serving its purpose, and the work that has gone into it will have been worthwhile.

Peter Lapsley May 1992

CHAPTER ONE

What's It All About?

Occasional statistical surveys identify angling as one of Britain's most popular pastimes. Of the four and a half million or so people who indulge in it, fewer than a third are 'game anglers'. The remainder prefer either so-called 'coarse' fishing or sea fishing.

I have nothing but admiration for those stalwart souls, the cod and whiting anglers, who huddle on bitter, windswept beaches in January, their rods curving upwards and outwards towards a grey, heaving sea; for those who rekindle memories of Dunkirk as they head their little boats out into the Channel in search of pollack, mackerel, flat fish or conger eels; for those who line piers and breakwaters on summer afternoons, often more in hope than in expectation; or for those who wade out into the tumbling breakers of a rising tide on a Devon beach, surf-casting for spiny bass. But differences between their sport and ours are so evident that they need no explanation here.

Coarse fishing versus game fishing

The division between coarse fishing and game fishing, though, and between game fishing for migratory fish (salmon and sea trout) and non-migratory ones (trout and grayling) may not be so immediately obvious to the novice fly fisher and merits a little elaboration.

Let me say at once that there is nothing coarse about coarse fishing. It is a delightful pursuit. Indeed, I can be as happy sitting by the glassy calmness of a pretty lake on a warm June morning, watching the tip of a tiny float and waiting for that tell-tale stream of bubbles – the indicator of an approaching tench – or spinning for pike on a crisp winter's day, as I can casting a fly to a waiting trout. But there are several differences between the two pursuits which set them apart from one another. Essentially, these have to do with the characteristics of the species being fished for and with the tackle, techniques and tactics used in the capture of those species.

While some coarse fish are edible, most coarse anglers fish chiefly for fun rather than for the table, returning the barbel, bleak, bream, carp, catfish, chub, dace, eels, gudgeon, perch, pike, roach, rudd and tench they catch to the water. In contrast, game fish – salmon, sea trout, trout and grayling – all make excellent eating and are often killed for this reason.

With two notable exceptions, the closed seasons for coarse and game fish are different, too. Closed seasons for angling are imposed to prevent interference with fish at spawning times. Salmon, trout and sea trout all spawn in the winter – albeit at slightly variable times – between October and February, and the closed seasons for them reflect this. In contrast, coarse fish spawn chiefly in the spring, between March and May, and are left in peace by anglers during that period.

The rainbow trout and the grayling provide the two exceptions to these rules. The rainbow trout is an importee into Britain from the west coast of the United States. While it can be bred and reared quite easily in British fish farms, few of our rivers provide the conditions necessary for it to breed in the wild, and it cannot spawn successfully in lakes or reservoirs. There is therefore no need to protect it at what would normally be its mid-winter spawning time. So the closed season often applied on rivers is there chiefly to protect brown trout, rather than rainbows that may live with them, and there is no statutory closed season for rainbow trout in stillwaters. The grayling, while belonging to the same family as trout and salmon, spawns with the coarse fish in the spring, and therefore shares its closed season with them.

It is the nature of the 'bait', though, and of the means by which it is cast, that really separates fly fishing from coarse fishing. Worms, maggots, bread paste, boilies and other baits, and the weights, floats, plugs, spoons and spinners used by coarse anglers – and by some salmon and sea trout anglers, too, from time to time – are sufficiently heavy to allow them to be thrown out into the water, pulling thin nylon monofilament or braided line off the reel as they go. Rods for this form of casting are therefore necessarily quite stiff.

An artificial fly is far less heavy and cannot be thrown. So the necessary weight is incorporated into the line itself, which is used to load a springy rod which then propels it out over the water. Because the fly line has to be quite heavy, it is necessarily quite bulky. For this reason, the artificial fly is joined to the end of it by a length of nylon fine, long and translucent enough to reduce to a minimum the risk of its frightening the fish.

There is one further significant difference between coarse fishing on the one hand and game fishing on the other. Generally speaking (and *pace* those who go spinning for pike and perch) coarse and sea fishing are relatively sedentary pastimes, the angler waiting for the fish to come to him – which accounts for the great green-umbrella'd encampments spread along canal banks and around gravel pits on summer afternoons. In contrast, game fishing is usually a mobile pursuit, the angler going in search of his quarry, very much the hunter.

This is important. Those who expect to fish in only one or two spots during the course of a day can afford to accumulate great quantities of piscatorial paraphernalia, and frequently do so. Tackle boxes, float cases, bait cans, stools, rod rests, picnic baskets and hurricane lamps, often trundled to the waterside on purpose-built trolleys, are all the legitimate accoutrements of coarse anglers. But the game fisherman must travel lightly laden, carrying all he needs upon his person and keeping it to a minimum.

Migratory and non-migratory game fish

Having identified the differences between game, coarse and sea fishing, we should also identify the division within game fishing between salmon and sea trout fishing on the one hand and trout and grayling fishing on the other.

Salmon and sea trout are born in freshwater but spend most of their adult lives at sea, returning to their native rivers only to spawn. When they do so, they stop feeding altogether. One cannot logically, therefore, fish for them with artificial flies designed to represent their natural food. Instead, the salmon or sea trout angler usually uses quite large or gaudy flies, lures or spinners which he hopes to goad his quarry into taking. For this reason, the real excitement of salmon or sea trout fishing is to be found chiefly in the playing of a fit, fierce and sometimes large wild fish, rather than necessarily in persuading it to take the fly in the first place.

In contrast, the essence of trout fishing has to do with the art of deception – in finding a fish or working out where it must be, in deciding what it is feeding on or what it is doing, and in placing before it an artificial fly or feathered lure in such a way that it is induced to take it, either as food or through curiosity or aggression. It is the pulling off of this confidence trick that provides much of the interest in fly fishing for trout, the playing and landing of the fish often becoming almost incidental.

The fun of fishing

So far, we have gone some way towards defining the sport, isolating the species fished for and, in the simplest terms, the means by which they may be caught. The trout we catch are important, but they are by no means everything. There are times – many of them – when they take second place to the sheer loveliness of the countryside to which they draw us.

I can sit by the little River Ebble for an hour and a half on an April morning, lost in wonderment at the ludicrous, chocolate-box prettiness of the orchard on the far side of the brook, with lambs prancing among the daffodils beneath the cherry blossom.

There are those marvellous spring days on West Country rivers, with leaf buds bursting, pale green on the trees, while fit, diminutive brown trout hurl themselves ferociously at bushy floating flies as though these seductive little objects are all they have ever wanted.

There are magical days on the chalk streams in late May and early June when huge brown trout, feeding on mayflies an inch or more long, will gobble down anything big and furry that comes their way. And there are similar days when they will touch nothing at all, or when, after much frustration, they prove to have been picking tiny gnats or midges from the armada of mayflies sailing towards them on the stream.

There are those warm, sunny, early summer mornings on lakes and reservoirs when the water is like glass, disturbed only by the languid, porpoise-like rolling of trout taking hatching insects and, just occasionally, by the hiss of a taut fly line slicing through the surface.

There are soft sunsets on the chalk streams in June and July, with droves of dead and dying insects drifting on the current, the trout sipping them down with metronomic regularity, or with skittering, moth-like sedge flies wrinkling the oily, orange-pink surface of the water, tempting the fish to cast caution aside.

And there are apparently identical evenings when nothing happens at all, when you sit by the river watching water voles paddling along the margins, moorhens squabbling endlessly among the reeds, the turquoise and orange flash of a kingfisher heading upstream, and the reed buntings and wrens settling down for the night, waiting for a rise which, inexplicably, never comes.

There are high-summer days on Highland lochs, mirror-flat under brassy skies, when you lie back in the boat idly watching the progress of the mobile specks on a distant hill – the sheep dogs skilfully rounding up their dim-witted charges and easing them towards the farm, ravens circling overhead.

There are those long lunch breaks by lovely rivers like the Kennet, the Test, the Itchen and the Wylye, and by Chew and Blagdon lakes, often extending until tea time, during which, in the shade of some great oak, with our hats over our eyes and a bottle of Something Special between us, we set the world to rights.

There are days spent afloat with anglers far more able than ourselves, from whom we may learn some of the intricacies of the sport, days spent with our peers, catching up on news we have failed to swap because we have been too busy chasing trout, and days spent with less experienced people to whom, we hope, we may be able to communicate some of the fun to be had from the sport.

Hackneyed though the phrase may be, there really is very much more to fishing than just catching fish.

One of the greatest delights of fly fishing for trout is that you can make of it what you will. At one end of the scale there are those who fish only on holiday, perhaps packing grandfather's venerable cane rod and an old tobacco tin with a dozen or so nameless flies in it into the boot of the car as they head off for some distant place. They may do no more than while away the odd afternoon or evening with this simple tackle, hoping idly that some passing trout may be absent-minded enough to take their offering into its mouth. Occasionally they will be rewarded, and it is the very 'occasionalness' of the reward that makes it so special.

At the other end of the scale are those fly fishers who turn their sport almost into a profession. They have at least two matt-varnished carbon rods for every possible type of water and weather, and half a dozen different lines for each one. Their fly boxes are little less than multi-layered, foam-lined suitcases, accommodating beautifully tied artificials for every occasion. They are often accomplished entomologists, well able to differentiate between a medium olive and a small spurwing at twenty paces and at a glance. With their eye shades and polarized sunglasses, they can spot a feeding trout four feet down in clear water long before it sees them, and they can land their artificial flies on a saucer, first time, at almost any range and in almost any wind. They rarely have blank days and tend to measure their success by the sizes of the trout they catch and by the difficulties they have overcome in catching them, rather than by numbers of fish taken.

In between these two extremes are the thousands of fly fishers who are more or less committed and more or less competent. They may head for the waterside once a week, once a fortnight or once a month. They may avidly devour the writings of the gurus who regularly hold forth in the angling press, striving constantly to emulate them, or they may be content to potter along at their own pace, seeing fishing as a pastime rather than as anything more earnest.

Fly fishing meets the needs of all these people, and each person's approach to it is as valid as the next. I have little time for anyone, especially the so-called and often self-styled experts, whose attitudes to those who fish less often than they do, or who are less able, is one of disdain. Nor have I much time for the successful fly fisher who keeps the flies and tactics he uses secret from those less skilful than himself. Fly fishing should be fun, and much of the pleasure in it is in sharing it with others.

Which brings us to the important question of sportsmanship.

On sportsmanship

I count myself greatly honoured that the late Dick Walker, arguably the most accomplished all-round angler this country has ever produced, and one of the nicest, should from time to time have described me as a friend. I once asked him to define sportsmanship in fly fishing. His answer was characteristically comprehensive and succinct. 'Sportsmanship in fly fishing,' he said, 'amounts to no more than obeying the rules of the fishery in the spirit as well as to the letter, and to doing nothing to damage the sport of one's fellow angler.'

The second part of this definition places a far greater range of obligations upon us than may be immediately apparent. At its simplest, it argues against hitching up one's waders, ploughing thigh-deep into a reservoir and then flogging away at the water with heavy tackle while other anglers close by are trying to fish delicately from the bank, and against groups of anglers bellowing ribaldries to one another, oblivious of the peace and quiet that others seek in their fishing.

It also has to do with the conservation of fish stocks and of the waterside environment as a whole, and with the protection of the sport against those who would deny it to us. These three issues go hand in hand.

The question of fish stock conservation is a complex one. The fishing pressure on waters in the most populous areas of Britain is so great that few of them can sustain self-perpetuating populations of wild trout. Indeed, many of them are not natural trout fisheries at all but have been pressed into service to meet growing demand for sport. Most of them are stocked with farm-reared fish which would be unlikely to reproduce even if left in peace, and which can be readily replaced when caught. Although some managers of such waters allow anglers to return some or all of the trout they catch, far more insist that all trout caught must be killed; they then replace them on a monthly, weekly or even daily basis. The angler's part in the 'conservation' of such stocks usually amounts to no more than paying for the trout that will replace those he catches.

Farm-reared trout are also used to supplement the native brown trout populations of some lochs and many hard-fished rivers. Necessary as this may be if good fishing is to be provided for those who want it, there is good reason to suppose that the newcomers may have a detrimental effect on the native population. Farm-reared trout, particularly wandering and voracious rainbows, tend to be greedy and may harass the wild fish unmercifully in their search for food. Where those who manage such fisheries decide that some farmed fish must be introduced, there is a case for seeking to conserve the native population by returning wild fish to the water but killing stocked fish for the table.

Fortunately – perhaps almost amazingly – there are still lochs, loughs, lakes and rivers in Britain that are able to provide fine fishing for truly wild brown trout. Such waters are our most precious assets. We owe it to ourselves, to our fellow fishermen and to those who will come after us to protect and preserve them, and to nurture the fish they sustain.

The threats to them are formidable.

The threats to angling waters . . .

Pollution comes in many forms. Pesticides, herbicides, chemical fertilizers, silage effluent and farmyard slurry; industrial waste and seepage; the outpourings from inefficient sewage works and from fish farms; the sulphurous emissions from factories and power stations, producing acid rain; even oil and lead residues washed from roads – all these poison lakes and rivers, de-oxygenating the water and killing not only the fish themselves but also the insects, crustaceans, snails and coarse fish fry they live on.

Abstraction – the pumping of water from natural underground reservoirs or from rivers for agricultural, industrial and domestic use – reduces water levels and flow rates and exacerbates the effects of pollution because it reduces the amount of water available to dilute the pollutants.

Land drainage schemes carry residual agricultural chemicals and effluent into lakes and rivers quickly, rather than giving them time to dissipate into the soil. The canalization of some rivers and draconian weed cutting on many hurries the water away to the sea, reducing already alarmingly low levels yet further.

And coniferous afforestation – the rapidly growing, get-rich-quick end of the forestry spectrum – excludes life-giving light from upland streams, acidifies the water flowing into those streams – the acidic water releasing aluminium from the soil, which is extremely toxic to fish – and denies fish the terrestrial insects upon which they so often depend for food.

But, however daunting all this seems, do not fall into the trap of thinking anglers are entirely powerless to do anything about it.

. . . and what we should do about them

As a starting point, every angler, however casual or occasional his involvement in the sport, should join the Anglers' Co-operative Association (ACA), which exists solely to fight cases of pollution in the courts and which has been extraordinarily successful in doing so. The subscription is modest but vital, and the Association's address is given in Appendix B.

Thereafter, we should take an active and intelligent interest in the welfare of the waters we fish. When we see deterioration in water quality or wild fish stocks, we should not simply bemoan the fact among ourselves and then head off in search of waters new. Instead,

15

we should take the matter up with the club concerned or with the riparian owner in the first instance, then with the National Rivers Authority, and then with anyone else who may be able to help -- fishery boards, associations or advisories, borough or district councillors, Members of Parliament or the ACA.

And, of course, we can do none of this with clear consciences unless we ourselves fully understand – and meet – our own obligations to the waters we fish and to the land around them.

Coarse fishermen aroused a good deal of public antipathy over a number of years because an idiotic few among their number consistently failed to take discarded lead shot, hooks and nylon home with them. Grazing wildfowl picked up the lead shot, which poisoned them, and birds became entangled in the hooks and nylon, often suffering dreadful and protracted pain before dying in misery. The coarse fishing fraternity had the wit and the wisdom to put their own house in order before it was put in order for them. They banned the use of lead shot and mounted a massive and persistent publicity campaign designed to discourage and deter such mindless malpractices, and it succeeded.

As fly fishers we should follow their example. Our aim should be to leave no evidence of any sort of visits to the waterside. And we should be conscious, too, of the public perception of our sport, most particularly as it relates to 'cruelty' and to 'gratuitous killing'.

If we are to fish at all, there must inevitably be an element of cruelty involved – the cruelty inflicted on the hunted by the hunter throughout nature – and it would be dishonest to deny that fact. But there is an absolute obligation on us to reduce that cruelty to a minimum. If fish are to be returned to the water, they should be handled carefully (or ideally not at all) and released at once. If they are to be killed for the table, they should be despatched quickly and as humanely as possible.

And it behoves us all to remember that a monstrous, over-fed and tailless rainbow, drooping from the arms of its smugly smiling captor is not a pretty sight. It may do wonders for the ego of the person who caught it. It may impress his fishing friends or fill them with envy. But by and large, the non-angling public finds it gruesome.

So be reasonably modest in your aspirations and reticent about the good days. If not, there is a very real risk that the small but vocal minority that opposes our right to go fishing will turn our successes against us.

All this is serious stuff, and necessarily so, because the very fact that we go fishing places moral obligations upon us, to the water, to the countryside and to our fellow anglers. But there is no reason why those obligations should spoil the fun. And that, after all, is what fishing is about – having fun.

I know of no other pastime so complete or absorbing, or in which so many different facets go to make up the whole. There are the history and traditions of the sport, which place it in perspective and which provide the framework within which we may experiment legitimately. There is the literature of the sport, the richest of any, which can transport us to other waters in other ages, and which so often serves to show those who think themselves innovators that there is really very little new under the sun. There is the satisfaction of buying and owning nice tackle, of setting it up 'just so', and of handling it competently. For those who want it, there is the fun of fly tying; can there be anything more rewarding than to take a trout on a fly of one's own tying, perhaps even of one's own invention? There is the endless fascination of learning about the trout and their behaviour, about the various tiny creatures they feed on and about the watery world in which they live. And, of course, there are the lovely places the sport takes us to and the friends we make through it.

Finally, do not be put off by the mumbo-jumbo and mystique with which some people surround fly fishing. Essentially it is a simple pursuit, the deceiving of a trout with an artificial fly, a glorious confidence trick, a protracted practical joke. And that is the fun of it. As in all worthwhile pastimes, consistent success comes through understanding and experience. But both are quite easily acquired, and I shall seek to provide a basis for the former in the chapters that follow. The latter you must provide for yourself.

CHAPTER TWO

Finding Fishing

An embarrassment of riches

From the grey, windswept vastness of Loch Harray in the Orkneys to
the sinuous serenity of the Test, meandering through water meadows
on its way to Southampton and the sea; from the heather-girt
blackness of Boliska Lough, above Galway Bay, to great Grafham
Water in the English Midlands, home or hostel to dabbling ducks and
divers, goosanders and great-crested grebes, redshanks, ringed
plovers, lapwings, mute swans and terns; from the tree-trapped
intimacy of the little Lyd in Devon, bubbling across the stickles
between one dark pool and the next, to the boldness of the Eden and
the Ure, tumbling two thousand feet, left and right, from the looming
mass of the Pennine Hills; from the Teifi, watched by Cambrian kite
and curlew as she babbles from the little lakes above
Pontrhydfendigaid to make her majestic way through Caron Bog to
Cardigan Bay, to the fens and flatlands of East Anglia, where gouged-
out gravel pits and agricultural reservoirs have been pressed into
piscatorial service; fly fishers in Britain are spoilt for choice.

It is a sad fact, though, that Britain's best wild trout waters are to be
found in its remotest corners, in Wales and the south-west peninsula,
in the west of Ireland and in the Highlands and islands of Scotland. The
most populous areas, the Midlands and the South East, afford
relatively little good, natural fishing. Magical as the southern chalk
streams may be, their capacity to provide good fishing is finite. Here,
the majority of trout anglers find their sport on man-made and man-
managed waters, lakes and reservoirs stocked with farm-reared fish.

The size and quality of the trout sustained by any particular water
will be dictated very largely by the quality of the water itself, and the
quality of the water will be dictated by the nature of the land in its
catchment area. Where rainwater spends months or even years in
porous rock full of readily dissolved mineral salts, eventually seeping
out through springs, it will be rich and fertile, water weeds will thrive
in it, myriad insects will thrive among the weed, and the trout will grow
fat. Where rainwater falls on hard, impermeable rock and runs directly
into lakes and rivers through decaying bracken and heather, it will be
poor in nutrients, there will be little plant life and few aquatic insects,
and the trout will be lean and hungry.

18

Soft, porous rocks – chalk and limestone – are easily eroded. The countryside in which they are found is therefore chiefly rolling downland, well worn by wind and weather, with wide, fertile river valleys meandering through it.

Chalk streams

The major chalk deposits in the British Isles are to be found in a band running from Hampshire and Wiltshire through Berkshire, Buckinghamshire, Hertfordshire and Cambridgeshire to Norfolk, in north Lincolnshire and in south-east Yorkshire.

Much of the rainwater falling on to chalk downlands sinks into the ground rather than running off it, and filters through into vast, natural, dome-shaped underground reservoirs or 'aquifers'. The tops of the aquifers, the 'water tables', rise and fall during the course of each year, rising as they are filled by autumn and winter rain and falling through the spring and summer as the water in them trickles out through countless springs. Spring and summer rain does little to replenish the aquifers, most of it being sucked up by thirsty plants and trees.

Springs high on chalk downland may run only in winter, bubbling brightly while the water table is high but drying up as it falls. The contributions made to the chalk streams by such 'winterbournes' are

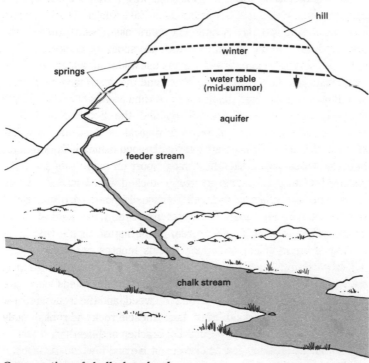

Cross-section of chalk downland

marginal; they bolster the flow in the spring and early summer. But it is their less temperamental counterparts lower down, running throughout the year, that really feed the brooks which eventually merge, one by one, to become some of the finest trout waters in this country – the Allen and the Piddle in Dorset, the Wiltshire Avon and the Wylye, the Test and the Itchen in Hampshire, the Kennet and the Lambourn in Berkshire, the Chess in Buckinghamshire, the Babingley, the Wensum and the Wissey in north Norfolk, and the Costa and Driffield Becks in Yorkshire.

All of these rivers have a number of factors in common. Because the rain tends to soak into the ground from which they flow, and because they are therefore fed chiefly from water tables – aquifers – rather than by water running straight off the land, they are even-tempered, rising and falling very little in response to rainfall and drought.

Because their water has seeped through soft rocks it is usually crystal clear, rich in soluble salts, hard and fertile, easily stripping suds from soapy hands and well able to support a mass of waving water weed that grows in the silt and shingle of the river beds. It is the water and the weed between them that support the insect life which abounds among the underwater greenery and in the gravel, and which feeds the fish.

So sturdy is the weed growth in a chalk stream that it must be cut back from time to time to make openings for fish and fishermen and to control the flow of water onwards towards the sea.

Weed cutting is a considerable craft and hard physical labour. The keeper, wading in the stream and working with his scythe, must cut the weed so that it spreads the current evenly from bank to bank, so that it provides lies and cover for trout, and so that it does not obstruct the flow of the river unduly. In normal years he will leave chequerboard blocks of weed with gaps between them. In drought years he may leave bars of weed from bank to bank, to slow the current and hold up the water level. He must establish a balance between those plants like the white-flowered water crowfoot, the shaggy marshwort and the pretty blue-bloomed brooklime, which harbour numerous insects and invertebrates but do not filter out great mounds of silt, and those like water milfoil and the little starwort which, while making marvellous larders for trout, do tend to gather silt around their roots and clog the river bed.

Cut weed drifts on the current in great, dense rafts, often covering the surface for as far as the eye can see and making fishing impossible. For this reason, chalk stream river keepers agree weed-cutting dates – usually one week a month from April to October – and publish them to their anglers in advance so that fishing may be planned.

Such is the demand for chalk stream fishing, and so limited the supply, that access to it can be both difficult to obtain and costly. Most lengths of the best chalk streams are in the hands of riparian owners who let them to individuals by the season or to clubs which often have long waiting lists. But some excellent stretches are let on a day-ticket basis, either privately or by businesses or hotels, and a few are managed by large clubs which are neither exclusive nor expensive.

Limestone rivers

Limestone rivers may be very similar to chalk streams in appearance and character, or they may be altogether more rugged and rumbustious, depending on the nature of the countryside in which they rise and through which they flow.

The main limestone deposits in the British Isles are to be found in a great swathe running from Gloucester across towards the Wash and thence upwards into Lincolnshire, in Derbyshire and the northern Pennines, and covering the whole of the centre of Ireland.

Limestone yields up mineral salts to water much as chalk does, and the differences in character between chalk streams and limestone rivers has more to do with the topography of the surrounding countryside than with the sources and chemistry of their water. Rivers like the Gloucestershire Colne and the Windrush – both rising on limestone – are virtually indistinguishable from the chalk streams a little further to the east. The countryside through which they flow may be a little less lush, and the villages past which they slide may have been built from yellow Cotswold stone rather than the imported red brick of the Avon and the Wylye valleys (you cannot build with chalk), but they are just as clear and fertile as the chalk streams and their trout are almost as fit, fat and happy as are those of the Test and Itchen, Kennet and Lambourn.

But journey northwards to Derbyshire, to the Dove, rising on Axe Edge and chattering down past Crowdecote and Pilsbury to Ashbourne, or to the Wye, as it tumbles fifteen hundred feet and more from its source above Buxton down past Bakewell and Haddon Hall to Rowsley, where it joins the Derwent. Fertile rivers these may be, and the Wye proves its point by being one of the very few in Britain in which rainbow trout have established self-sustaining populations, but they are hill streams, flowing through steep-sided valleys, and far more prone to sudden rises and colouring in response to heavy rainfall than any chalk stream.

And travel further to the north west, to the Ribble, the Hodder and the Lune in Lancashire, and to the Eden, pouring from its limestone source high in the Pennines and babbling down past Kirkby Stephen, Brough and Appleby, swelled by its lovely Ullswater-fed tributary the Eamont, and slowing and steadying as it flows out into downland above Carlisle. Above Langwathby there are stretches that look just like a chalk stream, wide and serene, well weeded, with an abundance of fly life and with a trout population among which a fish of a pound and a half is unremarkable. But it has many of the characteristics of a purely rain-fed river, too.

Wading at Warcop one warm summer's evening I failed to notice the water rising around me and very nearly took a ducking for my carelessness. A sudden storm up in the hills, wholly unseen from where I was fishing, swelled and coloured the river, raising its level by a foot or so in the space of an hour.

The three great Lancashire rivers start their lives as acid, upland streams, the Ribble and its tributary the Hodder in the Pennines and the Lune in the Cumbrian Fells. But they flow southwards and then westwards to the sea through broad, lush, limestone valleys, picking up calcium and increasing in fertility as they do so. Thus, while the trout in their headwaters may be small and wiry, those in their middle reaches may average three-quarters of a pound or more, and can provide splendid sport.

Limestone rivers in England are relatively few and far between and, as such, may perhaps be thought of as something of a curiosity. In Ireland, though, they are everything, for here it is limestone rather than chalk which provides the wherewithal for some of the finest trout fishing in the world.

Say 'Ireland' to the average fly fisher and his thoughts will turn at once either to the marvellous salmon and sea trout fishing to be had on the Ballynahinch, Blackwater, Corrib and Foyle river systems, and on the streams of Donegal and Kerry, or to the great trout loughs – Ennell, Gowna, Owel and Sheelin in the heartland of the country, and Conn, Corrib, Derg and Mask in the west and south west. But salmon and sea trout are not all, and nor are the loughs, marvellous as they may be. Ireland is blessed with some splendid trout rivers.

Do not be fooled by the peat bogs and low, rolling, heather-clad hills that dominate the island's western coastal counties. The rivers that run southwards and westwards from the Irish midlands – rivers like the Suir, rising in north Tipperary and curving south eastwards to enter the sea at Waterford, and those shimmering Shannon tributaries the Boyle, Deel, Fergus and Maigue – all have sources in and flow through lush pastureland, the emerald heart of Ireland, which is based on limestone. These are crystalline, highly fertile rivers in which insect life abounds and beautiful brown trout thrive. But, typically, they lack the continuity of flow of a chalk stream. They rise and colour quickly in heavy rain and their levels can drop dramatically in dry periods and in high summer.

Finding fishing on limestone rivers is often easier than it is on the chalk streams, and a bit less expensive, too. This is chiefly because most limestone rivers are found in somewhat less heavily populated areas than those through which the chalk streams flow, rather than because the fishing on the chalk streams is any better.

Profile of a trout stream

A few British rivers rise on upland shale or sandstone – sedimentary rocks which, while soft, contain relatively few mineral salts – and then flow through fertile agricultural land, accumulating nutrients as they do so. The Clyde and the Tweed are examples. In their upper reaches, where they race down to the north west and to the east from Broad Law, high in Scotland's southern uplands, they are mere bubbling burns. Here, the trout they sustain are hungry, wiry little creatures, greedy and incautious, rarely weighing half a pound when fully grown. But lower down, where the rivers are enriched by tributaries from the surrounding pastureland, the wild brown trout may average a pound apiece with two- and three-pounders being caught from time to time.

While they are among a minority of British waters, such rivers illustrate perfectly the classic profile of a trout stream. Pouring down from high hills, a mass of tumbling tributaries join successively to create a single river. The tributaries' pools may hold small trout but there will be few other fish species present. In its middle reaches, where it picks up nutrients from the land, the river will be larger but still fast flowing. Weed beds in its pools and runs, and the invertebrate life they sustain, will provide cover and food for larger trout, and other fish that feed on flies – grayling, dace and chub – may well be present too. Eventually, as it slides out into the coastal plain, it will slow and widen, depositing some of the silt that has been carried in suspension by the force of the current. Here, trout will give way to coarse fish, and the only game fish that will be seen will be transitory – juvenile salmon and sea trout making their way down to the sea and adults heading upstream to spawn.

Parts of this profile may be foreshortened or exaggerated. Usually rising on downland, and highly fertile from their sources, the chalk streams tend to have short tributaries, long middle reaches and quite short coastal stretches. In contrast, rivers that rise on high ground close to the sea may consist almost entirely of tributaries, becoming a single stream only just before they meet the salt water in their estuaries. Nevertheless, the species of fish sustained by any particular part of a river, and those fishes' sizes, will be dictated very largely by that part of the river's position in the overall river profile.

Rain-fed rivers

The least fertile British rivers, but some of the prettiest, are those that rise on heather-clad moorland, high on the fells or among towering granite mountains. The Americans call them freestone rivers; in Britain, less picturesquely but perhaps more accurately, we describe them as spate or rain-fed rivers.

The south-west peninsula is rich in such streams. In Cornwall the Camel and the Fowey bubble down from Bodmin Moor, turning north and south respectively towards the Bristol and English Channels. In Devon the Lyd, the Dart, the Teign, the Taw and the Torridge all have their sources within a few miles of each other among the golden bracken, dark heather and grey rocky outcrops of Dartmoor. And, travelling northwards and eastwards, the Exe, the Barle and the Lyn all rise on Exmoor, fifteen hundred feet above Foreland Point.

Most of these are quite small rivers, draining rainwater from limited catchment areas and hurrying it away to the sea, never far away. The rain runs straight off the unaccommodating moorland rock upon which it falls, seeping through a thin, acid topsoil of coarse, decaying vegetation, carving tiny rivulets, sliding around boulders, splashing into gravelly pools, chattering across stickles, rising and falling in direct response to downpour and drought, never giving itself time to accumulate riches even were there riches to be had. Even in their lower reaches, where they twist through green pastures under the baleful gaze of woolly bullocks, these little streams still hurry on.

The trout that live in them are fit, fierce and greedy, made hard by the sparseness of their surroundings. What they lack in size they usually make up for in numbers and in their eagerness to take almost anything offered to them. They may average three or four to the pound, and a twelve-ounce fish may be considered a monster, but hunger makes them incautious, they fight like demons and, with a couple of rashers of crisp-grilled bacon, they sit very well on a breakfast plate.

Bigger rain-fed rivers are to be found in the north of England, in Wales and in Scotland. The Wharfe rises high on Sike Moor in the Pennines, no more than three miles from the source of the Ribble, where hen harriers hunt low over purple heather and crimson-flowered bilberry.

While the Ribble heads west, the Wharfe drops down south and eastwards through Ilkley to be joined by the Ouse above Selby before pouring into the North Sea through the Humber estuary. The Ouse itself is an amalgam of three fine and very similar rivers, the Swale, the Ure and the Nidd, all of which have their beginnings among the bright green bog moss and white-tufted cotton grass of the West Yorkshire moors.

The Teifi, in Wales, is a brawling, bustling river, as are the Tay and the Spey in Scotland, whose tributaries drain the great Grampian Mountains. Especially in their upper reaches where their waters splash around dark grey, lichen-blotched rocks, and peregrines hunt elusive ptarmigan across the scree slopes of the high tops, these rivers are too acid and torrential, and their beds too stony, to afford nourishment and rooting for much vegetation or to sustain sizable trout. But they are not entirely devoid of insect life. Their fish are bright, lean, dark-backed creatures and, where the rivers steady in the foothills, they may average as much as half a pound or three-quarters of a pound apiece.

It is no coincidence that rain-fed rivers often have fine runs of migratory fish, salmon, slob trout and sea trout. Where food is always scarce it is inevitable that some fish will have dropped downstream in search of pastures new. It is equally inevitable that, over countless generations, such fish should have developed the ability to adapt to life in salt or brackish water and to do without food when they return to fresh water to spawn. The differences between brown trout, slob trout and sea trout are purely behavioural rather than biological. Brown trout spend their entire lives in fresh water. Slob trout and sea trout are migratory, the former usually going no further than the river's estuary to feed, the latter often travelling far out to sea, both returning to the rivers of their births to spawn.

Some rain-fed rivers, particularly those that are short and steep, with very little insect life, are exclusively salmon and sea trout waters, sustaining few if any non-migratory brown trout. The pretty Shimna River in Northern Ireland is one such. Clear and green, it cascades through narrow, rocky gorges from its headwaters in the Mourne Mountains to join the sea in Dundrum Bay no more than eight or ten miles away. Other examples are to be found in little rivers like the Dunn, the Glenarm, the Glenariff and the Glenshesk in the Glens of Antrim, the Eske, the Inver, the Gweebarra, the Owenea and the Owentocker in County Donegal, and in countless similar streams and small rivers along the west coast of Scotland.

The availability of trout fishing on rain-fed rivers varies. Those that have good runs of salmon and sea trout tend to be carefully protected and permission to fish them may be difficult or expensive to obtain. Many, though, are in the hands of fishing clubs or hotels which, although they may reserve the water chiefly for their members or guests, frequently offer day or weekly tickets at very reasonable prices. And, on many, the fishing rights are retained by the farmers or landowners through whose property they flow. Especially on lesser rivers in the quieter corners of Britain, such people may even grant permission to fish in return for no more than a courteous enquiry.

Just as rivers reflect the character of the land on which they rise and through which they flow, so do stillwaters reflect the nature of the countryside that surrounds them.

Limestone loughs

The Irish midlands and the west of Ireland provide some of the very finest wild brown trout fishing in the British Isles. Lower Lough Erne in County Fermanagh, Loughs Sheelin, Lene, Owel and Ennell in the heart of the country, Lough Derg on the Shannon, Lough Corrib in County Galway and Loughs Mask and Conn in County Mayo are all limestone loughs. Set in soft, rolling countryside, they are rich in mineral salts and have large areas of relatively shallow water into which the light, so necessary for life, can penetrate easily. They are positively crawling with insect life and their trout grow fit, fat and beautiful. What is more, the fishing on them is effectively free.

Ironically, it is the very fertility of the land around these fabulous loughs that places them under threat. Especially in the Irish midlands, farming is intensive, and where farming is intensive nowadays so too is the growth, cutting and use of silage as cattle feed and of nitrate fertilizers to promote crop growth. Silage effluent and excess nitrates both leach or run into watercourses and, eventually, into lakes and loughs. Such over-fertilization – 'eutrophication' – can have disastrous effects on fisheries, causing massive weed growth and the development of huge clouds of algae, especially in the summer, and seriously damaging or even destroying the insect life in the water.

Several once-magnificent trout loughs are now mere shadows of what they once were. Loughs Gowna and Derravaragh, particularly, have suffered severely from this sad side effect of intensive industrial farming.

It should also be said that, like most things Irish, the country's great limestone lakes do not give up their secrets easily. Many of them are huge. From Maam Bridge in the north to Galway City in the south, Corrib is thirty miles long. Lough Derg stretches more than twenty miles from Killaloe to Portumna. Lower Lough Erne covers 38,000 acres, Lough Mask 20,000, and even relatively intimate Lough Sheelin has a surface area of 4,500 acres.

The relative shallowness of these great loughs means that the fish can be almost anywhere, and the rocks and boulders that lurk just beneath the water's surface around the shoreline and even well out from it make them treacherous, especially in rough weather. On fine days, you may take a fish or two by drifting alone in their bays, but it is both safer and more sensible to engage the services of the local ghillie. He will keep you clear of hazards, put you over fish, advise and, if you are lucky, entertain you. Typically, Irish ghillies are gentle men, steeped in the lore of the countryside and of the loughs they love. Only the most arrogant of anglers spurn their services, and such people fully deserve the thin time they often have as a consequence.

Highland lochs

In contrast, many Scottish lochs are dark and dour, long ribbons of water set deep in steep-sided, conifer-clad valleys, with high granite hills towering above them. They are fed by black and amber rainwater cascading from high crags, seeping through dead heather and carpets of pine needles, collecting little or no nourishment on the way. They are often awesome places, silent and mysterious, marvellous settings for a few days afloat. Their names conjure up romantic images – Affric and Arkaig, Loyne and Lunn Da Bhra, Tay, Tummel and Rannoch. But the bleak beauty of the wild scenery that surrounds them is usually echoed underwater where scarcity of insect life makes for lean and hungry trout, rarely weighing more than half or three-quarters of a pound apiece.

There are exceptions. Lochs Boardhouse, Harray and Swannay in the Orkneys are shallow and fertile, with a wealth of shrimps and snails upon which the trout grow fat. Windswept Loch Watten in the flatlands of Caithness is similar, as is Loch Leven near Kinross, across the Firth of Forth from Edinburgh. Loch Leven is perhaps the most famous of all Scotland's many trout lochs but, like several similar waters in Ireland, it was severely damaged by eutrophication during the late 1970s and early 1980s, and it has taken a great deal of effort and determination on the part of the owners to restore it to something like its former glory.

There is a wealth of excellent loch trout fishing to be had in Scotland. You can tramp up through stands of capercaillie-inhabited Scots pine to the heather and red deer of the high hills, to fish for little trout in little lochans. More lazily, you can drift through rocky, fir-fringed bays, casting ahead of the boat and watching for the sudden flash of bronze beneath the surface as a trout turns to take your fly. With care, you can wade the gravel shallows where the clear water of a burn brings food into the loch and where, in late summer, mature trout foregather before heading upstream to their spawning grounds.

So wild and isolated are many of the myriad waters flecking a map of Scotland that it would be easy to presume that the fishing on them was there for the taking. It is not. All trout fishing in Scotland, apart from that in tidal waters, is controlled by those who own the land around it. Permission to fish may be freely given or there may be a charge, but you must seek permission. Tackle shops can always provide advice as to who owns which waters, and several good books and brochures contain the necessary details.

The English lakes

It is a little surprising that so few fly fishers realize that England has a substantial number of its own trout 'lochs' and 'lochans', very similar in character to those in Scotland, sometimes more accessible and every bit as pretty. Coniston and Crummock Water, Haweswater, Ullswater and Windermere, long, narrow strips of water threading their ways between the high fells of the Lake District, offer good and inexpensive fishing for wild brown trout, as do many of the area's smaller lakes – Brotherswater, Buttermere and Burnmoor Tarn, Devoke Water, and Sprinkling and Stye Head Tarns. The countryside surrounding these lovely lakes is as bleak and beautiful as the Highlands of Scotland and the waters themselves are only marginally more fertile than are those found further to the north. Generally, Lake District trout are not large, a three-quarter-pounder being a fine fish, and they often share their habitat with char, pike, perch, roach and rudd. But they are fit and wild, and can provide excellent sport.

The Midlands and the South of England have little or no such natural stillwater trout fishing, but that is not to say that they have no fishing at all or that what they have is in any way inferior. Keen to make the best possible use of the resources under their control, water authorities and private individuals stock reservoirs and lakes throughout the country with brown and rainbow trout, usually making the fishing available to the public on a season- or day-ticket basis.

Lowland reservoirs

Reservoir trout fisheries vary enormously in scale and scenery. Some are lovely – Blagdon, nestling in a Mendip fold, its bank carpeted with cowslips in the spring; some have a special intimacy – Ardleigh in Essex is one such, as is Eye Brook near Northampton; some, like Hanningfield Reservoir and Grafham and Rutland Waters, set under huge skies in low-lying countryside, have a wilderness feeling about them; some, like Farmoor II near Oxford, are bleak, featureless and concrete-sided but nevertheless have a mysterious appeal of their own.

The one thing that all these reservoirs have in common is their fertility. Lying in rich, agricultural land, or filled with water drawn from rivers like the Thames, the tributaries of which are chiefly chalk streams, they sustain a wealth of insect life, and fish introduced into them grow quickly. Typically, a rainbow trout weighing one pound when put into such a water in the spring will have doubled its weight by the end of the summer, and will have become truly wild.

Those fortunate enough to live in Scotland or Ireland sometimes pour scorn upon the 'tame, stew-pond trout' with which English reservoirs are stocked. There is little justification for their doing so. Few fish are prettier or more powerful than a reservoir rainbow that has been in the water for some time, and they are by no means always easy to catch.

Small stillwaters

The only lakes in which the fertility of the water has little or no effect on the size and quality of the trout they hold are the small stillwaters, large numbers of which have appeared as if by magic during the past twenty years. These fisheries range in size from about half an acre up to about fifty acres, anything bigger being classified – somewhat arbitrarily – as a reservoir. They may be very pretty – many of them are – and their water may be crystalline and crawling with good things for trout to eat. But the truth of the matter is that most of them are fished very intensively. As a result, trout stocked into them are usually caught quite quickly, in a matter of days if not hours. And fish that survive for more than about a week see so many artificial flies that they often become almost uncatchable.

In order to maintain a reasonable head of catchable fish, the managers of such waters usually ask their anglers to kill the trout they catch, restocking regularly to replace the fish that have been removed from the water.

From all this, it follows that there is little or no time in which the quality of the water can influence the size and condition of its trout. It follows, too, that day or season ticket prices on such 'put-and-take' waters must be markedly higher than those on reservoirs because the owner or manager of the fishery will have had to rear the trout himself or to pay a fish farmer to do so, rather than allow the fish to feed on free food as they do in lochs and reservoirs.

Where to begin?

So, where should the newcomer to fly fishing begin?

Obviously, the decision will be influenced quite heavily by geography and the depth of one's pocket. But there are certain considerations that, if taken into account, can make all the difference between a happy and successful introduction to the sport and languishing in frustration.

Firstly, I say it now and shall say it again, by far the best starting point is to be found on a fly fishing course or at a casting school, rather than in cantering off to the nearest bit of trout-filled water, either unaccompanied or with friends of questionable competence.

Like all worthwhile pursuits, fly fishing for trout involves certain basic skills. It is possible to acquire them on one's own, by trial and error over a period of time, or to learn them from fishing friends, along with those friends' faults and misconceptions. But a quicker, more certain and less painful way of acquiring them is by engaging the services of a qualified instructor. You can learn far more from half a dozen one-hour lessons or, better still, a two- or three-day course than you ever can from two or three seasons of untutored fishing.

Secondly, it is essential that the novice should catch fish – not many, perhaps, and not necessarily large ones. But the catching of a few trout can do wonders for one's confidence. This argues for choosing well-stocked waters that are neither too daunting nor too difficult to fish. Generally speaking, small waters are less daunting than large ones and stillwaters are easier to fish than rivers, where the constant movement of the stream can make it difficult to control the fly line on the water.

I understand the reservations some people have about small, put-and-take fisheries which, they say, offer entertainment rather than sport. But such waters do give the relatively inexperienced fly fisher, whose casting ability may be modest, the opportunity to cover fish for most of the time and to catch a few.

For those lucky enough to live in Wales or the West Country, the north of England, Scotland or Ireland, where there is first-class wild brown trout fishing to be had, or who can make holiday pilgrimages to such lovely places, the same principles hold true. To start with, at least, it would probably be sensible to seek out relatively small stillwaters, graduating to streams and burns or to larger lochs as skill and understanding develop.

CHAPTER THREE

The Fish and Their Food

Each winter, while fly fishers huddle at their vices in the lamplight, curtained against the early evening darkness, filling fly boxes for the season yet to come, the trout themselves are busy making good their numbers. In little brooks running darkly beneath skeletal trees; in peaty moorland burns where whisky-coloured water skips and gurgles between banks clad in the scratchy coarseness of last summer's ferns and heather; in chalk streams gliding past frost-rimed reeds; wherever clean, clear water washes through and over loose gravel, and especially where it does so at the tails of pools and in the river's margins, brown trout gather in their pairs to mate.

Brown trout

These mating fish are duller, drabber creatures than they were when we fished for them in early autumn. The males, the cocks, their grey-brown flanks flecked with copper-coloured spots, with lustreless cream bellies and sharply hooked lower jaws, are usually smaller than the females, who must do most of the work. The hens, heavy with spawn, will have an overall tinge of tarnished copper or gunmetal grey fading downwards to a dingy white, and the black spots on their heads and sides, so distinctive at other times, may barely show.

It is the swelling and cooling of the rivers by early winter rain that draws the trout upstream to their spawning grounds. When they arrive, the hens begin to cut 'redds', turning on their sides and fanning the gravel fiercely with their tails, washing pebbles away to leave shallow hollows in which they will lay their eggs. As they do so, the cock fish join them, squabbling among themselves and defending determinedly their claims to their chosen partners.

Once paired, and when the hen is satisfied with the hollow she has cut, she settles into it, her back arched, her mouth agape. The cock lies close alongside, emulating her, shuddering violently and spraying milky milt on to the stream of orange ova pouring from her vent.

This first mating is over in a trice. As soon as it is, the hen moves a foot or so upstream and starts to cut her next redd, the gravel thus displaced covering the ova in the first nest. She may repeat the exercise five or six times, depositing successively fewer ova into each hollow until, as she crouches over the last one, she has nothing left to give. Having sunk and been washed into gaps in the gravel, and having largely been covered by the pebbles washed down from the hen's next endeavours, most of the ova should survive the four to eight weeks it will take them to hatch.

The sowing of spring wheat and barley may be under way, and the first lambs will have been born, when the tiny trout, the alevins, emerge from the ova in February. Three-quarters of an inch long and with pendulous yolk sacs – their ration packs – hanging beneath them, they burrow further into the gravel, away from prying, predatory eyes. Only when their self-contained food supplies begin to run out and they have started to take on more fish-like form will they emerge as fry, to start feeding on tiny insects and crustaceans and to face the harsh realities of the world.

Those trout fry that survive the spring, summer and autumn, growing to perhaps three inches in length as they do so, will be the lucky ones. They will have seen the vast majority, perhaps 95 per cent, of their brothers and sisters providing protein for hungry pike and perch, rats, mink and water shrews, kingfishers, herons, cormorants, gulls and goosanders. Firm and fully finned, they will have begun to look like trout, although the 'parr marks' on their flanks, the fingerprints left by St Peter when he placed them in the water, will still bear witness to their youth.

Brown trout are wonderfully adaptable. Their size, colour and markings are governed almost entirely by the fertility of the water in which they live and by the hues and shades of their surroundings.

The size they attain as adults is wholly dependent upon the amount of food available to them. In acid, rain-fed streams, rivers and lakes, where food is scarce, the trout may average two or three to the pound, and a fish weighing a full pound may be counted as a monster. In chalk streams, where food is plentiful throughout the year, a fish of one and a half or two pounds may be unremarkable and a few four-, five- or six-pounders may be caught each season. And the most fertile lakes and loughs may well produce an occasional double-figure brown trout, invariably grown fat on a diet of smaller fish.

So diverse are the types of water in which brown trout are found, and so strongly is this diversity reflected in the appearances of the fish themselves, that it was only quite recently that fly fishers and biologists were able to conclude that the fish were all of one species. Yellow-backed, brown-blotched, vermilion-spotted 'gillaroo' from Irish loughs; dark, black-finned trout from Welsh mountain tarns and streams; sporting, silvery, black-flecked trout from Loch Leven; golden, sparsely marked little trout from moorland streams; bronzed and portly denizens of the chalk streams; even glittering, streamlined

The fly fisher's quarry: a wild brown trout breasting the current in the shallow, shingly margins

A wild brown trout

A fine rainbow trout. (Note the marrow scoop and dish used to examine the stomach contents of the fish, to make fly selection more certain)

BELOW: *Pound for pound, trout fight more fiercely than almost any other freshwater fish*

OPPOSITE PAGE ABOVE: *The fly fisher's tackle: the author's fishing waistcoat and its contents*

OPPOSITE PAGE BELOW: *Overall, attire at the waterside should be sober*

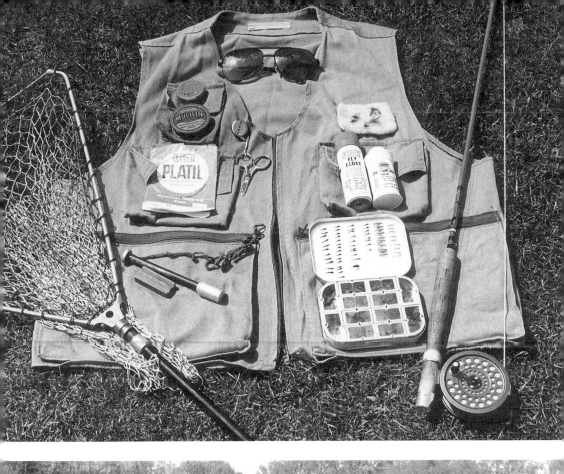

OPPOSITE PAGE ABOVE: *If you really want to learn to cast well, seek out a qualified, professional instructor*

OPPOSITE PAGE BELOW: *'On chalk streams, the slower you go, the more time you spend waiting and watching, the more successful will you be'*

Concealment is one of the keys to successful fly fishing, especially on small waters. Keeping low, wearing clothes that blend with the background, and using bankside vegetation as camouflage (BELOW), *are far more likely to yield results than standing up or wearing light-coloured clothes when fishing* (RIGHT)

OPPOSITE PAGE ABOVE: *Lifting into a fish: the action is very similar to the gradual acceleration into the up-cast*

OPPOSITE PAGE BELOW: *When playing a fish, keep the line tight and the rod tip up*

ABOVE: *A good trout comes to the net. (Note that the net is fully submerged and the angler is drawing the fish over it)*

LEFT: *Releasing a wild brown trout. When returning fish, they should be handled as little as possible, ideally not at all*

'Standing up when boat fishing is counter-productive and can be dangerous'

sea trout – the 'peal' of Devon, the 'herling' or 'finnock' of Scotland, the 'sewin' of Wales and the 'white fish' of Ireland – all these are, in truth, of one species, the brown trout, *Salmo trutta*.

Rainbow trout

Rainbow trout (*Oncorhynchus mykiss*) are markedly less variable in appearance than brown trout. At their best they are brilliant creatures, silver-dipped and lightly spotted, with wide, iridescent, pinky, mauve-green bands along their flanks.

I say, 'at their best' because many farm-reared rainbow trout are far less pretty than they would have been had they grown up in the wild. Although farming methods are improving, and although rainbow trout take on a bright, silvery sheen and grow full tails quite quickly when released into large reservoirs, some small stillwater fisheries still show rainbows at their worst, dull of flank, with twisted fins, poorly formed gill cases and tails worn to stumps by constant rubbing on the sides of concrete-lined stew ponds.

Rainbow trout were first introduced into Britain from the west coast of the United States in the mid 1880s and have established self-sustaining wild populations in only a very few of our rivers; the Chess and the Misbourne in Buckinghamshire are examples, as is the Derbyshire Wye. But they are more amenable to being reared in the somewhat cramped conditions of a stew pond than brown trout are and, being greedier, they may grow a third as fast again, which makes them ideal for farming, both for the stocking of angling waters and for the table. This, of course, is why you only ever see rainbow trout, rather than brown trout, offered for sale in fish shops and supermarkets. The very few brown trout that do find their way on to fishmongers' slabs are almost invariably rod caught, having been obtained from anglers.

Like their native cousins, rainbow trout spawn in the winter.

Some trout farmers trap mature rainbows migrating upstream from lakes and reservoirs; others maintain brood stock on their premises. Handling the trout with care, the ripe ova are extruded from the hen into a dry bowl, sprayed with a little milt from a cock fish and stirred gently. They are then covered with clean, cool water and left for ten minutes or so before being washed several times to remove excess milt.

The fertilized ova are placed in shallow trays through which spring water is run, simulating the water's percolation through the gravel in a redd. Provided the water continues to flow, the temperature is kept reasonably constant and the ova are kept clean, dead ones being removed, the alevins should appear a month or so later, beginning to feed three to four weeks after that. By the time they are eighteen months old, farm-reared rainbow trout will weigh about half a pound and will be ready to be killed, cleaned, frozen, boxed and packed for the trip to the supermarket.

It is not very surprising that non-anglers presume these somewhat grimly named 'portion-sized' fish to be fully grown. In fact, of course, they are not. It is quite easy to grow rainbow trout on until they weigh anything from two and a half to five or six pounds in their fourth summers and, by selecting the greediest and by careful husbandry in uncrowded stew ponds, to pump up a few until they weigh ten, fifteen, twenty or even twenty-five pounds apiece in their fifth or sixth summers. Unlike brown trout, which may live for twelve years or more, rainbows very rarely survive a sixth winter.

Colour and flavour

Two myths perpetuated by the ill-informed are that pink-fleshed trout necessarily taste better than pale-fleshed ones, and that wild trout necessarily taste better than farmed ones.

The colour of a trout's flesh is dictated by its diet. Pinkness in fishes' flesh – and, incidentally, the vermilion hue of some brown trout's spots – is caused by carotene in the diet. In the wild, carotene is present in shrimps and snails. Where trout eat a lot of shrimps or snails, their flesh will be pink; where they do not, it will be pale. In fish farms, trout are fed on pellets which may or may not be impregnated with carotene but which are usually identical in virtually every other respect. Where carotene-impregnated pellets are used, the trout's flesh will become pink; where they are not, it will remain pale. Carotene is a chemical which dyes the flesh pink but has no effect at all on the flavour of the fish. By feeding it on carotene-impregnated pellets, a pale-fleshed trout can be turned into a pink-fleshed one within about six weeks. If the carotene is then removed from its diet, its flesh will become pale again in about the same length of time.

Similarly, the texture and flavour of a trout's flesh is a product of its diet and, more particularly, of the 'plate' from which it eats. The pellets fed to trout by fish farmers provide the fish with a better and more balanced diet than would generally be available to them in the wild, and farmed trout should therefore taste better than wild ones. But it is not that simple. Where trout collect their food in clean water or from a clean, gravel bottom, they will taste 'clean'. Where they root around for food at the bottom of a silted river, a muddy lake or an ill-kept stew pond, they will take on a muddy taste.

I know of at least one trout lake which sustains what can only be described as an infestation of wildfowl. Naturally, the birds deposit huge quantities of dung into the water. The trout take much of their food from the lake bed. As a consequence they are quite inedible, tasting very strongly of the muck they have picked up with their food and in which the insects they eat have been steeped.

I also know of a small-scale fish farmer who went out of business because his trout were fed on sinking pellets which they grubbed for at the bottom of a muddy stew pond. They tasted of the mud they had eaten. He might have been able to solve the problem by feeding them on floating pellets, which they would have taken from the surface of the water.

Migratory trout

Few people would dispute that sea trout and slob trout taste consistently better than freshwater brown or rainbow trout, whether wild or farmed.

Sea trout are brown trout that go out to sea to feed, returning to the rivers in which they were born only to spawn. Living in well-oxygenated salt water, and feeding on a rich diet of shrimps, molluscs and small fish, their flesh becomes firm and pink with a wonderfully clean, delicate taste.

Slob trout are simply the sea trout's less ambitious brethren, which slip down river during the second or third year of their lives but rarely venture further than the estuaries of their home rivers. Feeding on sand eels, shrimps, shellfish and so on, they too grow fit and strong and make delicious eating.

The trout's diet

In lakes, lochs, reservoirs, streams and rivers, trout – both browns and rainbows – feed on a wide range of insects and other small creatures. Because we often see them taking hatching or adult winged flies from the surface of the water, it is tempting to presume that this is all they live on. It is not. Trout are voracious, opportunistic, carnivorous predators with remarkably catholic diets. They are also concerned with 'value for effort', usually feeding chiefly upon those creatures that are most readily available, which are most easily caught, and which offer the best deal in terms of food value gained in return for energy expended. The extent to which they feed at the surface will be dictated by the extent to which surface food is available to them. In most trout waters the vast majority of the food available to trout is to be found at the bottom and among the weed, only quite a small proportion – perhaps 10 per cent or less – being taken from the surface.

A trout's staple diet – and to some extent the times at which it feeds – will be dictated by the nature and fertility of the water in which it lives, and by the time of year.

In acid, infertile streams, rivers and lakes sustaining few aquatic creatures, the trout will be hard put to scrape livings for themselves. They may be incautious, taking almost any apparently-living creatures that come their way; they may rely heavily on terrestrial insects blown on to the water from the surrounding countryside; and they may be forced to feed throughout the day, simply to gather enough food to keep body and soul together. They are likely to be lean, muscular little fish, easily tempted but rarely big enough to keep.

In food-rich chalk streams, fertile lowland reservoirs and the marvellously productive loughs and lochs of western Ireland and northern Scotland, it is quite the opposite. Such is the mass and variety of edible goodies available to them that the trout can pick and choose. They may binge on one particular type of insect and then, without warning, change to another that temporarily tickles their taste buds. They may need to feed only quite briefly during the day, usually during the morning, and again late in the evening. And they may well average a pound and a half or two pounds in weight but prove fiendishly difficult to seduce.

Entomology

Much of the mystique that has been built up around fly fishing has to do with entomology, the study of insects. There is no surer way to daunt the novice, or to send him soundly to sleep, than to burble on about *Ephemeroptera, Diptera, Plecoptera* and *Trichoptera*, about *Crustacea* and *Coleoptera, Hemiptera* and *Hymenoptera*, or about *Lepidoptera, Odonata* and *Orthoptera*. Even the English names for the fishermen's flies are so multitudinous and esoteric as to leave the beginner with a sense of inadequacy. Can it really be impossible to catch trout without being able to tell a large dark olive from a lacewing, a pale watery from a pale evening dun or a green drake from a grannom?

No, of course not. Many perfectly competent fly fishers enjoy fine sport from the opening of each season to its close with no more than the sketchiest knowledge of what trout eat. But it does help to have a basic understanding of the quarry's dietary preferences, of what the fish feed on, where, when and why. Such understanding can add immeasurably to enjoyment of the sport and to success, and – what is most important – this basic understanding is not difficult to acquire.

Trout feed chiefly on four groups of aquatic flies, on shrimps, water bugs and one or two other wriggly underwater creatures, on snails and small fish, and on an assortment of land-bred insects.

The four groups of insects are the so-called up-winged flies (the *Ephemeroptera*, if you want to impress your friends), the flat-winged flies (*Diptera*), the roof-winged flies (*Trichoptera*) and the hard-winged flies (*Plecoptera*).

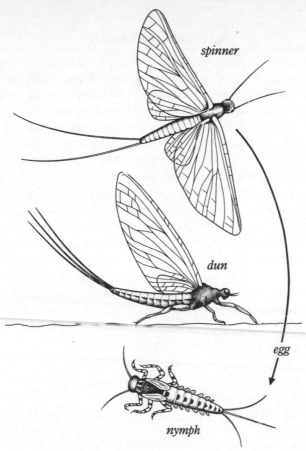

spinner

dun

egg

nymph

Life-cycle of an up-winged fly

Up-winged flies

The biography of an up-winged fly contains all the elements of a good drama. It is at once romantic and tragic, liberally seasoned with suspense, the ultimate Cinderella story of rags to riches.

Up-winged flies are more commonly seen on streams and rivers than on lakes and reservoirs, although a few are important to fish and to fishermen on the latter, especially on Irish limestone loughs. Their mothers lay their eggs either on the water's surface or beneath it, by crawling down bridge supports and the like, or down the stems of reeds and rushes. Surface-laid eggs sink and attach themselves to stones or weed; those laid underwater usually attach themselves to whatever they have been deposited on. In either case they eventually hatch to produce 'nymphs', the larvae of the up-winged flies.

Nymphs

Nymphs live on decaying weed and leaves and vary considerably in size, appearance and behaviour. Some, living on the silt in lakes and lazy rivers, are tiny creatures, less than a quarter of an inch long when fully grown, slow moving and perfectly camouflaged. Some are sturdy but idle, passing their days crawling about among the moss or rotting leaves on or between the stones on the river bed, and only occasionally swimming off slowly in search of pastures new. Many are strong and streamlined, with long, hair-fringed tails. Living among the weed, they dart from frond to frond, flexing their bodies rather like a swimmer doing the butterfly stroke. A few, the nymphs of the mayflies, up to an inch long and with pointed heads and JCB jaws, burrow into the river bed where they live in the tunnels they dig for themselves.

Trout love the nymphs of up-winged flies but tend to feed only on those that are most accessible to them. Nymphs that live and swim among the weed fronds are far more readily available than those that cling to the bottom or burrow into it, except when the latter leave the safety of their homes and head upwards to hatch, when they, too, become fair game for predatory fish.

Depending on their species, the nymphs remain in the water for anything from a few months to a year or even two. They outgrow their skins several times as they grow, shedding them in successive moults until, eventually, with humped wing cases on their backs, they are ready to hatch.

When conditions are right, the mature nymphs will float or swim to the surface where they will hang for a moment, their skins splitting along their backs to release adult, winged flies – 'duns' – into the waiting world.

Duns

Different up-winged flies hatch at different times of year and at different times of day. We do not know what triggers a hatch, but the way in which a mass of flies of one species will suddenly appear on the water, as if at a given signal, is quite astonishing. At one moment there will be no flies to be seen and no fish rising; five minutes later, a thousand identical little insects will be drifting on the current like a flotilla of tiny sailing boats, and the surface will be rippled with the ebbing rings of rising trout.

A hatch of up-winged flies may be quite brief, stopping as suddenly as it started, especially early in the season, or it may go on for an hour or more, petering out gradually. There may be only one species of fly hatching, or several.

Up-winged duns are rather drab creatures, dull of body and leaden of wing. They sit on the water's surface, their wings folded together above their backs, or fluttering slightly, only for as long as it takes them to dry themselves and take to the air. Trout do not mind this drabness at all, but often feed busily on the newly hatched flies, rising quickly lest their quarry escape or be stolen from them by marauding martins, wrens or reed buntings.

Those duns that escape the jaws of trout and the beaks of birds flutter off to the safety of trees, bushes, reeds or rushes at the waterside. They are unable to feed and can survive for no more than about a day, but their forbearance is rewarded with the most magical metamorphosis.

As it hangs on a reed stem or beneath a leaf, the dun's dull wings are held together above its back. Quite suddenly, it parts them and spreads them wide, shudders a little and then folds them back along its body. The skin of its back splits and there emerges a beautiful creature, bright and gleaming, with shining, diaphanous wings and long, slender, delicate tails – the 'spinner'.

Spinners

You can often see clouds of spinners dancing in the sunlight late on warm summer afternoons, flying upwards for a few feet and then falling, again and again, their glittering wings catching the sun's rays. Theirs is a mating dance and a dance of death. They mate on the wing, the male clasping himself to the female who must fight to keep them both aloft. Once they have fulfilled their purpose, they part, the males dying almost at once, the females seeking out a stretch of water to receive their eggs. They are far from selective, and rainy days are tragic days, for many of the spinners will lay their eggs on puddles that will be parched dry within hours and in which the eggs will certainly never hatch. But most of them will find the lake, stream or river from which they emerged as duns only a day or so ago, depositing their eggs there, most often in the evening. And then they will die.

Those that lay their eggs underwater will simply be swept away on the current. Those that dip to the surface again and again, leaving a tiny blob of eggs each time, will eventually tire, subsiding exhausted on to the water, fluttering briefly in protest at the inevitable. A dying spinner may sit proudly upright for a while, soaking up the last of the day's warmth. But soon the strength will drain from her; a wing will sag and catch in the oily surface; as she tries weakly to free it, the other wing will become caught. She may curl her protesting body up from the clinging fluid from time to time. Eventually, she will surrender. A tiny, trapped cruciform being, she will drift on the stream. Her glassy wings lit by the rays of the setting sun will refract fine beams of light down into the water, signalling her presence to the trout below. They have seen this before and know she cannot escape. Slowly and confidently, one of their number may rise to the surface and sip her down, a minute ring of ripples spreading outwards for a few inches to mark her passing.

Common up-winged flies, their appearance, distribution, seasons

(**Note:** Spinners included only where they are of consequence)

Angler's name	Body length	Body colour	Wing colour	No. of tails
Large dark olive	10mm	Dark olive	Light grey	2
March brown	12mm	Dark brown	Mottled brown	2
Sepia dun	10mm	Dark brown	Pale brown	3
Iron blue dun	5mm	Dark brown	Slate blue	2
Little claret spinner	5mm	Dark maroon	Clear	2
Medium olive dun	8mm	Medium olive	Grey	2
Medium olive spinner	8mm	Brown	Clear	2
Pond olive dun	12mm	Olive/ grey	Grey	2
Lake olive dun	10mm	Red- brown	Pale grey	2
Mayfly	15mm+	Cream	Grey	3
Spent gnat	15mm+	White	Clear	3
Caenis	5mm	Cream	Dull white	3
Pale watery	5mm	Pale olive	Light grey	2
Pale watery spinner	5mm	Buff	Clear	2
Blue winged olive	10mm	Olive/ grey	Dark grey	3
Sherry spinner	10mm	Amber	Clear	3
Small dark olive dun	5mm	Dark olive	Mid grey	2
Small dark olive spinner	5mm	Dark brown	Clear	2

Flat-winged flies – midges

Just as the nymphs, duns and spinners of up-winged flies often provide a substantial part of a river trout's diet, so does one family of flat-winged flies – the non-biting midges, the Chironomids – provide the bulk of the food eaten by trout in lakes, lochs and reservoirs. It is a huge family of almost four hundred species. Fortunately for the fly

and suggested artificials with which they may be represented

Water type	Time of year	Suggested artificial
Most rivers	March–April and Sept–Oct	Kite's Imperial
Stony, rain-fed rivers	March–April	Kite's Imperial
Acid lakes and slow acid rivers	April	Pheasant Tail
Most medium to fast rivers	May–Sept	Iron Blue Houghton Ruby
Most rivers (not Wales or Ireland)	May–June	Blue Upright Lunn's Particular
Small alkaline ponds and lakes	May–Sept	Blue Upright
Alkaline lakes	May, June and Sept	Blue Upright
Alkaline rivers and lakes in England and Ireland	Late-May/ early June	Any Mayfly pattern Deerstalker
All except Scotland	May, June and July	Last Hope
Rivers, mainly in southern England	May–Sept	Tups Indispensable Lunn's Yellow Boy
Most rivers	July–Sept	Blue-winged Olive (B-WO) Sherry Spinner
Welsh rivers	July–Aug	Blue Upright Lunn's Particular

fisher, they all look pretty much alike, varying only quite marginally in size and colour.

Midges thrive in water with a low oxygen content, either because it is very deep or because it is polluted. An increase in the number of midges in a particular water, often combined with a commensurate decrease in numbers of other insect species, usually indicates a decline in the quality of the water. Until quite recently, midges in Britain were

41

confined almost entirely to stillwaters, being found only in rivers, or stretches of rivers, that were both slow flowing and polluted. Since the Second World War, though, they have become numerous in many of our rivers, particularly in the chalk streams of southern England and in spate rivers in the West Country. There can be little doubt that this trend is the result of increased agricultural pollution, or that it is a sad reflection of modern attitudes to water quality. Whatever the reason, river trout fly fishers must now take as much interest in midges as their colleagues on stillwaters always have.

Clusters of eggs are laid on the water's surface by midges' mothers and usually remain there until the larvae hatch.

Midge larvae

Midge larvae – commonly known as bloodworms – vary in length from an eighth of an inch to half an inch and in colour from muddy green through buff to rusty or even bright red. They swim with a characteristic, figure-of-eight, lashing movement, making their way to the lake or river bed where they live among and feed upon the weed, silt and decaying vegetation. Vast numbers of them are eaten by trout and other fish.

Midge pupae

After a matter of months, the surviving midge larvae turn into comma-shaped pupae, with bulbous heads and thoraces, segmented bodies and fluffy white breathing and salt-absorbing filaments on their heads and tails. During the next few days, soft, pendulous wing sacs grow from either side of their thoraces. When they are ready to hatch, the pupae swim up to the water's surface where they hang for a while before stretching themselves out horizontally in the surface film, their backs split, and the adult midges emerge on to the top of the water.

Midge pupae swimming up and waiting at the surface to hatch are slow moving and succulent, and trout eat them in huge numbers. Indeed, so consistently do they feature in trout's diets that one rarely catches a feeding stillwater trout that does not have at least some midge pupae in its stomach. Trout also eat adult midges when they can but, as these winged insects usually take off and fly away very quickly after hatching, the fish have to content themselves chiefly with the stragglers, the stillborn, those that fail to escape from their pupal shucks, and those that are swamped by waves or fail to get airborne for some other reason.

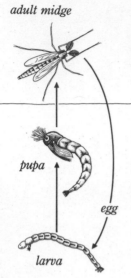

adult midge

pupa

egg

larva

Life-cycle of a flat-winged fly

Adult midges

Adult midges do not go through any further metamorphosis, as up-winged flies do. At rest, standing on their six long legs, they fold their two transparent wings flat across their backs, usually slightly overlapping.

Other flat-winged flies

Reed Smuts

Apart from the midges, only one other aquatic flat-winged fly, the reed smut, is of any real consequence to trout and to fly fishers. It is a tiny, dumpy little creature, black as your hat, and appears in prodigious numbers but only on rivers. Although trout love it, it is a source of constant frustration to fly fishers because, being so minute, it is almost impossible to represent on a hook.

Midges and reed smuts aside, several terrestrial or land-born flat-winged flies are eaten by trout when they fall or are blown on to the water.

Hawthorn flies

The hawthorn fly, a large, black, bumbling creature with two long, trailing legs, appears during the mornings in late April and early May. Hawthorn flies are quite often blown on to the water. When they are, the trout take them greedily.

Hawthorn fly

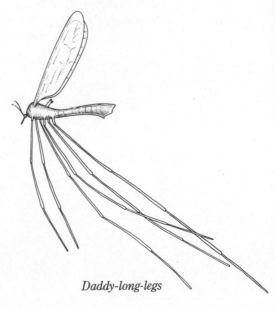

Daddy-long-legs

Black gnats

Black gnats – a generic name for several very similar species – look not unlike very small hawthorn flies. Although born on land, they may swarm over the water at any time between May and September. When they do, some of them will almost always fall or be blown on to it. Trout clearly regard black gnats as a welcome supplement to their diets and take them enthusiastically whenever they are available.

Daddy-long-legs

The crane fly or daddy-long-legs is a familiar sight almost everywhere in the late summer and early autumn. Wonderfully bad flyers, these gangling insects get airborne quite easily but are then almost entirely at the mercy of the wind, which may well carry them on to streams or rivers or, more frequently, lakes, lochs and reservoirs, often to be taken by trout.

Caddis flies

The third major group of insects eaten by trout in substantial numbers, in waters both running and still, are the roof-winged flies, traditionally known in Britain as sedge flies but increasingly referred to here nowadays by the title the Americans have given them, the caddis flies.

Female caddis flies may lay their eggs on the water's surface or by crawling beneath it, like the up-winged flies, or they may lay them on shrubs and rushes overhanging the water.

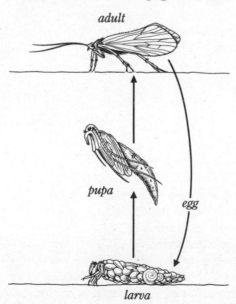

adult

pupa

egg

larva

Life-cycle of a caddis fly

Caddis larvae

When they hatch, the caddis larvae are juicy, succulent creatures, bulging with all the good things necessary for life, perfect for piscine picnics and terribly tempting to trout. Given the esteem in which the fish hold them, it is not surprising that the larvae seek to camouflage and protect themselves by building cases from bits and pieces they find on the lake or river bed.

The larvae of each caddis species – there are some two hundred in all – build distinctive and characteristic tubular cases. Those that live in streams and rivers, and which therefore risk being swept away by the current, tend to assemble their homes by sticking quite heavy sand and pebbles together. Those that live in lakes and ponds usually use vegetable matter which is light or even buoyant and which is therefore easily carried around. The few free-swimming varieties build tubular sheds on the undersides of stones, submerged tree roots and so on, retreating into them to rest when danger threatens or when the time comes for them to pupate.

The suits of armour the caddis larvae make for themselves may provide some protection from passing trout but certainly do not put off the fish altogether. Autopsies on fish often produce substantial numbers of these grubs, complete with their cases.

Caddis pupae

Having sealed themselves in, caddis larvae pupate within their cases, taking anything from a few days to a month or more to do so. When they emerge, the pupae are unable to feed but will have developed a strong pair of legs with which they can swim to the surface or crawl up emergent vegetation in order to hatch. Again, they are highly munchable morsels, much beloved of trout, and many of them perish as they move up through the water.

The adult caddis

Most caddis flies hatch in the evening, around dusk or just after dark. The grannom, which usually appears at about lunch time on early-season April days, is the only caddis eaten by trout which hatches in the daytime.

Adult caddis flies are somewhat moth-like insects, with two pairs of wings each and, generally, very long antennae. They vary in size from about a quarter of an inch to about an inch in length, and in colour from greyish yellow to plain or mottled brown. Perhaps surprisingly, the trout show no interest at all in most of them, but the thirty or so species they do eat seem to attract them chiefly because of the difficulty they have in getting airborne; they flutter and scutter about on the water's surface, making the most awful fuss and sending tell-tale telegraphic rings trembling out across the water. The trout appear to find such performances quite irresistible, and slash at the panicking flies with great excitement and ferocity.

Stoneflies

The flies in our fourth group, the hard-winged flies or stoneflies, are much more localized than those in the other three groups, being found chiefly in and around fast-flowing, rocky-bottomed rivers in the Midlands and in the north of England.

Stonefly creepers

Eggs deposited by female stoneflies on the surface of the water sink to the bottom and attach themselves to any solid object they may find there. The nymphs – or 'creepers' – that hatch from them are sturdy creatures which clamber around their rocky domains, looking not unlike large nymphs of up-winged flies except that they have only two tails as opposed to the up-winged nymph's three, and quite long antennae on their heads.

Trout like stonefly nymphs. Fly fishers do not, because their naturally confident crawling on stones and boulders buffeted by turbulent torrents is almost impossible to represent with an artificial fly.

Adult stoneflies

When they are fully grown, stonefly nymphs crawl ashore to hatch into winged adults which may live for days or even weeks among the rocks on the riverbank, on dry stone walls, on trees and posts, on almost anything that will provide them with adequate camouflage and with the shelter they need.

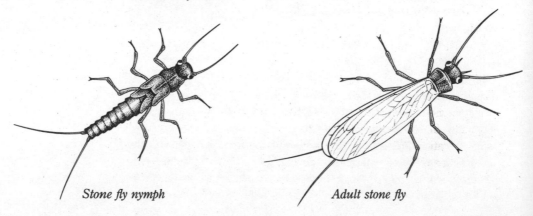

Stone fly nymph   *Adult stone fly*

Adult stoneflies have four hard, shiny wings each, which they fold over their backs almost like protective shells when at rest. The females' wings are generally much better developed than the males' which, in some species, are too small to be of any real use.

Stoneflies mate on the ground rather than in flight, the females then returning to the water to lay their eggs. It is this latter process that really endears them to trout and to fly fishers, for they usually make the most awful fuss about it, flopping down on to the water, scuttling along on the surface, bumping about and generally making a considerable commotion.

Etceteras

Beyond these four groups of flies there is an assortment of other aquatic and terrestrial creatures with which trout supplement their diets more or less opportunistically.

Small fish

It used to be thought that 'cannibalistic', fish-eating trout were necessarily old and cantankerous, ostracized elder statesmen of their communities, lurking in the depths and snapping, pike-like, at their nephews and nieces. In truth, though, most trout eat smaller fish from time to time. Lake and reservoir trout, in particular, are very partial to 'needle fry', the tiny, juvenile offspring of the coarse fish that abound in most stillwaters. The fry hatch in the spring and often shoal just beneath the surface in June and July, creating great glittering, shimmering clouds of protein which provide easy pickings for hungry browns and rainbows. And, in the autumn, when other food forms are scarce and the trout are building up their reserves of fat for the coming winter and for their breeding season, they will harry the larger coarse fish fry which congregate in the shallow margins of most big lakes, crashing through the shoals and returning at leisure to pick off small fish killed or injured in the initial charges.

Corixae

The corixa, the aptly named 'lesser water boatman', is a beetle-like creature no more than about half an inch long. It is equipped with two very prominent oar-like paddles with which it rows itself about. It is common in shallow water in lakes and reservoirs. Its personal administration presents it with a permanent problem, for it is air-breathing and has to visit the surface regularly to collect a bubble of air on the fine hairs on its stomach, and then, buoyed up by its bubble, to swim back down into the water, where it hangs on to a piece of weed

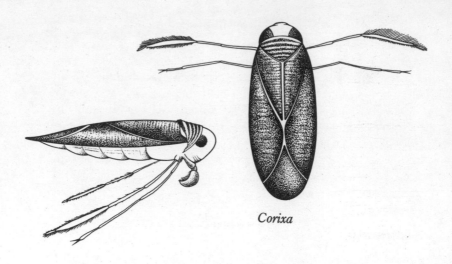

Corixa

or some such to prevent itself from floating to the top again. Trout eat significant numbers of corixae, especially in high summer when these little bugs are at their most active.

Damselflies and damselfly nymphs

Most people will be familiar with the dazzling damselflies that hover above and around most lakes and rivers throughout the early summer. The commonest – or perhaps the most obvious – are a vivid pastel blue. They differ from dragonflies in that they fold their wings along their backs when at rest, whereas dragonflies (which tend to be rather bulkier) hold their wings spread out. Stillwater trout frequently take female damselflies, which crawl down emergent vegetation into the water to lay their eggs, and will even slash at adults on the wing, flitting back and forth just above the surface. But it is the seductive wriggle of the slim, inch-long, pale green, brown or buff damselfly nymph that really excites them in stillwaters as it makes its way towards the shore to hatch.

Damselfly nymph

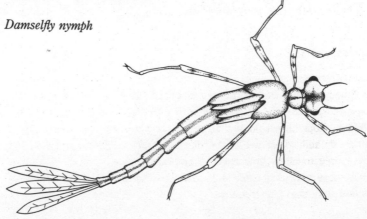

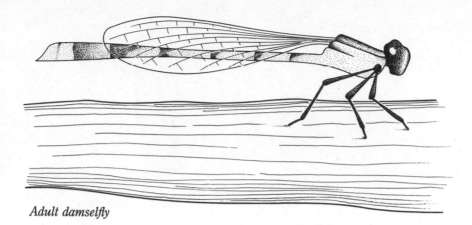

Adult damselfly

Freshwater shrimps

The freshwater shrimp is a busy little hunchback between a quarter and three-quarters of an inch long. It is a translucent, pale, fawnish colour for most of the year, but changes to opaque yellow ochre, often with rusty red blotches, during the mating season in the summer. Freshwater shrimps can be found in most fertile waters, both running and still, but trout tend to feed on them more often and more consistently in streams and rivers than in lakes and reservoirs.

Freshwater shrimp

Snails

Water snails can feature quite prominently in the diets of some trout, which feed on them both among the weed where they live for most of the year and, in stillwaters, when they float to the surface, as they often do when the water warms up in July and August. So preoccupied can trout become with snails during this annual migration that they may feed on them to the exclusion of all else. I have caught trout in high summer which felt like well-filled bean bags, their stomachs bulging and grating with the mass of molluscs that had been forced into them.

. . . and the rest

Alder larvae, ants, beetles, caterpillars, crayfish, dragonflies, earthworms, freshwater limpets and mussels, grubs, moths and zooplankton – clouds of myriad minute crustaceans and water fleas which multiply prodigiously in some stillwaters in the summer; all these can and do feature in the diets of trout from time to time, and serve only to show how catholic are our quarry's tastes – and how much more fun our fishing can be if we have some understanding of its predilections and preferences.

CHAPTER FOUR

Tackling Up

There is something magical about a proper tackle shop. By a 'proper' tackle shop, I do not mean one of those smart emporia with deep-pile carpet on the floor, a sparse selection of gleaming rods neatly arranged in polished racks along the wall, tended by besuited assistants who sidle up to ask how they can help you the minute you walk through the door. Such places make me nervous.

Nor – much as I respect coarse anglers and the shooting fraternity – do I mean those shops that deal chiefly in bait and bait boxes, rod rests, roach poles and great green umbrellas, or in shotguns and air rifles, cartridge belts and country clothing. Their concessions to game fishing are usually confined to a few ill-chosen trout rods, a choice of two or three reels and a largely depleted box of tatty flies all tucked away in one corner. As soon as you cross their thresholds, you know that they are unlikely to have what you really want, that – kindly and concerned as they may be – their staff will be quite unable to advise on choice of rod, line or fly, let alone on the state of the river or the prospects for tomorrow, and that you will leave almost at once having bought either nothing at all or, worse still, something you did not really want.

No, a proper tackle shop is one run almost for the love of it by people passionate about fly fishing. The piscatorial paraphernalia often inexpertly laid out in its cramped window acts as a magnet, drawing us from afar or stopping us in our tracks as we pass by. Inside, it may be a bit of a jumble, with dozens of rods, reels, fly lines, landing nets, leaders, scissors, zingers, priests, floatant, sinkant, mucilin, hooks, hackles, furs, feathers, silks and tinsels, and hundreds of flies in countless trays, all jostling for space. There will be no pressure to buy, and we will be allowed to browse indefinitely.

At quiet times, those behind the counter will be more than ready for a natter about what's new in tackle, who's fared how and where, and about how the local waters are fishing and which flies are doing best. Advice, when sought, will be sound, practical and freely given. And there will usually be some facility for trying a rod before buying it, which is essential if we are not to find ourselves stuck with one with which we are uncomfortable or which is unsuited to our purpose.

The range of rods, reels, fly lines and ancillary bits and pieces available to the fly fisher is vast and potentially daunting. The little rod and light line that may be perfect for flicking tiny flies on to small streams are less well suited to fishing lochs or reservoirs, where long casting may be called for. And the long, supple rod that is ideal for wafting a team of flies out ahead of a drifting boat would be irritatingly inefficient on a chalk stream, where high line speed is needed to dry a floating fly and accuracy is essential if we are consistently to be able to cover feeding fish.

Specialist trout fly fishers – those who almost always fish small streams, or chalk streams, or brawling rivers, or small lakes, or who spend most of their fishing time wading the margins of reservoirs, or drifting loch-style on large stillwaters – will arm themselves with tackle designed specifically for their purposes. If you know that you are likely to fish chiefly on one particular type of water, you should do the same. To help you, a catalogue of the most appropriate tackle and flies is included at the beginning of each of the fishing chapters in this book.

But if you are unsure about the sorts of waters to which your fishing will take you, or if you wish to be able to fish a variety of types of water in a variety of styles, it is perfectly possible to put together a set of tackle which should stand you in good stead in most circumstances, and that is what we shall consider here.

Since the fly fisher's rod is the most obvious item of his equipment, it may seem logical to choose a rod first. In fact, it is not. It is the type of fly line used that will be most closely related to the type of fishing we mean to do, and the fly line is therefore the cornerstone of our tackle. The rod and reel must be matched to it.

Fly lines

In the simplest terms, lines used for coarse and sea fishing are really no more than lengths of cord with which the terminal tackle – hooks, weights, floats and so on – is connected to the rod or reel, and thus to the angler. In casting, the coarse or sea rod is used as a lever, the terminal tackle being thrown out over the water, pulling the line with it as it goes. The essential requirements of lines for coarse or sea fishing are that they should be thin enough and smooth enough to be pulled easily from the reel and through the rod rings, and that they should be strong enough to handle the biggest fish the angler may expect to catch.

A fly line is very different. As we shall see when we come to consider casting, a trout fly and the length of nylon it is attached to weigh next to nothing and cannot be thrown any distance. The weight necessary to carry them out over the water must therefore be built into the fly line. To complicate matters further, various styles of fly fishing call for the weight to be distributed in different ways along the fly line's length. This distribution of weight produces different fly line 'profiles'.

Because very little of the fly line's weight is out beyond the tip ring of the rod when we begin to cast, a fly rod is designed as a 'spring' rather than as a 'lever'. Within obvious boundaries, a lever can throw almost any weight, from the lightest to the heaviest, without suffering damage. The same cannot be said for a spring: too light a weight will fail to load it; too heavy a weight will kill its springiness and may even cause it to break. For this reason, fly lines are available in a range of weights, and a line must be matched to a rod designed for lines of that weight.

And, because we may wish to fish our flies at the water's surface, just beneath it, in mid-water or deep down, fly lines are made in an assortment of densities, some floating, some sinking slowly and some sinking quickly. There are even composite lines in which the front part of the line sinks while the rest floats.

In order that it may be able to meet all these requirements, a fly line generally consists of a braided dacron core with a smooth plastic coating built up over it. The coating is sometimes impregnated with teflon or some other dry lubricant, to make it glide smoothly through the rod rings. All of which begins to explain why there is such a bewildering range of fly lines available and why they cost so much more than ordinary coarse or sea fishing lines do.

The fly fisher's choice of line is simplified by the tackle trade's use of a coding system. Every fly line is described by a series of letters and numbers – for example DT6F or WF7N – which are easy to read when you understand them. The first two letters indicate the line's profile; the number shows its weight, and must match the similar marking on the rod with which it is to be used; the last letter or letters indicate the line's density.

Profiles

A line may be described as DT (double-tapered), WF (weight forward), ST (shooting taper or, more commonly, shooting head) or L (level). Double-tapered lines are usually thirty yards (say, twenty-five metres) long. Their sixty-six-foot middle sections – their 'bellies' – are level and quite thick and heavy, tapering down for ten feet at each end to a fine, level, two-foot point.

It is often said that a double-tapered line will present a fly more delicately than a weight forward or a shooting head, and that it offers the added advantage of being reversible; when the plastic coating begins to wear and crack, the line can be turned around on the reel, the back end becoming the front end and vice versa. After many years of

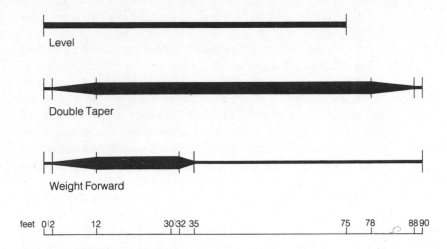

Level

Double Taper

Weight Forward

feet 0|2   12   30:32 35   75   78   88 90

Fly-line profiles

blind acceptance of these theses, I now question them. The difference in delicacy of presentation between a double-taper and a weight forward seems to me to be very marginal. And experience suggests that by the time the front half of a double-tapered line has begun to wear, so much of the plasticizer will have evaporated from the back half that its own life will have become strictly limited. In addition, much of the wear and tear on a fly line occurs around the middle of it, where it flexes close to the tip ring of the rod during casting; and the middle is the middle, whichever end you are using.

Weight forward lines are also around thirty yards long but, as their name suggests, the greater part of their weight is built into the front thirty feet or so, the back sixty feet being fine, level line which will slip easily through the rings of a fly rod. Their chief attraction is that, with a little practice, they enable the fly fisher to cast further than he would be able to with a double-tapered line. A weight forward line cannot, of course, be reversed on the reel.

Fly line manufacturers play around endlessly with the design of the bellies of weight forward lines, making them longer or shorter and adjusting their tapers, in a constant quest for improved performance. Such experimentation and refinement are of considerable benefit to the specialist fly fisher, but it must be said that some of the lines thus produced require a reasonable degree of proficiency on the part of the caster if they are to be used to best effect, and that the novice may find them a little difficult to control.

A shooting head is really little more than the front third to a half of a double-tapered line, fastened at its thickest point to a fine running line, usually of braided nylon or flattened nylon monofilament. To cast it, you work out line until the butt end of the fly line is a foot or eighteen inches beyond the tip ring of the rod, load the rod fully and then allow it to 'fire' the shooting head out across the water, towing the fine, smooth-running line behind it.

The advantage a shooting head offers is distance. The penalty paid is in lack of delicacy. Even the most expert caster will have relatively little control over a shooting head once he has launched it towards the horizon, and will be able to do very little about the splash with which it almost inevitably arrives on the water. It is also a fact that the backing – or 'shooting' – line used with shooting heads is often prone to tangles and that many people find it uncomfortable to handle.

Level fly lines are just what their name implies – simple lengths of level fly line. Because they offer no benefit of any sort over double-tapered or weight forward fly lines or shooting heads, they are almost unobtainable nowadays. They are occasionally used for trolling – trailing a lure deep down behind a boat, which involves virtually no casting and which can hardly be described as 'fly fishing'.

For the newcomer to fly fishing, I would suggest that an ordinary weight forward line or two will probably meet most requirements.

Fly line weights

The weight of a fly line is expressed in terms of the weight in grains of its first thirty feet, excluding the two feet of level line at the point. This weight is represented on fly lines and fly rods by the symbol #. Fly lines range in weight from #2 to #13. As approximations, lines in the range #2 to #4 are very light and are chiefly used for stream and small river fishing; lines in the range #5 to #7 may be termed 'general-purpose' and can be used on all sorts of waters, from small rivers to loughs and reservoirs; #8 and #9 lines are rather heavy and indelicate for trout fishing, but are sometimes used on reservoirs when the ability to cast long distances may seem important; and lines in the range #10 to #13 are intended chiefly for salmon fishing.

I own no lines lighter than #5 or heavier than #7. For a single, general-purpose set of tackle I would choose a #6 floating line, because surface fishing requires a little extra delicacy, and #7 sinking lines, because they might allow me to cast a yard or two further.

Fly line densities

In the past few years there has been an enormous increase in the range of fly line densities. Until quite recently we were limited to floating lines, slow sinkers, medium sinkers and quick sinkers.

Nowadays, even floaters float differently, some floating high on the

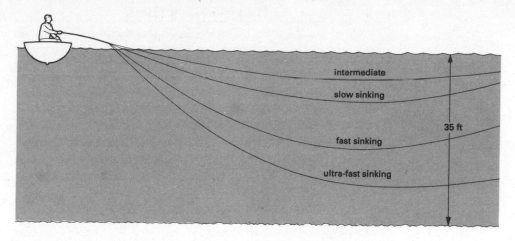

Relative sinking rates for sinking fly-lines – depths reached after one minute

water and others floating in the surface film. There are neutral density lines which float just beneath the surface; intermediate lines, which sink very slowly (1–1½ inches per second); slow sinking lines (1½–2½ inches per second); fast sinking lines (3½–4½ inches per second) and ultra- or super-fast sinking lines (4½–7½ inches per second).

In addition, there are so-called 'sink-tip' lines, of which the first ten feet sink, the remainder floating on the surface. They are useful for salmon and sea trout fishing, and for keeping one's flies in the water while at the same time retaining control of the line when fishing on windy days. Being made up from two lines of different densities, they are a little difficult to cast with and are therefore probably best left alone by the novice.

Returning to the line coding system, fly line densities are described as 'F' (floating), 'N' (neutral), 'I' (intermediate), 'S' (sinking – with no differentiation between sinking speeds, apart from the occasional use of 'UFS' for ultra- or super-fast sinking) and F/S (sink-tip).

The very casual and occasional fly fisher, or the person who only ever fishes streams and small rivers, can probably get by with a single floating line. But if you expect to fish stillwaters at all, and especially if you plan to fish them early or late in the season when the water is cold and the fish are deep down, you will need a fast sinker as well. And if you anticipate fishing chiefly or frequently on reservoirs, you may even find it necessary to add a super-fast sinking line to your armoury.

From all this, it should have become apparent that the DT6F and WF7N lines quoted as examples at the beginning of this section are a double-tapered, 6-weight floating line, and a weight forward, 7-weight, neutral density line respectively, and that the lines needed for a general-purpose set of tackle are a WF6F, perhaps a WF7S and, just possibly, a WF7UFS.

The last important factor when considering fly lines is colour. Fly lines are available in all sorts of colours, from drab grey through various shades of brown, green, blue and peach to some quite startling oranges, pinks and yellows. Some people delude themselves that light fly lines show up against the sky less than dark ones do or that mid-grey lines mimic the evidently effective camouflage of the heron's plumage. The truth of the matter is that, for most of the time, trout see a floating line not against the sky but against a reflected background of the underwater world – of dark depths, underwater vegetation or the lake or river bed. It follows, therefore, that our fly lines should match such backgrounds, which argues for mid browns and greens. The same goes for sinking lines, which also tend to be seen against dark backgrounds.

The only advantage offered by a light-coloured floating line is that it may be easier for us to see it against the inkiness of the water, which may help us to detect a trout's interest in our sunk fly.

For each fly line you buy, you will need an appropriate amount of backing line. Backing line is usually made of braided nylon. It acts as a reserve for when a particularly fit or ferocious fish tears line from the reel (oh, happy day!), and it serves to pad out the spool of the reel and to reduce the extent to which the fly line acquires 'memory coils' – those nasty, spring-like coils that develop if a fly line is wound too tightly round too small a drum for too long. You will want between fifty and a hundred metres of backing line for each fly line, depending upon the size of the reel you are using.

Having chosen your line or lines, you can now select a rod to match them.

Trout fly rods

Trout fly rods have been made from a wide range of materials over the years. The earliest recorded British rods, described in Dame Juliana Berners' *Treatyse of Fysshinge Wyth an Angle*, first published in 1496, were thirteen or fourteen feet long, with butts of blackthorn or medlar, middle sections of ash, hazel or willow, and tips of hazel. During the next two hundred years, lighter whole cane and whalebone replaced dense, native woods for middle sections and tips. But it was not until the nineteenth century, when greenheart became available and was then quickly replaced by built cane, that shorter, lighter, stiffer rods, not unlike those used today, finally ousted the longer, heavier and less wieldy ones that had gone before.

Built cane – male Tonkin bamboo cut and planed into triangular-sectioned strips which are then glued together – is still quite widely used by those who are prepared to accept a weight penalty in return for a rod which has a natural and traditional feel to it. But most fly fishers welcomed the introduction of man-made materials in the 1970s – fibreglass and then carbon fibre, boron and kevlar. Of these four, carbon fibre has proved the most popular. It can be fashioned into extraordinarily light and slender rods which can comfortably be used all day, which cut through the wind without effort and which, in the hand of a competent caster, can deliver a fly over considerable distances with great accuracy and delicacy. Nowadays, the vast majority of rods on offer to fly fishers are made of carbon fibre, and so good and reasonably priced are they that there is little to be said for buying one made of anything else.

A trout fly rod is characterized by its length, the weight of the fly line it is designed to be used with and by its 'action'. Rods may be anything from six to twelve feet long. The shortest are really intended for use only on small, overgrown brooks; the longest are designed for casting teams of flies ahead of drifting boats on large lakes, lochs and reservoirs.

One of the commonest and saddest mistakes made by the well-intentioned is to buy a very short rod for a boy or for a novice woman fly fisher in the belief that it will be lighter and easier to handle than a longer one. In truth it will not, or, rather, the weight saved will be very slight and will be cancelled out completely by the rod's inferior performance. It is very much easier for anyone to put out a reasonable length of line with a rod of between eight and a half and nine and a half feet than with a six- or seven-foot 'toothpick', and the slightly longer rod will offer an added advantage in its ability to lift line cleanly from the water over bankside vegetation that may be three or four feet high.

The ideal general-purpose rod for fly fishers of any age or either sex will be made from carbon fibre and will be within three inches on either side of nine feet long.

As we have already seen, the rod must be matched to the weight of the fly line we shall use with it. Every worthwhile rod made today has the line weight or weights to which it is best suited marked on it, just above the handle, thus: #6 or #5–7. The former rating indicates that the rod is designed to be loaded with a #6 line, the latter that it will work efficiently with a #5, a #6 or a #7 line.

When people talk about a rod's action, they are talking about its springiness and about the points along its length at which it flexes most freely. Some rods - rather too many, in my view – are somewhat soft and soggy, their flexibility starting almost at their handles and increasing progressively towards their tips. Rather fewer are very stiff, their flexibility being confined largely to the third of their length nearest their tip. And, of course, there are some with 'medium' actions, with only modest flexibility in their bottom half and progressively more from their half-way point to their tip.

While a very soft rod is an abomination, giving the sensation of

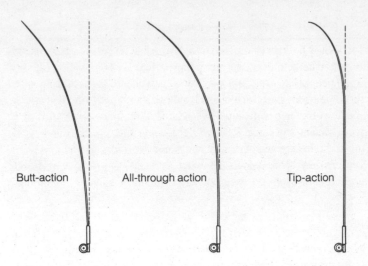

Butt-action   All-through action   Tip-action

Fly rod actions

casting with nothing more than a length of rubber hosepipe, moderately soft rods do often have the lazy action that is ideal for boat fishing on lochs and reservoirs. Stiff rods make the fly line move quickly through the air and describe tight arcs, which helps with casting into or across the wind and with the drying of floating flies, but they tend to be a little more physically demanding to use than softer rods.

The ideal all-purpose rod will be of carbon fibre, about nine feet long, rated #6–7 and with a medium action. With it, there is no reason why you should not manage perfectly well on streams and rivers, on small stillwaters and on lochs, loughs and reservoirs, both from a boat and from the bank.

Fly reels

Coarse and sea anglers cast from their reels and retrieve line on to them at the end of every cast. Fly fishers do not. Before he starts casting, the fly fisher strips line from the reel either on to the ground or into a line tray fastened to a belt around his waist. He uses this loose line to cast with and retrieves the line on to the ground or into the line tray. Even when playing trout, many fly fishers simply trap the line between the forefinger and the handle of the rod, pulling it in with the free hand and allowing it to fall, loose, around their feet.

All this being so, it must be evident that a fly reel is little more than a receptacle for line that is not in use. The essential requirements of a fly reel are that it should be big enough to accommodate the fly line and as much backing line as may be necessary, that it should have holes in the face of the drum to ventilate the line and to enable it to dry out, and that it should be light and mechanically reliable. If it has a reasonably efficient, adjustable drag, so much the better.

Some people like multiplying fly reels, in which the spool turns twice or three times for each turn of the handle, or automatic reels, in which the pulling off of line winds up a spring which can then be released by a trigger, winding the line in for you. Personally, such contraptions seem to me to be heavy, unnecessary and potentially unreliable.

You can buy spare spools for most fly reels, and will need either another reel or an extra spool for each additional fly line.

Leaders

A leader, which used to be called a 'cast', is the length of nylon monofilament used to attach the fly or flies to the fly line. It is a vital link in the chain between the fish and the fisherman and is worthy of careful consideration.

A leader must be long enough to distance the fly from the potentially fish-frightening fly line and short enough to be manageable. It must be fine enough to be effectively invisible to the trout and strong enough to withstand the sudden shock of a fierce take or a surging run. It must act in concert with the fly line, rolling over neatly and transmitting the power stored in the line right down to the fly at its tip. And it must present the fly to the fish in as natural a manner as possible.

People use all sorts of leaders, from simple lengths of level monofilament to extraordinarily complex creations made by knotting together a number of lengths of nylon of different thicknesses. While the former are only really of use for fishing lures on sinking lines, where delicacy and invisibility may be of relatively little consequence, the latter have the disadvantage of numerous knots; knots weaken nylon by up to 50 per cent and tend to pick up weed, which often puts fish off.

The simplest effective leaders are those sold in tackle shops ready made – knotless, tapered leaders, seven, nine or twelve feet long, for use with just one fly, or knotted leaders with 'droppers' (short lengths of nylon sticking out from them) for use with a team of two, three or more flies.

Especially on stillwaters, ready-made leaders can almost always be improved by putting a length of eighteen- or twenty-pound nylon monofilament between the leader and the fly line. And the 'braided butts' that are now widely available - lengths of tapered, braided nylon which go between the fly line and the leader – undoubtedly help to transmit the line's power to the leader and thus to turn the leader over neatly on to the water.

Specifications for the leaders most suitable for particular styles of fishing will be found at the beginning of each fishing chapter.

Landing nets

Although you can land trout by hand, a landing net makes the job very much easier, especially when you are fishing from a boat or a high bank, or across bankside vegetation.

I have to say that I find landing nets a damned nuisance. They tend to be unwieldy, they are awkward to carry, they always seem to be irresistibly attracted to every thorn, thistle and bit of barbed wire, they become unhooked from their fastenings with monotonous regularity and they usually refuse absolutely to unfold at just the wrong moment, when you are standing, precariously balanced on some slippery, mid-stream rock with the leviathan of a lifetime thrashing around in the raging torrent below. But we can scarcely do without them.

For river fishing and for fishing from the banks of lakes and reservoirs, I use a net with quite a short handle and two folding arms joined by a length of oiled cord. I hang it from a ring sewn high on to the back of the left shoulder of my fishing waistcoat, where it is out of the way, (almost) immune to the temptations extended to it by passing briars and brambles, and where it is readily accessible when I need it.

For boat fishing, I use one with a rigid frame and a telescopic handle which extends to about four feet. I don't hang it on anything; instead, I set it up as soon as I am in the boat and keep it optimistically to hand throughout the day.

Bits and pieces

Beyond these bare essentials – a fly line, a fly rod, a reel, a leader and a landing net – there are all sorts of bits and pieces that will prove more or less useful to the fly fisher. You will need a priest – a small club with which to administer the last rites – and a pair of scissors or snippers for cutting nylon. A pair of artery forceps is useful for removing flies from fishes' mouths. You will want a small tin of mucilin with which to keep leaders afloat; buy the red tin, not the green one, the contents of which are said to damage fly lines. For fishing with a floating fly, you will need some fly floatant – available in a bottle or as a spray – and a tub of silica gel for drying drowned flies. A putty-like mixture of Fuller's Earth, washing up liquid and glycerin is better than mud for making leaders sink; you can make it up yourself, or you can buy a tiny tub of it for an astonishing price. You will find a soft, rubber eraser useful; draw a nylon leader smoothly and steadily across it, trapping the nylon with your thumb, and you will find you have removed most of the coils from it. And, of course, you will want some flies and a fly box or two, but we shall deal with those in the next chapter.

Putting it all together

Most of those who have been fishing for some time will probably have worked out how to prepare their tackle and put it together. However, several years spent teaching newcomers to the sport suggest that rods, reels, fly lines and leaders often come with far too few instructions, and that a few notes jotted down here may save them some confusion and frustration.

When you bring your new rod home from the shop, its cork handle may well be shrink-wrapped in transparent, protective plastic. Remove it. If you do not, the grip will be hard and slippery rather than soft and comfortable, and water will seep in between the plastic and the handle, eventually causing the cork to rot.

Take the stub of a candle and rub it briskly up and down the male ferrule (or ferrules) of the rod. This will cause the male ferrule to fit smoothly, snugly and firmly into the female one and give you a secure joint. The process should be repeated at the beginning of each season.

When you put the rod together, there should be a gap of between an eighth and a quarter of an inch at the foot of the male ferrule. This is intentional and allows for gradual wearing of the ferrule without the joint becoming loose. Push the joints of the rod together firmly but without forcing them, and make sure that the rings on each section of the rod are carefully aligned.

Useful knots are illustrated in Appendix A.

If it has not been done for you in the shop, the backing line should be secured to the hub of the reel spool with a slip knot. The way in which you wind the backing – and, subsequently, the fly line – on to the reel will dictate whether you wind the reel with your right hand or with your left; this is entirely a matter for personal preference.

The backing line should be fastened to the back end of the fly line with a nail knot. (Obviously, there is no 'back end' to a double-tapered line; both ends are the same. But it is essential to get a weight forward line the right way round on the reel. Most new fly lines come wound on to plastic spools with their back ends outermost.)

I recommend strongly the use of braided butts or shorter braided loops for attaching leaders to fly lines. In either case, the tip of the fly line should be pushed two to four inches into the wide, open end of the braid – think of it as pushing a leg into a stocking. The soft plastic sleeve provided with the braided butt or loop should then be threaded on to the braid (over the 'foot') and then worked up it until it covers equal amounts of 'stocking top' (the top end of the braid) and 'thigh' (fly line). This will prevent the top end of the braid from fraying and catching in the rod rings. While not strictly necessary, you may think it helps to put a dab of superglue on the top end of the braid before running the sleeve up over it.

If you are using a braided loop, the leader can be joined to it with a 'loop-to-loop' joint, which is secure and simple, both to make and to undo.

If you are using a braided butt without a loop at the end of it, a length of eighteen- to twenty-pound nylon monofilament should be secured to its point with a nail knot, and the butt of the leader itself should be tied to this length of nylon with a four-turn blood knot.

When tying knots with nylon monofilament, always suck them for a moment or so, wetting them thoroughly, before pulling them tight and snugging them down. This lubricates the nylon and stops it abrading and forming itself into nasty little kinks.

Place the reel into its seating below the rod handle so that the line comes forward from the bottom of the drum. Seat the reel securely and tighten the fastenings – usually a pair of threaded locking rings. When you have tightened the fastenings, wiggle the reel a little and re-tighten them; if you do not, there is a risk that they will eventually come undone during casting.

Draw the line from the reel to the butt ring of the rod by the most direct route, without passing it around or across any of the bridges on the reel cage.

When threading the line through the rod rings, it helps to have the rod horizontal, with the handle resting on a table, a car boot or some such. If you rest the butt of the rod on the ground you may damage the reel, and if you let go of the line it may slip back down through all the rings, which can be irritating.

It also helps to pull some line from the reel and to fold it over, threading the folded end, rather than the point of the line or leader, through the rings. A folded end is easier to see and tends to open if released, preventing the line from slipping back down through the rings. Make sure you thread the line through each ring in turn, and that you do not take a turn around the rod between two rings. A missed ring or a turn around the rod both make casting much more difficult.

When you have threaded the line and leader right up to and through the tip ring of the rod, tie a fly to the point of the leader and either hook it to the keeper ring (the tiny ring just above the handle of most rods) or take the leader round behind the leg of the reel and up the rod again, hooking the fly to one of the rod rings. This latter system is useful when you are using long leaders because it should keep the tip of the fly line out beyond the tip ring of the rod, which will make things easier when you start to cast.

Finally, never lie a rod flat on the ground; if you do, you may be sure that somebody will tread on it eventually, which is likely to break it. And always carry a rod with its tip pointing backwards. If you carry it with the tip pointing forwards and then dig it into the ground or stub it against a tree or a post, you will break it; touching the ground with a backward-pointing tip should do no damage at all.

Clothing

There was a time when the fly fisher wore uniform – a trilby hat, a tweed jacket, a vyella shirt and a tie – and he invariably went forth with a wicker creel slung across his back. Today we are less formal, even on the smartest stretches of chalk stream, but certain simple practicalities are worth mentioning.

Overall, waterside attire should be sober and, as far as is possible, it should blend in with the backgrounds against which the fish are likely to see us. This objective is more readily attainable when we are fishing among the greens and browns of trees and bushes than when we must inevitably appear silhouetted against the sky, as when fishing from a boat, for example, or from a bank devoid of vegetation.

A broad-brimmed hat or a cap with a large peak will shade the eyes and make it very much easier to see into the water.

You will need a pair of polaroid sunglasses, both to protect your eyes from flying flies and to reduce glare from the water's surface – essential if you are to see the fish you are fishing for.

Waders should have felt or studded soles rather than cleated ones, which tend to slip. And they are as useful for kneeling in mud or on damp grass as they are for keeping one's legs dry in the water.

You may choose to carry your tackle in a bag or in a multi-pocketed fishing waistcoat. Many people find bags a bit cumbersome; a good fishing waistcoat will enable you to organize your tackle efficiently and to have it ready to hand. It should have a three-inch square piece of sheepskin pinned to it to accommodate used flies while they dry out; the hooks of flies returned to their boxes while still wet will rust, as will those adjacent to them.

Do remember that it is almost always much colder out on the water than on the shore. Far better to put on too many layers of clothing to start with and then to shed them successively than to spend the day miserably seeking refuge from a biting wind. And don't forget a waterproof jacket and a pair of waterproof over-trousers. Warmth and comfortable dryness are essential if fishing is to be fun.

Finally, do remember that you must have a National Rivers Authority rod licence before you may fish for trout anywhere in England or Wales, whether or not the water you are fishing is private. A licence may be obtained from almost any tackle shop or, often, from the fishery itself. No rod licence is required for trout fishing in Scotland. The rules in Northern Ireland and in the Republic of Ireland are a little complicated; details of current requirements may be obtained from The Fisheries Conservancy Board for Northern Ireland, 1 Mahon Road, Portadown, Co. Armagh and from The Department of Fisheries and Forestry, Agriculture House, Kildare Street, Dublin 2.

CHAPTER FIVE

Trout Flies

Trout flies are seductive little objects, often as seductive to fly fishers as to trout. Made of fur, feather, floss and tinsel, they are tied in an almost infinite variety of colours, shapes and sizes, a variety as likely to bemuse and confuse as to present the fly fisher with his panacea, the answer to his prayers.

Befuddled by the profusion of patterns to be had, the novice tends to indulge in brief love affairs. He has a good day with one fly and sets it on a pedestal, extolling it above all others until it fails him. When it does so, he will blame the weather, the state of the water or the dourness of the fish – anything except his 'infallible discovery' – until some other confection catches his fancy.

Gradually, it will dawn on him that no one pattern offers certain success, that changing conditions call for changes of flies. Intelligent fly selection requires logical reasoning, and the ability to reason logically is born of experience. With little experience to guide him, he will indulge in a lucky dip, picking this pattern or that on a whim. And he will start to collect flies, tying or buying an endless succession of patterns, arranging them in neat, serried ranks, preening and admiring them, adding box after box until he almost needs a wheelbarrow in which to cart them to the waterside.

Eventually, when he is able to apply reasoning based on real experience, he may conclude that it is the 'driver', as much as the fly, that catches fish, that good presentation is every bit as important as sensible fly selection, perhaps more so, and that the range of dressings needed for any particular type of fishing is really quite limited. Perhaps he will rationalize his collection, abandoning variety for variety's sake. He may reach a point at which he is content with a dozen or so flies stuffed into an old tobacco tin, or he may even become a 'one fly' man, content to see the season through with but a single pattern.

But let us start at the beginning.

In what follows, I shall seek only to explain the differences between various types of flies and the circumstances under which each type is most commonly used. Lists of specific patterns for particular kinds of water and for particular fishing styles will be found at the beginning of each of the five fishing chapters and in the colour plates.

Dry flies and wet flies

Even non-anglers have usually heard that there are 'dry flies' and 'wet flies'. The difference between the two groups is simple – a dry fly is a fly that is intended to float and to be taken by fish from the surface of the water; a 'wet fly' is a fly that is intended to sink and to be taken beneath the surface. Between these two groups there is now a third one, 'damp flies', which is gaining rapidly in popularity. These are flies designed to float in, rather than on, the surface film, or to hang from it.

In the interests of lightness, dry flies and damp flies are usually dressed on hooks made of fine wire. Wet flies are generally dressed on relatively heavy hooks.

It was the practice at one time to tie dry flies on hooks the eyes of which were turned upwards – up-eyed hooks – and wet flies on down-eyed ones. This differentiation is much less widely used nowadays and the direction in which a hook's eye is bent is no longer a certain indication as to how a particular fly is intended to be used.

Dry flies tend to be light and fluffy, with bushy hackle fibres spread out as collars around their necks to help them float. Damp flies may use teased-out fur to keep them just afloat, or they may be more or less sparsely dressed with a tuft of deer's hair or a small ball of ethafoam or some other buoyant material tied in at their heads. Wet flies are usually streamlined in shape, to help them penetrate the water's surface and sink quickly.

Most dry flies are 'imitative' patterns, designed to imitate or suggest insects that trout take habitually from the water's surface – the duns and spinners of up-winged flies, black gnats, daddy-long-legs and adult caddis flies, adult stoneflies, ants, beetles, moths and even small fish, which often float at the surface when recently killed or injured.

Similarly, damp flies are usually intended to represent the hatching, stillborn or drowned creatures that trout so often feed on – hatching up-winged nymphs, hatching midge or caddis pupae, drowned adult midges, hawthorn flies (which tend to sink very slowly having been blown on to the water), or snails hanging from the surface film.

Wet flies may be intended to represent or suggest the creatures trout feed on beneath the water's surface – the nymphs of up-winged flies, midge or caddis larvae or pupae, small fish, corixae, damselfly nymphs, freshwater shrimps, or alder larvae – or they may be 'attractor patterns' or 'lures', designed to take advantage of the trout's natural curiosity or aggression rather than its feeding habits.

Imitative patterns

Of course, it is effectively impossible to imitate a natural creature accurately by spinning fur, feather, floss and tinsel on to a hook. Less obviously, serious attempts to do so very rarely enhance our chances of catching fish. From time to time, imaginative, inventive and skilful fly dressers have assembled what, to human eyes, appear to be astonishingly lifelike representations of various insects. Ingenious as they may be, such artefacts are often ignored by trout which tend to prefer more impressionistic offerings.

The Chinaman

The late Dick Walker, a most talented, observant and analytical angler, suggested that an imitative pattern's success depended upon the inclusion in its dressing of one or more 'trigger points'. He used to illustrate this by drawing a very simple caricature of a face – no more than a U-shape with a squashed triangle for a hat and two short lines sloping inwards and downwards for eyes. Everyone he showed it to identified it as a chinaman. He would then explain that the 'trigger points' were the conical 'hat', the slit eyes and, to a lesser extent, the rounded face shape, which acted as a vehicle for the other two features.

The same principles, he said, applied to imitative trout flies. So long as the general size, shape and colour were about right, and provided the pattern incorporated a couple of 'trigger points' – the breathing filaments at the head of a midge pupa, for example, the gangling legs of the hawthorn fly or the daddy-long-legs, or the flash of silver in the body of a corixa or a small fish – trout would generally take it without a second glance.

It should also be said that 'trigger points' can be behavioural rather than physical. If an artificial up-winged dun drifts on the water's surface just as the natural does, if an artificial caddis fly scutters convincingly, if a midge pupa can be made to hang inert, immediately beneath the surface film, or if artificial shrimps, corixae or damselfly nymphs can be made to swim almost exactly like their living counterparts, these behavioural characteristics will play at least as great a part in deceiving the fish as the flies' appearances do. Which is why experienced fly fishers place as much emphasis on presentation – the manner in which a fly is presented to the fish – as on the fly itself.

It is the effectiveness of impressionistic rather than strictly imitative trout flies, and the importance of the ways in which they are presented to trout, that has led to the development of widely differing styles of fly dressing in different parts of the country.

In Wales and the West Country, where rain-fed spate rivers stumble and tumble across countless stickles, it is more important that a dry fly should stay afloat than that it should resemble closely the insect it is intended to imitate. West Country dry flies tend, therefore, to be bushy and fully hackled, so that they may bob on the stream without being drowned.

On smooth southern chalk streams, though, where the water slides, gin clear, towards the waiting fish, giving them all the time in the world to study would-be food before accepting or rejecting it, a dry fly must be as sparse and delicate as its natural counterpart if it is to pass muster.

And on brawling northern rivers, where – for reasons we do not fully understand – up-winged flies seem to hatch and fly off in an instant, offering the trout little opportunity to take them as they float, there is a tradition of fishing imitative wet flies, sparse spider patterns, in or just beneath the surface film.

Appropriate imitative patterns, whether dry, damp or wet, can be effective on all types of water, from lakes, lochs, loughs and reservoirs to streams and rivers in their various forms. Interestingly and apparently inexplicably, strictly imitative wet flies – midge and caddis pupae, as examples, and shrimps and corixae – usually prove less useful on Highland lochs and Irish loughs than more general food-suggesting or traditional patterns.

Food-suggesting patterns

Some flies designed to be taken as food by trout are markedly more impressionistic than others, to the extent that they may be intended to represent a range of food forms or even simply to look edible. Many of the dry caddis flies fall into the former category, as do patterns like the Dambuster, the Stick Fly and the Ombudsman, all of which are reminiscent of caddis larvae. The Black and Peacock Spider is a classic general food-suggesting pattern, as are such dressings as Eric's Beetle, Tom Ivens' Green and Yellow Nymph and the Orange Partridge.

Traditional and attractor patterns

Almost all traditional and attractor patterns are wet flies. They fall into two broad groups. The majority have quite neat, cigar-shaped bodies of floss, fur or tinsel, wings – usually of quill or other feather fibre – sloping back across their bodies, and somewhat stylized 'beard' hackles sweeping downwards and backwards from their 'throats'; they may also have feather fibre tails. Rather fewer are tied 'palmer', with a hackle wound up the lengths of their bodies from tail to shoulder. The bushiest of these are often called 'bumbles'.

The origins of traditional wet flies are varied. Many were designed specifically for loch fishing in Scotland and Ireland, the angler drifting on the breeze, casting a team of three, four or even five flies on a short line ahead of his boat. Some are scaled-down salmon or sea trout patterns, used for the same purpose. While they can sometimes be useful on rivers or fished from the banks of lakes, lochs or reservoirs, they are chiefly used for boat fishing.

Winged traditional wet flies are usually fished on the point of a leader, or on one or more of the middle droppers. Palmered patterns and bumbles are usually fished as 'bob flies' on the top dropper in a team.

Some winged traditional patterns are intended or imagined to represent natural insects. The Blae and Black and the Invicta are examples, the former being particularly useful during early-season hatches of black midges, the latter doing stalwart service on summer evenings when trout are feeding on hatching caddis pupae. Others, like the Alexandra, the Butcher, the Cardinal, the Dunkeld and the Parmachenee Belle, neither represent nor suggest any creature known to nature. One can only suppose that they rely for their effectiveness upon the extent to which they arouse the trout's curiosity or aggressiveness.

Lures

I suppose it could be argued that all trout flies are 'lures', but nowadays the word is widely understood to mean a pattern dressed on a long-shank or tandem hook (two hooks tied one behind the other) which is not intended to represent or suggest any particular item of the trout's diet.

Modern lure fishing is chiefly a product of an enormous increase in interest in stillwater trout fishing since the Second World War. Although they are used for sea trout fishing on rivers, and perhaps for salmon fishing, if a salmon fly is counted as a lure, lure fishing for trout is confined chiefly to lakes and reservoirs.

There are those who say that, even on reservoirs, lure fishing is not fly fishing at all; some, huffing and puffing, and likening it to mackerel fishing or spinning, say it is not 'sporting'. I even know one charming and eminent elder of the sport who asserts that fishing an imitative wet pattern is not fly fishing but 'fly-rod fishing' or 'artificial bait fishing' – because 'flies have wings and anything without wings cannot therefore be a fly'.

Such petty pedantry serves our sport ill, provoking only sterile argument and causing divisions where there should be none. Fly fishing is meant to be fun and, at the right time and in the right place, lure fishing can be every bit as much fun as any other form of fly fishing. I would only be concerned if an angler fished lures to the exclusion of all else – not because to do so would be 'unsporting' but because I would fear that he was missing much of the fun to be had from (sometimes) more imaginative forms of the sport.

With a vast range of silks, furs, feathers, chenilles, hair, tinsels, wires and other materials available to them, countless fly dressers have run riot over the years, creating an astonishing number of apparently different lures. I say 'apparently' because the truth of the matter is that most lures are really no more than variations on themes.

By and large, a black lure is a black lure whether you call it an Ace of Spades, a Black Bear's Hair, a Black Chenille, a Christmas Tree, a Black and Orange Marabou, a Poodle, a Sweeny Todd or a Viva. On days when the trout are predisposed to take black lures, they will probably take any of these, provided the chosen pattern is fished at the right depth and speed. Similarly, the Appetizer, the Baby Doll, the White Marabou, the Missionary and the Persuader are all essentially white lures. And there are further ranges of gaudy lures, like the Breathalyser, Chief Needabeh, Goldie, the Leprechaun, Mickey Finn, the Murk-Meister, the Nailer, and flashy lures, like the Orange Bucktail, the Squirrel and Silver and the Whiskey Fly. Pick any one from each of these four groups and you will be well on the way to having a selection of lures with which to see the season through.

Relatively recent developments in stillwater trouting have produced separate groups of heavily leaded lures and buoyant ones.

Lead-headed 'jigs' have been used in the United States for many years. They were introduced into Britain as Leadhead patterns by the late Richard Walker and as Beastie lures by Geoffrey Bucknall, and then popularized as Dog Nobblers by Trevor Housby. Their tantalizingly sinuous up-and-down movement in the water can be irresistible to trout, but even the most liberal minded admit that they are on the margins of what constitutes 'fly fishing' and they are actually banned on some waters. And, beware; so heavy are they that they can be very difficult – and sometimes dangerous – to cast.

The opposite of the Dog Nobbler is Gordon Fraser's so-called Booby Nymph and a growing number of other buoyant lures. These patterns enable reservoir anglers to fish their flies right on the bottom, where trout often feed, without becoming caught in the weed and other obstructions that are so often found there. They are almost always fished on quick-sinking lines. When the line reaches the bottom, the buoyant lure floats above the end of it, diving temptingly with each pull on the line. Again, barely 'fly fishing', but a fascinating and effective way of catching reservoir trout that might otherwise be uncatchable, especially early and late in the season.

Mini lures

The boom in competitive reservoir fly fishing over the past ten years or so has produced dramatic changes in flies and fly fishing tactics. Rules for most competitions are based on those that have governed international matches for fifty years or more and – having their roots in the traditions of loch-style fishing – they are strict, particularly with regard to the sizes of hooks and flies that may be used; in most matches, long-shank and tandem hooks are banned.

Keen to press proven reservoir lures into service, competitive fly fishers have developed a range of 'mini lures' – standard lure patterns tied on ordinary shanked hooks, which meet the requirements of match rules. Such dressings defy our definition of a lure as 'a pattern dressed on a long-shank or tandem hook'; equally, they cannot be considered to be traditional wet flies. So perhaps we should place them in a group of their own.

Hook sizes

Trout flies are tied on hooks ranging in size on the Redditch scale from 4 (enormous) to 24 (minute). Hooks are generally available only in even-numbered sizes.

Those who tie their own flies will know that manufacturers seem to delight in producing a constant stream of new hook shapes – keel hooks, nymph hooks, sedge hooks, grub hooks, mayfly hooks, midge hooks, emerger hooks, hooks named after well-known anglers – the list is almost endless and serves only to complicate an already somewhat complex problem. The making of quite ordinary hooks against the Redditch scale seems to be a very approximate business, apparently similar patterns from different makers varying quite significantly in size. The addition to the range of more and more gimmicky (and unnecessary) new hooks only adds to the confusion of sizes and shapes.

Such irritations should be of little concern to those who buy their flies rather than tie them. Most commercially tied flies are dressed on sensibly shaped standard-shanked or long-shanked hooks, the shank of

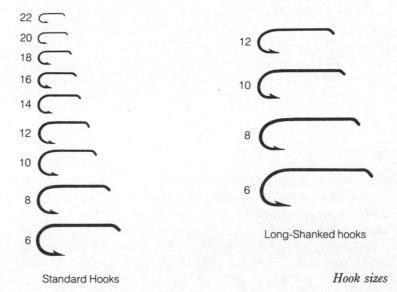

Standard Hooks

Long-Shanked hooks

Hook sizes

the former being about half the length of that of the latter.

Flies for stream and river fishing are generally tied on standard-shanked hooks in the range 12 to 18. Mayflies, which are much bigger than most of the other creatures trout eat, may be represented on special mayfly hooks or on 10 standard-shank or 12 long-shank ones, and some tiny artificials may be tied on 20s, 22s or even 24s. But, again, beware; seductive as these minute offerings may be, it can be difficult to obtain a firm hold with such small hooks, and the very fine wire of which they are necessarily made is likely to bend or break if a large or lively fish is played roughly.

I think there is a tendency for lake, loch and reservoir fly fishers to use flies tied on hooks that are rather too large. Most of my stillwater flies are tied on hooks in the size range 10 to 16 with those tied on 12s and 14s being used for perhaps 90 per cent of the time. Virtually all of the lures and long-bodied nymphs I use are tied on long-shanked 10s and 12s.

Fly boxes

I know some people who carry their half-dozen or so flies in tatty tins in their pockets and others who stagger to the waterside weighed down by huge, beautifully varnished wooden boxes which open up to display layer upon layer of foam-lined trays, each containing hundreds of neatly arranged patterns. Presumably, the former sees his flies as no more than a means to an end while the latter takes some pride in his collection. It is, of course, a matter of preference. Most of us find compromises somewhere between these two extremes.

My own view is that a fly box should be small enough to fit into the largest pocket of a fishing waistcoat – say, not much more than six inches by four; that it should be rigid enough to protect its contents against crushing – soft 'fly wallets' are hopeless in this respect; that the flies in it should be well ventilated (as a guard against rusty hooks) and clearly visible; and that the flies should be sufficiently securely held or contained to prevent them from being blown away when the box is opened.

It seems to me that different kinds of fly require different types of box if all these objectives are to be met. For river fishing I have a couple of boxes, each with a dozen dry fly compartments with transparent, spring-loaded lids in one half, and a flat ethafoam lining for nymphs in the other. Three boxes with ridged ethafoam linings on both sides hold my stillwater nymphs, dry flies and lures. And a single box with sixteen transparent flip-lid compartments in the base (for palmers and bumbles) and about fifty clips in the lid (for winged patterns) holds all my traditional and attractor patterns for boat fishing on lochs and reservoirs.

Tying one's own

All the fly patterns mentioned and illustrated in this book are available from tackle shops and mail order firms, and they will stand you in good stead. But there is enormous pleasure and satisfaction to be had from tying your own flies, perhaps even flies you have designed yourself. It really is not difficult – anyone who can tie his or her shoelaces and thread a line through the rings of a rod can tie flies that will catch trout; and doing so offers a number of advantages.

Cost is one of them.

Although the initial capital outlay required for the purchase of a set of tools and the materials to tie a reasonable range of patterns may seem quite high, the tools will last a lifetime (I have had almost all of mine for over thirty years) and you will be able to tie literally hundreds of flies from an assortment of hooks, a couple of spools of silk, a few packets of furs and feathers and a small range of wires and tinsels.

Quality is another.

The professional fly dresser must work quickly and cannot afford to discard usable materials. The amateur can usually take as much time as he wants to get his patterns absolutely right and, because he uses relatively small quantities of materials, he can afford to use only the best. Professionals must also tie flies that fishermen will buy, which often leads them to over-dress their patterns, using too much fur for the bodies, too much feather for wings and tails and winding on hackles that are altogether too bushy and bulky.

Variety is a third.

A professional fly dresser must limit the range of flies he ties. He will tend, therefore, to avoid patterns that are complicated or time consuming, or that are not widely known. With time at his disposal, the amateur can fiddle around with the most intricate and esoteric artificials for the sheer fun of it.

There is no space here to give detailed instruction on fly tying, but it is a craft that can be learnt from books; a few of the best of them are listed in the Bibliography at the end of this one. And fly-tying classes are run by and for enthusiasts throughout the country.

Do try 'rolling your own'; it is an intriguing hobby in its own right and a wonderful vehicle upon which to transport yourself to the waterside, if only in imagination, during the long, dark, closed-season evenings.

CHAPTER SIX

To Cast a Trout Fly

It is worth going to the Country Landowners Association Game Fair just to watch the casting demonstrations. Here, under late-July skies and before thousands of people united by common concern for interests as diverse as angling and archery, coursing and country crafts, hunting and hawking, shooting and saddlery, masters of the fly rod put themselves through their paces for the benefit of the crowd.

A lone figure at the end of the casting platform takes up a rod and flicks out twenty yards of line on to the water in front of him. Slowly he lifts the rod, tips it slightly to the side, pauses for a moment and taps it downwards; apparently taking on a life of its own, the line slides across the surface towards him, rolls into the air, unfurls, straightens and falls like a feather, precisely on target.

He lifts the rod once more; the line flies high and fast behind him, and hovers. A slight tug with his left hand sends it arrow-straight to the second target, ten yards beyond the first.

Roll-casts, overhead casts, side-casts, double-hauls, trailing loops and nymph pitches, right-handed and left-handed, follow in smooth succession. He casts with two rods at once, then four, holding two in each hand, the lines paralleling each other as they waft out, effortlessly, over the water.

A virtuoso performance for an awed audience.

Ignore the gimmickry and watch the evident ease with which the master propels a fly to a predetermined point thirty yards or more away. Few of us have any interest in being able to cast with more than one rod at a time; almost all of us would like to be able to cast further, more accurately, more delicately and with less effort.

Fly fishers spend huge amounts of money in pursuit of this objective, buying new, stiffer and more powerful rods and sleeker, slicker and more aerodynamic fly lines. In doing so they are, perhaps unconsciously, indulging in the bad workman's habit of blaming his tools. Certainly, it is difficult to cast well with an indifferent rod and line, but the truth of the matter is that it is good technique, rather than superior tackle, that sets the competent caster apart from his fellows at the waterside.

If we accept the truth of all this, it must seem strange that the one thing that fly fishers seem reluctant to buy is technique – strange, because it is readily available at quite modest cost and because, once purchased, it is far more durable than any rod or fly line.

Game angling instruction

Just as you can buy driving, tennis or golf lessons, so can you buy casting tuition. Half a dozen lessons with a qualified, professional instructor can make the difference between easy, effortless and effective casting on the one hand and many seasons of frustration on the other. But far too few fly fishers are prepared to make the investment. Instead they struggle on, trying to teach themselves – usually with only the sketchiest understanding of the principles involved – or to learn from more or less competent friends, absorbing those friends' faults as well as such useful advice as they may have to offer.

So if you really want to learn to cast well, seek out a qualified, professional instructor and get him to teach you. I emphasize the word 'qualified' because anybody can set him or herself up as a fly fishing instructor, faults and all. Only by going to somebody who has been tested and approved by the Association of Professional Game Angling Instructors – the APGAI – or the National Anglers Council can you be sure that his knowledge is sound and, just as important, that he has proved his ability to communicate it to his students.

I would be among the first to acknowledge that, where casting instruction is concerned, the written word is a very poor substitute for demonstration, practice and personal fault correction. But if you are unable to seek proper tuition, what follows should help.

The mechanics of casting

A trout fly and a nylon leader weigh next to nothing and cannot be thrown. Try it, if you like. Bunch them up in your hand and throw them as hard as you can; they will go no more than a couple of yards. Pull a few feet of fly line off your reel and try to throw the fly line, the leader and a fly using the rod as a lever; it simply does not work. Casting a trout fly has nothing whatever to do with 'throwing'. Nor, incidentally, does it have anything to do with cracking a whip.

Now think back to when you were at school, to the wad of blotting paper you chewed, held against the tip of a ruler, drew back and fired at the neck of a fellow pupil three rows in front of you; think how it stung him. It is this principle – the use of the ruler (the fly rod) as a spring – that makes the casting of a trout fly possible. A number of essential truths flow from it.

Firstly, we must load the spring. With the ruler, this was done by holding it upright by its base, and pulling back on the top of it. With a fly rod, we must use the fly line to load the spring, propelling it high and fast behind us and then allowing its weight and velocity to bend the rod. And it follows from this that we must have enough line out beyond the rod tip, enough weight, to bend the rod. It also follows that it is the back-cast (or more correctly the up-cast) rather than the forward-cast that provides the power to propel the line out over the water.

Secondly, if the spring (the fly rod) is to be loaded to best advantage, it must stop in, or as near as possible to, the upright position. The further back its tip is allowed to go, the less will the line be able to bend it and the less well loaded will it be.

Thirdly, we must give the fly line time to load the spring – to unfurl behind us and to pull the rod tip back.

These are the basic principles. Now let us look at the practice.

Before we begin

It is best to learn to cast or to practise casting on grass, rather than on water which may contain fish and is therefore a distraction.

Attach a short (say, four-foot) leader to the end of your fly line and tie to it a half-inch tuft of brightly coloured wool to represent a fly. (If you use a real fly it will catch in the grass; using nothing at all will cause the leader to crackle unpleasantly.) Rest the rod on a tackle bag or some such – do not lay it flat on the ground where you may tread on it – and pull off ten yards or so of line on to the grass straight in front of you.

If you are right handed, stand with your right foot forward and pointing straight ahead of you. Your left foot should be about a foot behind it and parallel to it. Lean into the cast a little, biasing your weight towards the right foot. Obviously these positions, and all others that follow, will be reversed if you are left handed.

Pick up the rod and lay the handle across the palm of your right hand. How you hold the rod is very largely a matter of personal choice. Some people like to have the 'V' between forefinger and thumb uppermost on the handle; others prefer to have the thumb on top. Either is acceptable. The grip one occasionally sees, with the index finger stretched out along the top of the handle, is inefficient because it causes the rod to be held with the last three fingers rather than chiefly with the index and middle ones. Whichever grip you choose, hold the rod comfortably in the middle of the handle and tuck the butt up quite tightly beneath your wrist.

For the moment, trap the line against the handle of the rod with your right index finger.

In explaining the various casts, I shall use the now traditional 'caster's clock-face' to describe the positions of the rod.

The overhead cast

The up-cast

Starting with the rod at about eight o'clock, its tip about eight inches above the ground, with your right elbow comfortably against your side and with the butt of the rod tucked firmly in beneath your wrist, begin to lift the rod upwards by bending your arm at the elbow, bringing your rod hand up close to your right eye and lifting the elbow until the upper arm is at about 45 degrees to the ground. The action is very similar to the one you would use when preparing to throw a dart at a dartboard.

The movement should be progressive, starting slowly and speeding up as the rod approaches the twelve o'clock position, where you should check it. Done correctly, the line will begin to travel towards you, accelerating as it does so, and then fly high and fast above the rod tip and behind you.

The rod tip will almost inevitably drift backwards at the top of this up-cast - perhaps to about one o'clock – and it is right that it should do so; too sudden a stop will cause the rod to shudder and will destroy the fluidity of the cast. But it should be allowed to go back no further than about one o'clock, and the butt of the rod should drift away from the wrist by no more than about an inch.

Far too many people cast with their wrists; some even seem to believe that casting is necessarily a 'wristy' action. It is not. The muscles controlling the wrist are not strong enough to control a fly rod properly, especially for protracted periods, and flexing of the wrist almost always allows the rod to travel too far back on the up-cast. If you find it difficult to keep the butt of the rod close to the wrist, try

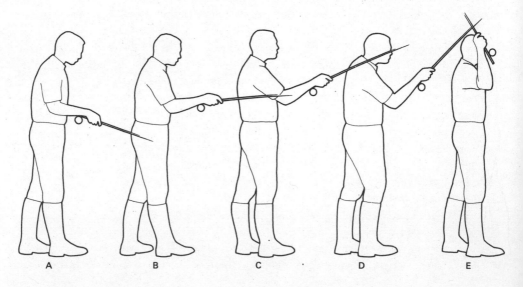

A   B   C   D   E

strapping it there with a handkerchief or a length of webbing with a velcro fastening.

The further the rod is allowed to drift back beyond the twelve o'clock position, the less will the line be able to load it, and the more will the situation have to be retrieved by using the rod as a lever with which to throw the line forward. As we have already seen, this is inefficient.

So we have lifted progressively into the up-cast, propelling the line high and fast behind us, stopped the rod at the upright position and allowed it to drift back to about one o'clock.

The pause

Now you must pause, to allow the line to straighten in the air behind you and to load the rod. If you do not, if you start to move the rod forward as soon as it reaches the vertical, it will not be loaded and you will simply pull the line out of the air. And if you do this quickly, the effect will be a whiplash, the fly quite possibly being cracked off as it snaps around.

Novices are often surprised at how long the pause at the top of an up-cast can be. Of course, it varies with the length of the line in the air – the longer the line, the longer the pause. But pause we must if the rod is to be properly loaded.

The forward tap

Once the line has straightened, simply tap your rod hand forward to about eleven o'clock or ten-thirty, much as you would if you were

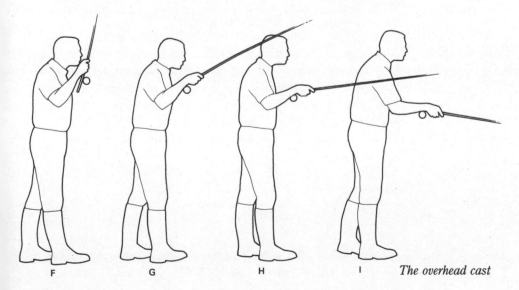

F   G   H   I   *The overhead cast*

throwing a dart, and then lower the rod back down to the eight o'clock position quite gently.

If you have timed everthing correctly, the line should flow out in front of you, hover briefly a couple of feet above the grass and then drop gently on to it. If it goes out too high and then stalls, try taking the 'tap' a little further forward. If it slaps down on to the ground, stop the 'tap' just a little earlier.

Shooting line

Obviously, the purpose of casting is to extend line over the water. Continuing to trap the line against the handle of the rod with the index finger of the rod hand, pull three or four feet of line from the reel and allow it to hang down loose.

Do another overhead cast – a progressive up-cast; check at the vertical and allow the rod to drift a little, pause while the line straightens, and tap forward. This time, as soon as the 'tap' has been completed, release the index finger of the rod hand; the weight and impetus of the line beyond the rod tip should pull the loose line out through the rings, lengthening the cast by a yard or so.

The timing of the release is critical. Let the line go too early, before you have completed the forward tap, and you will simply slide the rod down the line, dissipating the energy stored in the process. The line may still travel forward, but it will do so in a loose, sloppy fashion, and will probably fall in a heap in front of you. Let go too late, when the fly line is almost fully extended in front of you, and it will have insufficient impetus to pull the loose line through the rings.

Nobody can teach you this timing; it is a matter of practice and experience.

When you can extend line confidently and consistently like this, release the line from the index finger of the right hand and hold it in the left hand instead. At the start of each cast, the line should be quite tight between the left hand and the butt ring of the rod and, crucially, the left hand should remain close to your left hip throughout the cast; it *must not* be allowed to move up and down with, or in sympathy with, the rod hand. To start with, at least, you may find it helpful to tuck the thumb of the left hand into your left-hand trouser pocket, to prevent the left hand from moving.

You should now practise extending line by releasing it from the left hand as soon as you have completed the forward tap.

False casting

False casting involves checking the line in the air on the forward cast and going straight into another up-cast before it touches the water (or grass). It is used for a variety of purposes – to extend more line than can be extended with a single forward-cast; to dry a dry fly; for changing direction; and for timing the presentation of a fly perfectly when casting to feeding fish.

A fly line flickering back and forth in the air has considerable fish-frightening potential. Many fly fishers do far too much false casting. With good technique and timing, it is perfectly possible to extend 25 or 30 yards of weight forward or double-tapered fly line with no more than three or four false casts.

Make a normal up-cast – accelerating steadily from eight o'clock to twelve, allow the rod to drift back to one o'clock but no further, pause, tap forward and release line. As soon as the line is fully extended in front of you, but before it touches the water, trap the line again with the left hand and go into another up-cast. The exercise can be repeated several times, extending a little more line with each forward cast. The more line you extend, the more line weight and velocity will there be to extend line and the more line will you be able to extend. With practice, you should find that twelve to fifteen yards of line out beyond the rod tip will tow out the remaining fifteen to eighteen yards of a standard double-tapered or weight forward fly line quite easily.

You will find that you can only extend line on the forward-cast, not on the up-cast. The reason is simple; on the up-cast you need the weight and velocity of the fly line to load the rod. If you dissipate that energy by using it to extend line, you will have none left with which to load the rod. The same does not apply on the forward-cast, from which you pull the line into the up-cast rather than using the rod as a spring.

Whatever you do, do not get into that laziest and most fish-frightening of habits, using the weight of the line on the water to bend the rod and to extend line. You are likely to see someone doing it at every fishery. Perched on his stool, he lashes a line out on to the water, heaves it off into an untidy back-cast and hurls it forward again, extending perhaps four or five feet of line as he does so. Then he repeats the process, hauling the line up again, sending shock waves out across the water, gaining another yard or so on his next forward throw. Desperate. Follow the fishes' example and give him a wide berth.

The roll-cast

It is tempting to teach beginners the roll-cast first. It is immensely useful for getting out of all sorts of difficulties, and it is extraordinarily easy to do. It just takes a little courage, especially when you are using a new rod.

You can use a roll-cast to straighten line out on the water or to cast in confined spaces or where there are high trees or bushes

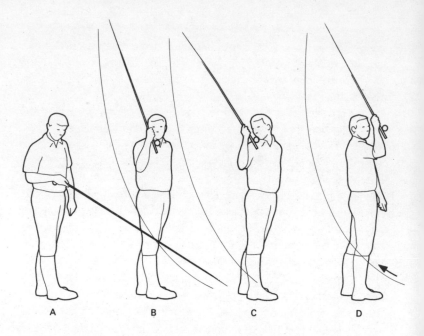

A   B   C   D

immediately behind you. You can also use it to bring a sinking line up to the surface before re-casting with an ordinary overhead cast. (If you try to lift a sunk line straight out of the water and into an up-cast, there is a real risk that you will break your rod. But a preliminary roll-cast will lay the line out on top of the water, reducing the drag when you lift into the up-cast and thus making it safe to do so.)

Start with about ten yards of line out in front of you. It does not need to be straight; indeed, it can be as wiggly as you like. Bring the rod slowly up to the one o'clock position and tip it away from your body by about 15 degrees. The line should hang from the end of it, curving downwards and forwards towards the water.

Now – and this is where courage is called for – strike the rod sharply downwards, as though you were using a hammer to drive a nail into a board in front of you and at about waist height. Hit the nail hard; you will not damage your rod. The line should slide towards you, curve up into the air and roll out in front of you, laying itself out neatly on the water's surface.

A high roll-cast, stopping the forward 'hit' at about ten-thirty, should extend the line in the air and then drop it on to the water. A low one, stopping at about nine o'clock, will lift off more line but will roll it out across the surface.

When you are using a roll-cast to lift a sunk line to the surface, you should go into the up-cast as soon as you have completed the roll-cast, before the line has time to start sinking again. But do make sure that the whole of the line has been laid out on the surface by the roll-cast and that none of it is still underwater.

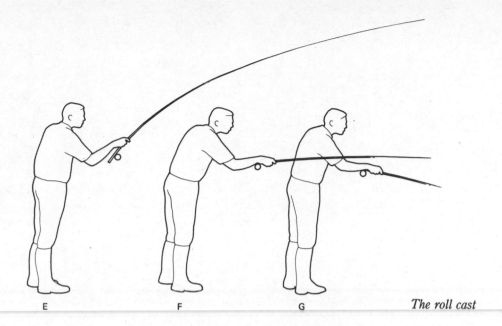

The single-haul

By implication, we have already seen that the most important thing for good casting is high line speed. Line speed can be increased – and casting therefore improved – by judicious 'hauling' on the line with the left hand.

Execute a perfectly ordinary overhead cast with some slack line below your left hand, ready to be extended. As you reach the top of the up-cast, but not before, allow the weight of the line extending behind you to 'pull' your left hand up from your left hip to within about a foot of the butt ring of the rod. Now, as you tap forward, pull down sharply with the left hand and then release the loose line, which should slip forward through the rod rings much more quickly; you may even find it tugging on the reel at the end of the forward-cast.

Apart from increasing line speed, this single-haul will narrow the loop of the line as it travels forward, which is useful when you want to cut into a wind.

The double-haul

Double-hauling is a technique used to gain extra casting distance, especially with shooting heads.

The badly executed double-haul is widely used as a form of macho war dance by some reservoir fly fishers. That most of them can reach no further with it than the competent caster can with a perfectly ordinary overhead cast usually seems to escape their notice. They seem to believe that because they are using all their muscles and

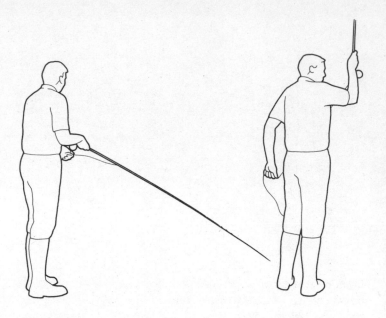

expending a great deal of energy they must be casting as far as it is
possible to cast. In truth, though, and as we saw earlier, good casting
has little or nothing to do with physical exertion. Double-hauling *is*
effective, very, but only if done correctly – which does *not* include
stretching your right arm high behind you and flailing like a demented
windmill.

Before starting a double-haul, place your left foot very slightly in

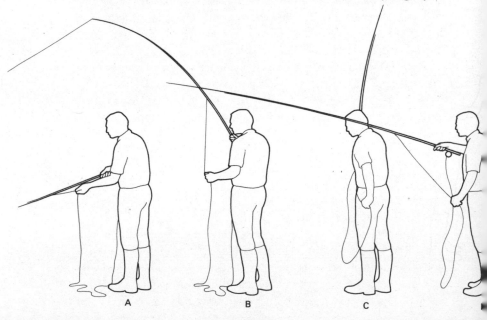

A   B   C

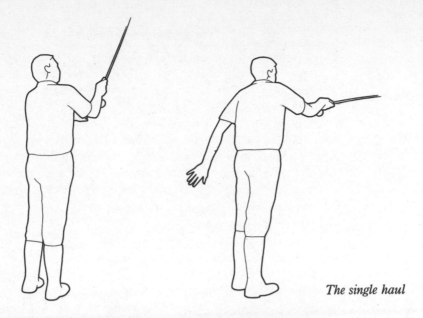

The single haul

front of the right one to enable you to 'loosen up' a little. With twenty or twenty-five yards of backing or fly line hanging slack from your left hand and coiled loosely in a line tray or at your feet, work your shooting head out until its butt is six to eight inches beyond the tip ring of the rod, or until the whole of the belly of a weight forward line is in the air.

Lift into a high, fast up-cast and allow the line to pull your left hand

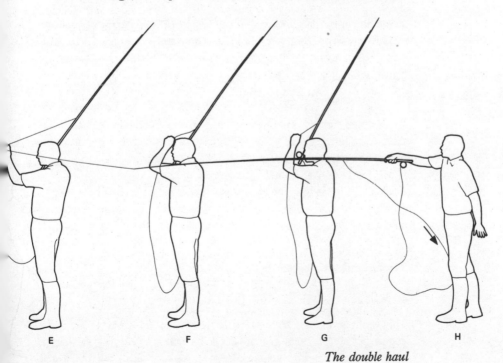

E   F   G   H

The double haul

up to within about a foot of the butt ring of the rod. Haul down with the left hand as you tap into the forward cast and, instead of releasing the line, allow its forward movement to pull your left hand up towards the butt ring again. As you start to pull the rod up into the next up-cast, haul down with the left hand. This movement, combined with a well executed up-cast, should send the line whistling high and fast behind you, fast enough to pull your left hand almost up to the butt ring of the rod. Tap forward again, hauling with the left hand as you do so, and release the line with the left hand. Done well, this will send the line scorching out over the water, trailing the backing line or the running part of the fly line behind it.

The rod-arm movement when double-hauling is exactly the same as for an ordinary overhead cast except that you may wish to lift the arm just a little more and to extend it forward on the follow-through, pointing the rod along the line's line of flight.

Double-hauling is a disciplined exercise the purpose of which is to load the rod more fully than is possible with an ordinary overhead cast. Do not fall into the trap of trying to throw the line, instead of simply tapping forward. It can be terribly tempting but will do you no good; indeed, it is the one mistake that is guaranteed to reduce the distance you cast rather than increase it.

Side-casting

A rod and a fly line flickering back and forth in a vertical plane are terribly visible to trout, especially in clear-water rivers and lakes. The same rod and line moving backwards and forwards in a horizontal plane, at waist level or lower, are far less visible.

There is nothing difficult about side-casting. You simply tip the rod out sideways and execute a perfectly normal overhead cast. Remember, though, that all the same principles still apply. Keep the casting arc tight, allowing the line to extend backwards and to load the rod on the back-cast, and aim the back-cast high, in order to keep it clear of vegetation, barbed-wire fences and the like.

When side-casting, you may find it a little difficult to land the fly accurately to start with. Practise and persevere. The dividends paid by competent side-casting will far more than repay the effort invested.

Tricks and wrinkles

Casting into the wind

The wind is the fly fisher's most persistent adversary. However competent a caster may be, he will never find it as easy to cast into a head wind or across a strong side wind as he will to put out a line downwind with a gentle zephyr behind him. But it is perfectly possible to cast into or across a stiff breeze and, once again, the principles involved have everything to do with technique and timing and nothing whatever to do with brute strength.

Those who do not understand the mechanics of casting almost always do battle with the wind by trying to *throw* the line into it, putting more and more effort into the forward-cast. But we have already established that you cannot throw a fly line any distance, even in calm air; still less can you do so with the wind against you. The harder you try to throw the line, the more will it land in a tatty heap on the water in front of you, and the more frustrated will you become.

The trick to beating the wind is to load the rod more fully by increasing line speed on the up-cast, stopping the rod in the vertical position and then tapping forward to project the line low and fast across the water. However strong the wind, it is almost always lightest close to the water's surface; by aiming the forward-cast a little lower than usual, you should be able to take advantage of this, rolling the line out beneath the full force of the wind.

Changing direction

There are two ways of changing direction while casting, one ungainly and time-consuming, the other quick and efficient. Most self-taught fly fishers use the former – lifting the line from the water and then moving round about 5 degrees with each successive false cast. The infinitely preferable alternative is to point the rod at the new target *before* lifting the line from the water and then simply cast as normal. The line should be virtually on course for the new target as it straightens at the top of the up-cast, and one false cast should have it aimed precisely.

Cutting corners

There are times, especially when fishing on rivers, when you may need to put a steep curve into the fly line as it lands on the water. The trick is particularly useful when casting to a fish tucked in beneath the bank from which you are fishing, or when you must cast across the current and still want the fly to drift down on the stream without being skidded or dragged across the surface by the weight of the water on the fly line.

There is nothing difficult about this. Simply make a perfectly ordinary overhead cast and then, as soon as you have tapped forward, tip the rod over to the side, so that it is parallel to the ground, in the opposite direction to the one in which you wish the line to curve. If you want the line to curve to the left, tip the rod to the right, and vice versa.

It takes a little practice to put a curve into the line and still to drop the fly on target, but the ability to do so is well worth the effort involved, and you will find that the steepness of the curve can be adjusted by reducing or increasing the degree to which you tip the rod over to the side.

Common problems

The line crawls towards you and fails to get into the air on the up-cast: you have not been positive enough in accelerating the line into the up-cast. The acceleration should be progressive, and the movement from ten-thirty to twelve o'clock must be quite brisk.

The line leaps from the water but still fails to climb into the up-cast: you have snatched the line from the water rather than accelerating it into the up-cast progressively.

The fly catches an obstruction behind you or hits you in the back as it travels forwards: you are taking the rod too far back – perhaps to two or three o'clock, very probably because you are allowing your wrist to break at the top of the up-cast. Lock the butt of the rod tight against the underside of your forearm, using a strap to keep it there if necessary. And concentrate on stopping the rod in the twelve o'clock position at the top of the up-cast.

The power is dissipated from the rod as you tap forward when shooting line, or the cast falls short of an attainable target: you are probably releasing the line too soon; tap forward and *then* release the line.

The line crashes on to the water's surface: you are aiming *at* the target rather than two or three feet *above* it. Aim at a point above the target.

You keep getting 'wind knots' in the leader, or the line hits the ground behind you and the water in front of you during false casting: you have resorted to a 'throwing' action – either because, perhaps subconsciously, you believe it will enable you to cast further (which it will not), or because you are allowing your wrist to break on the up-cast. Concentrate on tucking the butt of the rod up beneath the forearm, getting a high, fast up-cast, and checking the rod in the twelve o'clock position.

You hear a whiplash 'crack' as you go into the forward cast; perhaps it even breaks the fly from the leader: you are starting the forward tap too early, before the line has had time to extend in the air behind you. *Pause* at the top of the up-cast.

The fly or the fly line catches on the rod during false casting: you are almost certainly moving the rod fore and aft through too narrow an arc. While checking it at twelve o'clock on the up-cast, allow it to drift back to one o'clock thereafter; and allow it to drift forward to eleven o'clock or even ten-thirty on the forward-cast.

The line leaps from the water and then falls in a heap during the first movement of a roll-cast: you have carried out the movement too quickly and forcefully. It should be a slow, deliberate action.

The line fails to extend fully and to roll out over the water during a roll-cast: you are not making the downward hit with the rod sharply or strongly enough; it must be a crisp, positive action.

The cast falls short of an attainable target while double-hauling: there are two possible reasons for this.

(a) You may be taking the rod too far back on the up-cast, and thus inducing that caster's curse – a throwing action. Rod movement and control for double-hauling is almost exactly the same as that used for a normal overhead cast. Keep the butt of the rod tucked up tight beneath your forearm to prevent wrist break, and check the rod in the upright position, allowing it to drift back no further than one o'clock thereafter.

(b) You may be extending your rod arm and working from the shoulder. This is as inefficient as it is tiring. Work from the elbow, lifting your upper arm by no more than about 45 degrees.

Finally

Three positive things you can do to improve your casting dramatically.

Firstly, if you are a beginner, or if you are in any way dissatisfied with or frustrated by your casting, do seek help from a qualified professional. The financial investment will be modest and the dividend should be out of all proportion to it.

Secondly, try to engrave the mechanical principles of casting in your mind; they are all about loading springs, and have nothing to do with throwing.

Thirdly, aim every cast you make *at something*, even when you are confronting the featureless expanse of a large lake, a loch or a reservoir. Such constant practice will stand you in good stead when you really need to be able to drop a fly accurately, in front of a rising fish.

CHAPTER SEVEN

Catching Trout

It was with some difficulty that I persuaded my father to start trout fishing when he retired some twenty years ago after a long and distinguished career in the Royal Air Force. I gave him a basic set of tackle for Christmas, but he was a keen golfer and ornithologist and it took much cajoling to get him to accompany me on occasional visits to a large gravel pit fishery near Reading during the following season. He caught nothing on the first three trips, which discouraged him, and he came on the fourth almost reluctantly.

It was a hot, bright June day without a breath of wind. The sun glared down from a pale, pale sky, stunning the water and the air above it. After lunch, the fish and I took our siestas, they sulking deep in weedy darkness, I with my hat over my eyes in the welcoming shade of a low-boughed oak. Father fished on in a half-hearted and desultory sort of way.

Suddenly, he shouted. I leapt to my feet and stumbled down to join him at the waterside. His rod was hooped over and a rainbow trout of about a pound and a half was somersaulting at the end of his leader twenty yards away. Father fought frantically to reel in the slack line lying around his feet. Eventually he brought the fish under control and, little by little, drew it towards him. He said he wanted to land it himself, so I handed him the net.

By now, the trout was tiring. We could see it in the clean, clear water, bright and silvery, making ever shorter and more desperate runs. At last it came to the surface where, still upright, it swam in slow, apparently resigned circles, almost suspended at the end of the leader. With a look of rapt concentration on his face, father slid the net into the water and drew the weary fish towards it.

Summoning all its remaining energy, the trout set off across the lake again, making one final bid for freedom. Father hung on tight. Down and down went his rod tip until it was pointing directly at the fish. There was a 'ping' and the line went slack. Half a minute later, a fish jumped thirty yards away. Rippling rings ebbed outwards across the still, shining surface. Father just stood there, his rod hanging from his hand, a picture of despondency.

The following spring, he joined me for a week's fishing on a lovely

Devon stream. So numerous and hungry were its tiny trout that I was certain he would catch at least a few of them. I tied a bushy little Blue Upright on for him, explained the principles of upstream dry fly fishing and watched as he waded into the water at the foot of a stickle. A dark, sinuous run, three feet wide, slid between the rough water and the bank that rose high above it.

Slowly, father began to work his way upstream, casting a short and remarkably accurate line on to the glide. The fly bobbed and span on the current. A bronze flash, a plop at the surface, and it vanished. Father did nothing. He cast again and the same thing happened. Another trout snatched the fly, drowned it and was gone. Quite clearly, he was not seeing the splashy little rises among the general hubbub of the stream. We conferred and agreed that I should lie on the bank above the glide, watching his fly on the water. When I called 'strike!' he would do so without hesitation.

I took up my position and he climbed back into the water. For the first two or three casts, nothing happened. Then there was a rise. 'Strike!'

His reaction was instantaneous and awesome. As he heaved the rod back ferociously, the smallest brown trout in the south-west peninsula was yanked from the water like a cork from a bottle, arced into the air and plopped into the stream behind him. Loose line festooned his hat and shoulders as he stood, bemused, calf-deep in the torrent.

We sorted him out and wound in the line, only to find the obliging little fish at the end of it, still firmly attached. Had I not slid my hand down the leader to the hook shank and shaken the tiny trout off, I rather suspect that father would have cudgelled it to death and insisted on eating it for breakfast the next morning.

No matter how sound the novice's tackle may be, or how competent a caster he may have become, the hooking, playing and landing of his first few fish always seem to be fraught affairs, tinged with panic, probably because little thought is given to the problems involved until they have to be overcome.

Striking

Although widely used, 'strike' is a less than perfect word with which to describe the action required to set a hook in a fish's mouth without breaking the leader; it implies far more violence than is either necessary or desirable. 'Tighten' is a far better word, the action involved being very similar to the gradual acceleration into the up-cast.

Most breakages occur when striking rather than while fish are being played, and they are almost always the result of striking too hard against a leader that is too fine or against a poorly tied knot.

From time to time, you will hear a fly fisher say, with rueful pride, that a trout has broken him. Both his assessment and his pride are misplaced. Fish do not break leaders; fishermen do. And to break on the strike, allowing a trout to swim off with a hook in its mouth and perhaps several feet of nylon trailing behind it, gives cause for concern rather than for pride. All of which argues for always using a leader strong enough to cope both with our enthusiasm and with the biggest fiercest fish we may reasonably expect to encounter, and for using the right knots, tying them carefully, moistening them before snugging them down and testing them once we have done so.

Where you must use a very fine, two- or three-pound leader to avoid frightening fish, on a chalk stream for example or a very clear stillwater, you may be able to cushion it against too fierce a strike by tying in eight inches or so of 'power gum' – an elasticized monofilament – between the butt of the leader and the braided butt or between the leader and the butt length of heavy nylon attached to the fly line.

The timing of the strike is crucial.

When you are fishing a wet fly or a nymph, there is no problem; you should strike as soon as you see the leader or fly line pull forward, see the flash of a fish beneath the surface in the vicinity of your fly or feel a tug on the line. And the faster your reactions, the better will be your chances of success. The speed with which a trout can detect the falseness of fly and spit it out is astonishing. Hesitate and all is lost.

It is essential to learn to *see* takes, to spot the tell-tale underwater glint, the almost imperceptible movement of nylon slipping down through that little hole in the surface film, or the slight checking and straightening of a wind-curved floating line laid out across the ripple, rather than simply to wait until you feel the pull of a fish. Deep lure or wet fly fishing aside, the vast majority of takes are so subtle that you will never feel them, so those who *watch* their lines and leaders on the water, and the water itself, will almost always do far better than those who gaze around them, waiting for a fish to hook itself.

Timing the strike is a little more difficult when you are fishing a dry fly.

In order to take a fly from the surface, a trout tips itself upwards, rises through the water, opens its mouth, engulfs the fly and a small amount of air with it, turns downwards with its mouth still open, allowing the water flowing in through its mouth and out through its gill covers to expel the air and to carry the fly back into its mouth, and then shuts its mouth. If you strike while its mouth is still open, there is a very real possibility – amounting almost to a certainty – that you will pull the fly out of it.

People will tell you that you should count to three or say 'God save the Queen' before striking to a rise to a dry fly. Such guidance works well on medium-paced chalk streams, but it builds in too much delay when we are confronted by the quicksilver rises of the little trout that live in tumbling rain-fed rivers, and its use would cause us to strike too quickly to the lazy, languid rises one so often sees on Irish loughs. Eventually, experience and instinct will enable you to hook trout rising to dry flies on any type of water. In the meantime, you should be able to achieve a reasonable degree of success by matching the speed of your strike to the pace of the water, striking almost instantly to rises in fast-flowing streams and waiting much longer than may seem necessary on calm days on lakes and loughs. And when you do strike, try to make the action a progressive one, 'feeling for the fish' and then tightening into it, rather than simply giving it a hearty thwack.

Playing fish

Pound for pound, trout fight more fiercely than almost any other freshwater fish, apart perhaps from their brine-hardened cousins the sea trout, whose strength and acrobatic ferocity can leave even experienced fly fishers trembling. Brown trout tend to fight doggedly, tugging and boring with great determination and stamina. Rainbows often fight more spectacularly, leaping and making long runs but tiring more quickly. Our objective should be to bring the trout to the net as quickly and surely as possible.

The two golden rules in playing trout are to keep the line tight and the rod tip up. If we allow the line to go slack, there is a real risk that the hook will come loose, allowing the fish to escape. A tight line will usually prevent this, and the tighter we keep the line the more quickly will the fish tire and come to the net. Equally, of course, if we put too much pressure on a fish, there is a risk that a sudden leap or run will break the leader, which is why the rod tip must be kept up.

When playing fish, the springiness of a fly rod is used to cushion the leader against sudden shocks; in a sense, it acts in exactly the same way as the length of 'power gum' we may have tied in between the leader and the fly line. The more the rod is kept at right angles to the fly line, the better it will be able to flex and to cushion the leader. Many beginners lose trout because they hang on too tight, allowing the fish to pull the rod tip down and down until it is pointing straight down the fly line and no longer offers the leader any protection at all. If a trout makes a determined run, keep the rod tip up by allowing line to slip out through your hand or to be pulled from the reel; as soon as the run ends – as eventually it must – you can retrieve the line, bringing the fish back towards you, still keeping the rod tip up. Only if the fish jumps should you drop the rod tip momentarily, to slacken the line a little and reduce the risk of the leader snapping as the fish drops back into the water.

There is an endless debate as to whether trout should be played 'from the reel' or 'by hand', with loose line being allowed to fall on to the bank or into the bottom of the boat. Personally, I usually choose the latter course, partly because the job of recovering ten or fifteen yards of loose fly line on to the reel before establishing proper contact with the fish seems to me to be an unnecessary distraction, and partly because I feel that I can control the fly line more sensitively by hand than by checking the reel or winding in with it. But this is really a matter of personal preference. If you do play fish by hand, you should always seek to ensure that the line is free to run out – that you are not treading on the loose coils on the ground and that they do not become caught around thistles, tree roots, boat fittings or other obstructions.

Once a trout is under control, you can tire it quickly and control its movements – keeping it away from weed beds and other obstructions – by applying side strain, simply tipping the rod over to one side and keeping tension on the line. If you do this quickly and are firm with the fish, you will find that you can throw it off balance and make it much more biddable; you may even be able to walk it downstream or along the bank to a convenient landing point, like a dog on a lead.

If a hooked trout heads for cover, try to turn it away before it gets there. Some fly fishers swear that a trout will seek to wrap the leader around a submerged tree root or some other underwater obstruction, or even that it will actually hold on to a weed stem with its teeth to avoid being brought ashore. I do not believe fish are so calculating, but they can certainly cause problems if they bury themselves in weed beds as they often do, particularly in rivers. If a trout does entangle your leader in the weed, try letting the line go slack; he may come out of his own accord. If he does not, point the rod directly down the line and pull on him gently by hand – being prepared to lift the rod tip quickly and to reapply tension to the fish if and when he comes free.

If you allow a trout, particularly a heavy one, to get downstream of you when you are fishing a stream or river you will find that playing it becomes very much more difficult, because its own strength and weight will be added to by the weight of the current. Even when it is exhausted, you may find that drawing it upstream towards you puts an unacceptable strain on the hook hold and on the leader. If a fish tries to move downstream from you, it will almost always pay to try to prevent it from doing so, either by applying side strain and pulling it off balance, or by moving downstream with it and keeping below it.

The same principle applies when you are fishing from a boat drifting on a stiff breeze. Because you will be casting downwind, ahead of the boat, this is where fish will be hooked. As long as they stay downwind of you, with the boat drifting towards them, playing them should be quite straightforward. But if you allow them to get upwind of the boat, you will effectively be dragging them along behind you and, again, the weight of the water added to the strength and weight of the fish will make playing them that much more difficult.

Releasing trout

If we mean to release the trout we catch we must be careful to tire them as little as possible and to harm them not at all before doing so.

Whether or not trout can be released safely will depend on the tackle used, the way in which the fish is played and the ways in which the flies are removed from their mouths and the fish returned to the water.

The huge amounts of energy expended by trout when they are being played causes potentially lethal lactic acid to accumulate in their muscles. If they are played to exhaustion, they may appear to recover before swimming away but may die within a day or so, before the acid has had time to disperse. It is therefore essential to use a leader that is strong enough to bring the fish to hand quickly, before they have tired themselves out. The bigger the trout you may catch, the more important it is to use a strong leader if they are to be released. On clear lakes and rivers it may be that so strong a leader will make the fish cautious and reduce the number that take your flies, but that is the price to be paid if those you do catch are to be released safely.

You must also use barbless hooks or hooks with the barbs broken down – easily done with a pair of fine-nosed pliers or the flat tips of a pair of fishing scissors. Some people who have not used them are afraid that barbless hooks may come free while fish are being played. In fact, their fear is unfounded; even if the fly line is inadvertently allowed to go slack for a moment or so, its weight as it is towed through the water is usually sufficient to hold the hook in place.

You must play a fish hard if it is to be released, looking for the earliest opportunity to slip the hook out before it has become exhausted, and you should seek to remove the hook while the trout is still in the water, without handling it at all. It is often possible to do this by running the tip ring of the rod right down the leader to the hook and then just wiggling it a little, or by running your hand down the leader and twitching the hook free. If you have to handle a trout that is to be released, always wet your hands first – to avoid wiping off any of the protective mucus that covers its skin and scales – and cradle it gently on its back in one hand while you slip the hook free with the other. If you hold a trout the right way up, it is likely to flap, which may cause you to tighten your grip, which may damage the fish's internal organs. If you cradle it on its back, it will lie still while your remove the hook.

Once the hook is free, return the fish to the water carefully and as quickly as possible. You should hold the fish upright in clean, unmuddied water, facing it into the current if you are fishing a stream or river, and continue to hold it there until it has regained its composure. Once it is fully recovered, a very gentle push should be enough to wake it up and encourage it to swim off.

Landing trout

If you mean to kill a fish for the table, you must first bring it safely ashore. If you have not already done so, prepare the landing net and keep it ready to hand, but do not be in too much of a hurry to use it. We shall never know what goes on in trouts' minds, but the reserves of energy they can summon on first seeing a landing net in the water can be remarkable. It is quite common for a seemingly almost exhausted trout to panic when it sees the net and to head off on a long, powerful, surging run, which can easily pull the hook out or break the unwary or inexperienced angler's leader.

To start with, at least, you should deem a trout to be exhausted only when it has rolled over on to its side and the tension on the line is keeping its mouth just clear of the water. At this point, you should slip the net into the water quietly, making sure that the whole of the mesh and at least the front three-quarters of the frame are submerged. Then, with the rod tip well up and the fly line trapped with the fingers of the rod hand, draw the fish towards you and over the rim of the net. There are very few occasions in fly fishing when we can safely use the words 'always' or 'never', but this is one of them. *Always* keep the net still and draw the fish over it; *never* scoop at the fish with the net – if you do, you may well alarm the fish, dislodge the hook hold or get tangled up with the other flies on the leader.

Trout that are to be killed must be despatched as quickly and humanely as possible. It is not acceptable to set off in search of some more or less suitable stone or piece of wood while a fish lies flapping and gasping on the bank, or to try to kill it by beating it against a tree root or a fence post. If you plan to take trout home, you should have a purpose-made priest secured to your belt or fishing waistcoat by a reasonable length of cord so that it is always ready to hand. And the fish should be killed while it is still in the landing net, *before* the hook is removed. Using the mesh to give yourself a sure grip, hold the fish upright and rap it firmly on the top of its head, just behind its eyes, four or five times; treated thus, its death will be certain and instant, even though its nervous system may cause it to continue to twitch or flap for a few minutes more.

Keeping fish fresh

Some years ago, when I was running a trout fishery of my own, one of our season rods telephoned me and said she thought there was something wrong with our fish – those she had just brought home were flabby and the flesh was coming away from their bones. I asked her at what time she had caught them – all before noon; and how she had kept them – in a polythene bag on the bank beside her, throughout a long and blisteringly hot afternoon. She could scarcely have cooked them more thoroughly if she had put them in the oven.

If they are to stay fresh, trout should be kept as cool as possible from the moment they are caught until eventually they are transferred to fridge, freezer or frying pan.

I usually take an insulated cool-bag to the waterside with me. I keep my picnic and cold drinks in it, covering or surrounding them with four or five ice packs from the freezer. In order to keep the cool-bag's liner clean, I place each trout I catch in a large plastic carrier bag and then put it in the cool-bag, covering it with ice packs.

An acceptable alternative is to use a canvas (*not* wickerwork) fish bass to hold the fish you've caught and keep them fresh by soaking it frequently and hanging it in the sun or wind. The effect is similar to that obtained with the canvas chaguls used for cooling water in the Middle East; rapid evaporation of water from the chagul's surface cools the contents dramatically – if you hang a full chagul from the wing mirror of a vehicle and then drive steadily at forty miles an hour or so, you can almost freeze the water in it.

A commonly used but less effective means of storing fish is to place them in a canvas or wickerwork fish bass – or, worse still, a plastic carrier bag – and hang them in the water, attaching them either to a rowlock on the boat or to a peg on the bank. This keeps the fish at the temperature of the surrounding water, which may be quite high on a hot day, especially at the surface of a lake or reservoir. The same goes for 'stringers', lengths of cord upon which trout are strung and then hung in the water.

The most damaging way of keeping fish is to leave them in a plastic bag on the bank or in the bottom of a boat. It is tantamount to leaving them in a greenhouse.

If you wish to freeze your fish, you should freeze them *ungutted*. Simply hold them by the gills and squeeze them firmly along the lengths of their flanks, squeezing the contents of their intestines out through their vents. Then wash them in cold water, wipe them dry, place them in individual polythene bags marked with the date and place of capture, and put them in the freezer whole. The reason for this is that a fish's skin is an excellent hermetic seal. If you cut it down the length of the fish's belly in order to remove the contents of the body cavity, the fish's flesh will dry out quite quickly. If you leave the skin intact, cleaning the fish on the day on which you mean to eat it, the flesh will retain its moisture. Typically, a cleaned trout can be kept frozen for around four to six months while an uncleaned one should keep for up to a year. As a bonus, cleaning a trout while it is defrosting is much easier and less messy than cleaning an unfrozen one, the innards coming out as a single, frozen lump.

CHAPTER EIGHT

Spate River Fly Fishing

There always seems to be a queue for decent housing in the trout's world. The speed with which vacated lies are re-occupied, often by fish of similar size to the previous inhabitants, is quite remarkable. Remove a trout from any comfortable and identifiable lie and it is an odds-on bet that the spot will be occupied by another comparable fish the next time you pass by. This is why I do not know whether it was the same fish that taunted me through springtime expeditions to the Torridge in north Devon over three consecutive years, or whether the original trout had one or more equally fussy successors.

I first met her on a still, warm, blue-sky morning in May.

The cool water bubbled across the bleached boulders and scoured stones of the stickle and into the oily-smooth glide below. Dried debris trailing from the lowest branches of overhanging trees bore witness to the previous winter's floods, but the river was low now, and muttered to itself beneath its breath as it pottered on. The glide ran round a bend. The stream was deep, dark and mysterious where it slid along the foot of the vertical far bank upon which a couple of small bushes had managed to grab toe-holds; slower, shallower and apparently clearer where it lapped against the crescent-shaped shingle spit which formed the near bank, on the inside of the bend.

I sat on the bank at the foot of the shingle spit and watched the water carefully. A pulsing ring ebbed out from beneath the branches of the nearest bush and faded on the current. I moved on to the gravel and crouched down; there it was again, a confident, glopping rise and an elliptical disturbance rippling out from beneath the bush. The fish was tucked in tight against the vertical wall worn away by the current, shaded and sheltered by the overhanging leaves which dipped towards the silky surface.

There was a constant trickle of medium olive duns floating down on the stream, their grey wings held high. Occasionally, one of the tiny flies would take off hesitantly and flutter upwards, seeking the safety of the bankside vegetation. I watched one being carried towards the bush. It disappeared into shadow. A second later, the trout rose again.

I had already tied a size 14 Blue Upright to the point of my leader, dipped it in floatant and allowed it to dry. Keeping low, I moved

Adult Damselflies

Alder Larva	Bloodworm (Wobble-Worm)	Midge Pupae (Buzzers)	Sedge Pupa	Corixa

Damselfly Nymph	Gold-ribbed Hare's Ear Nymph	Mayfly Nymph	Montana Nymph	Olive Emerger

Phantom Larva	Plastazote Corixa	PVC Nymph	Sawyer's Pheasant Tail Nymph

Shipman's Buzzer	Shrimp	Suspender Buzzer	Stick Fly	Water Hog Louse

MOSTLY NYMPHS

Flies provided by Cook's of Datchet

Appetizer

Black Chenille

Booby Nymph

Jack Frost

Missionary

Muddler Minnow

Rassler

Viva

Whiskey Fly

White Chenille

LURES

Flies provided by Cook's of Datchet

CDC
Black
Gnat

Blue
Upright

CDC Blue-Winged
Olive Dun

Cinnamon
Sedge

Coch-y-
Bonddu

Daddy-
Long-Legs

Deerstalker

CDC Emerging
Buzzer

G&H
Sedge

Ginger
Quill

Gold-Ribbed
Hare's Ear
(Parachute)

Greenwell's
Glory

Hawthorn
Fly

Hopper

Houghton
Ruby

Iron
Blue
Dun

Kite's Imperial

Lunn's
Particular

Palmered
Sedge

Red
Ant

Rough
Olive

Shadow
Mayfly

Sherry
Spinner

Tups
Indispensable
(Parachute)

Wickham's
Fancy

DRY FLIES

Flies provided by Cook's of Datchet

Alexandra *Bibio* *Black & Peacock
Spider*

**Black
Pennell** **Blae
& Black** **Blue
Zulu** **Butcher** **Connemara
Black** **Dunkeld**

**Fiery
Brown** **Greenwell's
Glory** **Grenadier** **Invicta** **Mallard
& Claret** **March
Brown
Spider**

Murrough **Olive
Bumble** **Orange
Partridge
Spider** **Green
Partridge
Spider** **Yellow
Partridge
Spider** **Peter
Ross**

**Poult
Bloa** **Silver
March
Brown** **Sinfoil's
Fry** **Snipe
& Purple** **Soldier
Palmer** **Sooty
Olive**

**Teal
& Blue** **Teal
& Yellow** **Waterhen
Bloa** **Watson's
Fancy** **Williams
Favourite** **Zulu**

MAINLY WET FLIES

Flies provided by Cook's of Datchet

CHECK LIST – SPATE RIVER TACKLE

RODS:

Small streams: 7ft–8ft 6in: #4–6: medium-to-tip action

Larger rivers: 10–11ft: #5–6: medium action

LINES: Weight forward or double-tapered, floating, #4–6

LEADERS:

Small stream/dry fly

Larger rivers/wet fly

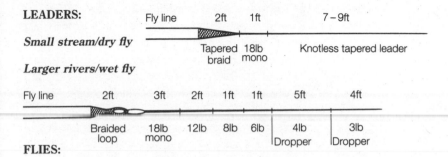

FLIES:

Dry flies and nymphs – for small streams and larger rivers; all in sizes 14–16

March/April Kites Imperial, Rough Olive, PT Nymph

May/June Blue Upright, Greenwell's Glory, Ginger Quill, Iron Blue, Black Gnat, Houghton Ruby, Lunn's Particular, Coch-y-Bonddu, Cinnamon Sedge, PT Nymph

July/August Blue Upright, Ginger Quill, B–WO Dun, Greenwell's Glory, Houghton Ruby, Lunn's Particular, Sherry Spinner, Cinnamon Sedge, Red Ant, Daddy-Long-Legs, PT Nymph

September Rough Olive, Kite's Imperial, Blue Upright, Ginger Quill, Houghton Ruby, Lunn's Particular, Cinnamon Sedge, PT Nymph

Wet flies – chiefly for North Country and Scottish rivers

March/April Blae and Black, Snipe and Purple, Orange Partridge, Waterhen Bloa, March Brown Spider, Silver March Brown

May/June Snipe and Purple, Greenwell's (wet), Poult Bloa, Williams Favourite (or Black Spider)

July/August Snipe and Purple, Poult Bloa, March Brown Spider, Williams Favourite

September Waterhen Bloa, Poult Bloa, Snipe and Purple, March Brown Spider

And do not forget scissors or snippers, artery forceps, silicone floatant, mucilin (red tin), sinkant (Fuller's Earth, washing-up detergent and glycerin), hook-hone, spare leaders or leader material, landing net and priest.

Note:
The flies listed above are general suggestions; local advice should be sought whenever possible.

cautiously down to the water's edge eight or ten yards downstream from the bush and unhooked the dry fly from the keeper ring of the seven-foot cane rod. The cast was not a difficult one. All I had to do was to drop the fly on the water tight in against the far bank and just above the overhanging foliage. The current would do the rest.

I worked out the line, paused on the final up-cast and tapped the rod forward. The line and leader unfurled, hovered for a moment and then dropped on to the water. The fly, sitting up nicely on the surface, was carried into the dark cave beneath the bush. I heard a 'glop' and tightened. There was a sharp tug on the rod tip and then nothing; the water beneath the bush rocked and an ebbing ring spread and faded.

I tried the Blue Upright again, and then the other patterns that might have been deemed sensible for the place and the time of year: a Greenwell's Glory, a Ginger Quill, a Black Gnat and an Iron Blue. Nothing; not a flicker of interest. Clearly, I had frightened the fish which by now was presumably lurking in its bolt-hole, nursing a sore lip.

I returned to the spot several times during the remaining ten days of the holiday and during the same periods in the two following seasons. More often than not, there was a fish feeding under the bush. Whether it was the same one I cannot say, but the repeated sense of *déjà vu* became intensely frustrating. On each visit, I put a carefully chosen fly on to the water, close to the bank, above the bush. On each occasion it drifted steadily down into the darkness. On almost every occasion, the fish rose, I struck, there was a brief tug, and the line went slack.

On the last morning of the third successive spring holiday, I set out to go through the ritual again, more through force of habit than in expectation of success. I put up a little Black Gnat, crept into position on the shingle bar, waited and watched. Within moments there came that now-familiar 'glop' and a bulge in the water's surface, which turned into a give-away ring eddying outwards.

Predictably, after so much practice, the little fly landed in precisely the right spot before beginning its short journey into the shadows. Almost as predictably came that carefree sound as the trout took it. Up went the rod tip, there was the familiar tug, but this time, to my astonishment, the rod arced into a tight, satisfying curve and the nylon leader hissed through the smooth surface of the water as one very angry brown trout charged out into the pool and began boring away towards the stickle above it.

I tipped the rod over to the side and brought the fish's head round. It sidled back towards me and then set off downstream towards the fast water at the tail of the pool. Again, I turned it, with more difficulty this time, and it hung on the current below me, doing nothing, a deadweight bowing the rod over and testing the light, two-pound leader almost to breaking point.

Any fish that gets downstream of you while you are playing it can present problems because the weight of the current is added to its own weight. The bigger the fish, the faster the water, the greater the problem.

Keeping the rod tip up and the line tight, I trotted along the bank until I was level with the trout, which appeared by now to be weakening.

Most of the brownies in these Devon streams are little fish, rarely weighing more than about half a pound, their numbers, voracious appetites and the ferocity with which they fight making up for their lack of size. Apart from the odd one kept for breakfast, I slip the vast majority of them back, using barbless hooks which can be tweaked free under water. This fish was different, though, a veritable leviathan. I freed and extended my landing net, sank it into the water, drew her over the rim and swung her up on to the shingle beach. Holding her upright in the mesh, I tapped her sharply three or four times on the back of her head, just behind her eyes. She quivered and lay still, golden, gleaming, dark spots in pale haloes, with perfect fins and tail, the now drowned Black Gnat embedded firmly in the 'scissors' at the corner of her mouth. She pulled the spring balance down to a fraction over one pound four ounces – a respectable fish by any standards and a monster for this relatively inhospitable little river.

Upon reflection, the reason for my consistent failure to hook the fish before probably had to do with striking too quickly. Little fish in tumbling streams tend to dart up to dry flies and to turn down on them very quickly. One's response must therefore be quick. But, unknown to me, this was not a little fish, nor was it lying in fast water. In striking as soon as I heard the sound of its rise, rather than waiting for a second or so, I was probably pulling the fly from its still half-open mouth.

Another place, another day.

The Tweed at Caddonfoot is sheltered from the south-west wind by Minch Moor, across which shepherds once strode as they drove their flocks to market at Selkirk. Despite the high hills around, this is water far less intimate than that of the Taw or Torridge, the Dart or Teign, the short, bubbling streams that drain the Devon moors. Here, the Tweed is thirty or forty yards wide and awesome in a spate, its red-brown waters tumbling and brawling around the worn grey pillars of the bridge. As the April downpour thinned to a drizzle over Broad Law and the Lowther Hills, and then died, the river began to fall. Daffodils along its banks nodded golden in soft spring sunshine; pale primroses glistened in the grass; the rippling song of a white-bibbed dipper, perched on a rock, rose above the babble of the stream.

Chest waders are better than thigh boots here, and a wading staff is essential, as is a long rod, ten feet at least (eleven is better), with which to control and maintain contact with the flies.

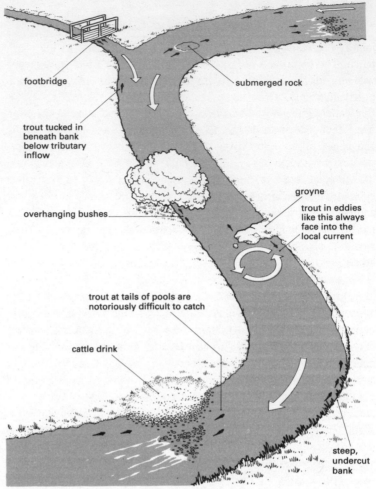

The trout's lies in a spate river

Sitting on the bank beneath the trees, I made up a sixteen-foot leader with two droppers, tested the knots carefully and tied a size 14 Blae and Black on the point, a Snipe and Purple on the middle dropper and an Orange Partridge on the top one.

The water raced along the near bank, lurching over sunken stones and swirling around clumps of grass which would stand high and dry in a few hours' time when the flood had abated fully. Further out, over deeper water, the surface was smoother, and a long, deep glide slid sinuously away from me beneath the trees along the far bank.

I started cautiously, kneeling at the river's edge, wafting out no more than six or eight yards of line and allowing it to swing round on the current before retrieving and recasting. The first few casts brought no response but then the flies dropped a few feet upstream of a short stretch of slack water. As they were carried into it, there was a sharp tug on the rod tip – and then nothing. I repeated the cast, giving just a little slack as the team of flies reached the head of the slack patch. The tip of the fly line pulled away sharply; the rod went up and was immediately hauled into a bow. Less than a minute later I drew a pretty quarter-pound brown trout into the shallows, ran my hand down the leader, grasped the Blae and Black by its shank and tweaked it free. The little fish remained static for a moment, breasting the current and regaining its composure before darting off into the dark water whence it had come.

I stepped into the stream and waded carefully towards a just-submerged ridge in the middle of the river, feeling for each foothold and casting as I went. I had a number of pulls and slipped back two more small brown trout before reaching the ridge, from which I knew I would be able to cover the deeper water beyond. Once there, I took stock.

The pebble bar on which I was standing was quite steep sided and no more than a couple of yards wide. Downstream, it appeared to slope away gradually. Immediately upstream of me the rounded peaks of an outcrop of grey rock just broke the water's surface. The water between the bar and the far bank was dark and swirling, flecked with flotsam from the fading flood, calmer beneath the trees fifteen yards away than in midstream.

I lengthened line gradually, covering the whole width of the stream until, eventually, the flies were tucking in beneath the branches of a silver birch and dropping tight in against the bank. Then I began to move downstream, along the bar, one pace at a time – cast across the stream, allow the flies to settle and to swing round on the current, retrieve them, one pace downstream, cast again.

Suddenly, only a few seconds after the flies had landed and while the floating line was just starting to curve on the current, there was a fierce pull. As I lifted the rod tip, it was hauled downwards by a fish far larger than the three I had already caught. It jumped twice and then bored away downstream, tearing line from the reel as it went. I could not follow it. The rod was bowed into a fierce arc, the line tight as a harp string, the leader and hook hold tested almost to destruction. Eventually I was able to check and slow the fish, to turn its head and to ease it gradually upstream towards me. At last, and after what seemed an eternity, it came to hand, bronze on top, an irregular pattern of neat black circles breaking up the gilded silver-gold of its flanks, a perfect brown trout of just over a pound. I released it and continued fishing.

After half an hour or so I had reached water at the foot of the bar so deep that I could go no further. I turned and began to try to wade back upstream, but the push of the current made progress difficult and heaped water high against my chest. The gradient of the river bed was steeper than it had felt as I had moved slowly downstream and the pebbles and small stones gave and scrunched away as I tried to climb it. A length of black and sodden timber washed away by the preceding night's flood was pushed against me and then became caught in the landing net hanging from a ring on my jacket. As I turned to free it, I stumbled and almost fell. My heart thumped; I was breathing hard.

In the end, I did not take the ducking I deserved. My wading staff saved the day. I regained the shallower water below the rocks and was then able to make my way cautiously back to the bank. But it had been a hard ten or fifteen minutes and had reminded me of an essential lesson – that it is always easier to wade downstream than up, and that as you enter the water you must always know how you intend to get out of it.

Wading difficulties aside, fishing across and down is the simplest method for the beginner and one widely practised by many anglers in Scotland and in the north of England. The water does the work for you. A team of three or four sparsely tied wet flies – a size 16 Orange or Yellow Partridge, perhaps, a Williams Favourite, a Snipe and Purple, a wet Greenwell's Glory, a Greenwell's Spider or a Blae and Black – is cast across the current and allowed to swing round on the stream before being lifted off and recast. Concentrating on good fish-holding water – the heads and tails of pools, undercut banks, overhanging trees and bushes, the slack areas above and beside rocks and boulders, bays and eddies – work slowly downstream, one pace at a time, watching the curve of the floating line on the surface of the water, striking at the slightest sign of its straightening or checking.

Where the stream is deep and powerful, the leader can be attached to the fly line by a sinking braided butt, which will act like a 'mini-sink-tip', carrying the flies down a foot or two and allowing them to work there much more naturally than they would were we to attach split shot or lead wire to the leader, or to use weighted flies.

My own reservation about fishing across and down is that it seems to me to prick more fish than it catches. Time and again, the line checks or straightens a little, or there is a tap or a tug at the rod tip, and that's all. This may be because the trout sense the tension in the line as they grab at the fly, rejecting the fraud instinctively and immediately, or because, inevitably, we will almost always be striking upstream, literally pulling the fly from the fishes' mouths. Whatever the reason, the frustration caused is more than sufficient to persuade me that it is better to work upstream, casting ahead of me, retrieving line and lifting the rod to maintain contact with my flies as they are borne back towards me on the current.

Upstream wet fly fishing is a more calculating and precise exercise than is fishing across and down. Because the flies will travel only relatively short distances in quite straight lines, rather than long ones in great sweeping arcs, they should be cast accurately to likely lies, each lie being explored carefully before moving on to the next. And do not concentrate only on the obvious lies, those associated with rocks, groynes, trees or banks protruding from the water or standing above it. Every sizable feature on the river bed – each boulder, each hollow – can provide a home for fish, an area protected from the full force of the current in which a trout may lurk, waiting for its food to be borne to it on the stream. Such features create turbulence, humping the water upwards, often right to the surface where the river is of modest depth. Learn to 'read the water', to identify the places that will be attractive to fish, and concentrate on them.

Whereas there may be advantage in using a team of three or four wet flies when fishing across and down, I prefer to use only two when

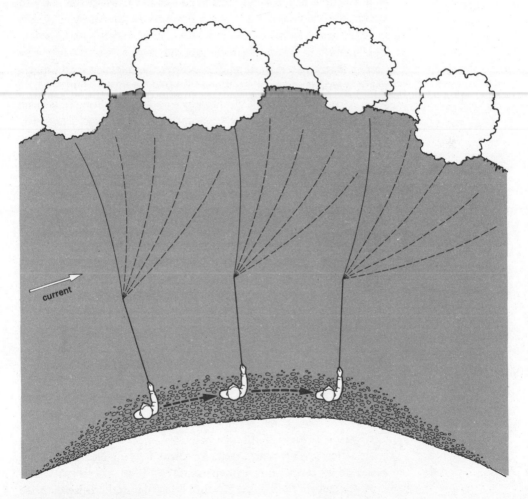

Fishing across and down
1. *Start at the head of the pool, casting a short line and fanning the water*
2. *Extend line until you are tucking the flies in under the far bank*
3. *Take two or three paces downstream every two or three casts*

fishing upstream wet – perhaps a small (size 14 or 16), lightly-leaded March Brown or Gold-Ribbed Hare's Ear nymph, a Sawyer's Pheasant Tail nymph or a wet Greenwell's Glory, March Brown or Silver March Brown on the point, and a spider pattern, maybe a Black Spider, a Snipe and Purple or an Orange Partridge, on the dropper, about four feet above it.

Upstream wet fly fishing requires greater concentration than does fishing across and down. Your flies will begin their downstream journey as soon as they land on the water, and you must keep in touch with them. In relatively slow, streamy water, you may cast up to ten yards ahead of you, recovering line by drawing it across the index finger of your rod hand and either allowing it to fall loose or, rather better, bunching it into your free hand with a figure-of-eight retrieve.

Keep closely in touch with your flies and watch the water, hawk-like, where you believe them to be, tightening at the first hint of a bronze or silver flash beneath the surface, the tell-tale glint of a fish rising or turning to take a fly. When the tip of the fly line is four or five yards from you, begin to lift the rod tip steadily. And when it reaches the ten-thirty or eleven o'clock position, flick the line up behind you, recasting with no more than one or two false casts.

Allow the speed of the current to dictate the length of line you cast; the faster the flow, the shorter the line. When the water is running so quickly that it is effectively impossible to keep pace by retrieving line, cast no more than six or eight yards and begin to raise the rod as soon as the flies alight on the surface. With a minimum of practice, you will learn how to maintain delicate contact with the flies without dragging them through the water, casting, raising the rod, flicking it up and recasting in a controlled, rhythmic sequence.

Sometimes in the spring, but more frequently in the summer, from late May to September, you may do as well on the Tweed with a dry fly as with a wet one. The same goes for all the spate rivers – the Deveron, the Don, the Spey and the Tay in Scotland, where wonderful wild brown trout so often have to play third fiddle to salmon and sea trout; the Nidd, the Ure and the Wharfe sweeping down from the Yorkshire moors; the Lune and the Ribble pouring into Lancashire from the Pennines; the Teifi and the Usk in South Wales; and those lovely Lilliputian Devon streams the Dart, Exe, Taw, Tamar and Torridge.

Such rivers, especially those in the north of England, are often described as 'classic wet fly waters', and so they may be. You may even hear people say – especially in respect of Yorkshire rivers – that up-winged duns hatch, dry their wings and fly off so quickly that the trout tend to ignore them, concentrating instead on nymphs and drowned spinners, and that to fish them with a dry fly is therefore no more than an exercise in futility. That is not my experience, nor the

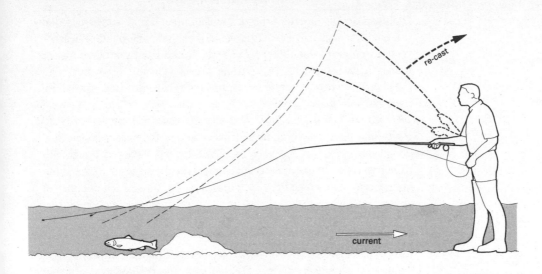

Upstream wet fly fishing

experience of my Yorkshire friends, many of whom take some of their best trout of each season on dry flies cast to rising fish, or on modern emerger patterns which hang in the surface film, representing hatching insects.

The history of river trout fly fishing over the past hundred years or so is one of quite irrational 'regionalization' of fishing styles.

Several books published in Scotland and Yorkshire during the second half of the nineteenth century developed and promoted the art of wet fly fishing. Among the best and best known of them were W. C. Stewart's *The Practical Angler*, published in 1857, and *Yorkshire Trout Flies* by T. E. Pritt, published in 1885 and then republished as *North Country Flies* in 1886. These and other works by writers like John Jackson and Michael Theakston seem to have established in fly fishers' minds the view that North Country fly fishing and wet fly fishing were necessarily one and the same thing.

It is perhaps an unhappy coincidence that the great chalk stream fly fisher F. M. Halford should have published his first work, *Floating Flies and How to Dress Them*, in 1886, just as Pritt's book was becoming widely known. Halford was an articulate and convincing advocate of the dry fly for use on chalk streams – not because he saw it as more 'sporting' than wet fly fishing but simply because he found it to be the most effective means of taking trout feeding on duns, spinners and caddis flies.

Halford followed *Floating Flies* with six more books, including *Dry Fly Fishing in Theory and Practice* (1895), *Dry Fly Entomology* (1903), *The Modern Development of the Dry Fly* (1910) and *The Dry Fly Man's*

Handbook (1913). By the time of his death in 1914, he had become a cult figure. It was Halford's disciples, rather than Halford himself, who promoted the concept of 'dry fly purism', seeking to turn fly fishing for chalk stream trout into a mysterious and esoteric art.

By 1916, when Harfield Edmonds and Norman Lee published privately their marvellous but now very scarce book *Brook and River Trouting: A Manual of North Country Methods*, the divide between North and South was complete; chalk stream fly fishers fished dry flies, North Countrymen and Scotsmen fished wet ones, and the Devonians and Welsh, bewildered and then indifferent, went on pragmatically, matching their fishing styles – dry or wet – to the water and the weather.

It is extraordinary how long it takes to dislodge prejudice from the subconscious. Even today, and despite the efforts of successive fine and respected anglers – George Skues, Frank Sawyer and Oliver Kite among them – to restore wet fly fishing to the chalk streams in the guise of nymph fishing, which requires every bit as much skill as dry fly fishing does, there is still a form of snobbery associated with these rivers which has much to do with dry fly purism and which is often reflected in fishery rules which disallow the use of nymphs for all or part of each season.

The polarization has been completed and compounded by the widespread belief, usually articulated by southern anglers with little North Country experience, that Yorkshire and Scottish rivers are wet fly waters and that to fish them with dry flies is always to waste one's time.

'Always' and 'never' are dangerous words to use where fishing is concerned. Fishery regulations apart, there is really no hard and fast rule as to whether or when one should use a sunk 'wet' fly or a floating 'dry' one. On all rivers, from the chalk streams of southern England and Yorkshire, through the limestone ones of Gloucestershire, the southern Pennines, Cumbria and Ireland, to the spate or freestone rivers of Wales, the West Country, north-east England and Scotland, it is a fact that most trout take most of their food from the river bed, from mid-water or from beneath the surface, and that only a relatively small proportion of their diets is made up of surface food. Of course, these proportions will vary from month to month and river to river. In warm weather on fertile streams, huge hatches of duns and caddis flies and great falls of spinners may tempt the fish to take much of their food from the surface and relatively little from beneath it. Similarly, and while the wet fly may be the better bet on them through much of the season, even the least fertile spate rivers will produce respectable hatches of large dark olives and March browns in April, iron blue duns and (save in Wales and Ireland) medium olives in May and June, and pale wateries, blue-winged olives and assorted caddis flies in high summer, hatches to which the trout will rise when conditions are right and which can present the angler with excellent opportunities to fish the dry fly with every expectation of success.

And we should not forget the terrestrial insects either, those hatched in the ground or in bankside vegetation and which are then blown on to the water, providing welcome pickings for opportunistic trout. I do not know of a river in the British Isles that does not have falls of black gnats from May to August, that does not have beetles and caterpillars dropping into it from overhanging trees or bushes, that does not see occasional falls of flying ants on hot, humid July or August days, or on to which no daddy-long-legs are ever blown towards the back end of the season.

The less fertile a river, the less aquatic insect life it sustains, the more important are terrestrial insects to the trout that inhabit it. It matters not where you fish, it is always a good idea to have some Black Gnats in your fly box, half a dozen dry Coch-y-Bonddu with which to represent beetles, a few dry Red or Black Ants, two or three floating Daddy-Long-Legs and even, perhaps, an artificial caterpillar or two.

While it is an inescapable fact that chalk streams and limestone rivers are more fertile than spate rivers and therefore support a greater profusion of aquatic insects, there is one group of flies – the stoneflies – which is confined almost entirely to the rough streams and rivers of Scotland, northern England, Wales and, to a lesser extent, the West Country. It is a group which presents some special problems of its own.

As we saw in Chapter 3, stonefly nymphs or 'creepers' are sturdy, earwig-like creatures which cling tenaciously to rocks on the river bed, crawling about in search of food. It is their behaviour, rather than their appearance, that is almost impossible to suggest with an artificial fly. Countless convincing imitation stonefly nymphs have been tied by inventive fly dressers; few if any of them have offered consistent success. The problem is one of presentation. Stonefly creepers are found only on or very close to the river bed, and most of them prefer craggy, jagged, rocky river beds and fast water. It is very difficult to fish even a heavily-leaded artificial right on the bottom in a powerful stream, and even were you to succeed in doing so, there is every likelihood that you would then spend more time with your fly caught in nooks and crannies than actually fishing.

When the trout are feeding on creepers, many northern anglers shed such inhibitions as they may have, collect a tin full of the natural insects and fish them as bait.

You do not get a 'hatch' of stoneflies in the fly fisher's sense of the word. Stonefly creepers crawl ashore, and it is there that the adult hatches out, so the trout are given no opportunity to take hatching adults at the water's surface. But, having hatched and mated, female stoneflies do fly back to the water to lay their eggs, dipping on to it repeatedly as they release little clusters of them or even paddling about on the surface, making quite a commotion as they spread their eggs around, and it is here that the trout will often take them enthusiastically.

Whether you use a dry fly or a wet one to represent the egg-laying or dying female stonefly is a choice that will be dictated chiefly by the nature of the water. Where it is smooth and calm, the natural insects may stay afloat for some time, the trout will take them from the surface, and it will pay to use a dry fly. There are several patterns available tied on hooks ranging in size from 14 to long-shanked 10 and with bodies ranging in colour from drab brown through amber and orange to bright yellow.

What almost all of them have in common is a pair of wings sloped low across their backs and a bushy hackle which may be wound 'palmer', down all or part of the body, giving a flue-brush effect and helping the fly to float well. You should allow the size and body colour of any dry stonefly pattern you use to be dictated by the appearance of the natural flies on and around the water.

Where the water is fast and tumbling, the female stoneflies are likely to be drowned very quickly, the trout will be used to taking them beneath the surface, and it makes sense therefore to fish a wet fly, or a team of wet flies. There are numerous patterns to choose from, many of them long established and well proven. Among the best known are the Orange Partridge, the Snipe and Yellow, the Waterhen Bloa, the Yellow Sally, the Dark Spanish Needle and the Woodcock and Yellow. The differences between some of them – especially between the 'yellow' patterns – may appear marginal, but it is a strange fact that one will often work when another fails. The answer for the newcomer to a particular water is to take informed local advice, either from a tackle shop or from a fellow angler at the waterside.

Drowned adult stoneflies drift, inert, on the current, and that is how the artificials should be presented to the trout. Fished across and down, our flies would swing across the current as a natural never does. So cast them upstream, either directly or diagonally, and allow them to be carried back towards you while you watch for the slightest evidence of a fish's interest in them.

Finally, a few words about conservation.

Our Victorian forefathers gauged the success of their days on the river by the numbers of trout they slaughtered and carried home. Catches of twenty, thirty or more fish a day were far from uncommon, and rarely does the angler appear to have considered returning fish to the water. This may not have mattered much. Most Victorians had less free time than we have nowadays, and they were less mobile, so pressure on angling waters was relatively light and the trout had adequate opportunity to replenish their numbers.

Today, with longer weekends and holidays, and with most people having access to motor cars, fishing pressure on all but the wildest and remotest waters is very much greater than it used to be, and the trout's natural capacity for regeneration cannot compensate for the numbers of fish killed each year. As a consequence, most readily accessible waters now have to be stocked with farm-reared trout. This is an expensive exercise which must be paid for by the angler. It is also a somewhat unsatisfactory one, in that farm-reared fish rarely look as pretty, fight as well, taste as good or spawn as readily as wild ones.

The only way in which we can enhance stocks of wild fish and reduce the need to introduce farm-reared ones into our rivers is by practising self-restraint. I have little time for the 'holier than thou' attitude often displayed by the crusading catch-and-release brigade, those who claim to see the killing of fish as an anathema. It seems not to have occurred to them that by returning all the fish they catch they are effectively making a plaything out of a living creature, which cannot be right. But there is certainly merit in setting our sights high, in imposing demanding size limits on ourselves, in returning all fish that are undersized by our standards and in killing only as many trout as we need for supper tonight or breakfast tomorrow. Those who boast of filling their freezers or of selling trout in order to defray the cost of petrol and permits have only themselves to blame when the wild trout they are used to fishing for are replaced with farmed ones and ticket prices rise yet again.

CHECK LIST – CHALK STREAM TACKLE

ROD: 8ft 6in–9ft: #4–6: stiff, tip-actioned

FLY LINE: Weight forward or double-tapered floating, #4–6

LEADER:

Fly line	Braided loop	1ft	Knotless tapered leader 9ft
	18lb		tapered to 2 – 3lb

FLIES:

	Morning	*Afternoon/evening*
April	Kite's Imperial (14)* Cinnamon Sedge (12 or 14)	
Late April/early May	Hawthorn Fly (14) Kite's Imperial (14)* Blue Upright (14 or 16)	
Mid May to Mid June	Shadow Mayfly (10) Blue Upright (14 or 16)* Gold-Ribbed Hare's Ear (14 or 16) Black Gnat (16 or 18)	Deerstalker (1/s 10) Lunn's Particular (16)
Mid June to Late August	Gold-Ribbed Hare's Ear (14 or 16) Blue-Winged Olive (14)* Black Gnat (16 or 18) Tups Indispensable (14 or 16) Pheasant Tail Nymph (14 or 16)	Lunn's Particular (16) Sherry Spinner (14) Cinnamon Sedge (12)
September	Kite's Imperial (14)* Blue Upright (14 or 16)* Gold-Ribbed Hare's Ear (14 or 16) Cinnamon Sedge (12 or 14) Pheasant Tail Nymph (14 or 16)	

And do not forget scissors or snippers, artery forceps, silicone floatant, mucilin (red tin), sinkant (Fuller's Earth, washing-up detergent and glycerin), hook-hone, spare leaders or leader material, landing net and priest.

Notes:
1. Numbers in brackets represent hook sizes (1/s – long-shanked).
2. Any of the flies marked * can be replaced with a CDC Olive Dun.
3. A Cinnamon Sedge may be expected to serve perfectly adequately as a grannom, a summer sedge or a caperer.

CHAPTER NINE

Chalk Stream Fly Fishing

A cuckoo's call echoes over clouds of bluebells carpeting the woodland floor. In the meadows, the rare fritillary's purple bells nod on slender stems; ducks doze in spring sunshine among golden celandines and pale pink lady's smock. It is mid April. The countryside is coming to life and the trout season is opening on the chalk streams.

Opening-day excitement brings me too early to the waterside. During winter weekends and evenings, rods and landing nets have been checked, lines and reels cleaned, flies replenished and rearranged in their boxes, nylon renewed. The night before the 'off' always finds me fussing about, baking chicken legs, making sandwiches, stowing tackle in the car, laying out fishing clothes washed, pressed and put away last autumn.

I wake early, peer out at the weather, shave with my mind miles away by the river, munch a piece of toast, scald myself with my coffee, pour soup into a flask. I *know* there is not the slightest possibility that even the first of the grannoms or large dark olive duns will hatch before midday, but closed-season patience turned to impatience more than a month ago and has now evaporated completely. I can wait no longer.

The drive to the river is like a reawakening. White cow parsley makes lacework beneath pale leaf buds in the hedgerows. Clumps of late primroses glow soft yellow from the roadside verge. Cotton-wool cumulo nimbus sail across a sharp blue sky.

It's ten o'clock. A brisk, cold, south-easterly breeze chills the valley. There are two other cars in the car park, their owners boiling a kettle in an ancient clapperboard fishing hut which stands by one of the carriers, a side stream from the main river, cut in the days when the water meadows were flooded in winter to increase their fertility or to enable the growing of reeds for thatching. We stand outside the hut, blowing steam from mugs of coffee cupped in cold hands, mumbling about the winter past and the prospects for the season ahead, watching the dark water sidling towards us for the first flutter of fly life, the first tantalizing, tell-tale, rippling ring pushed outwards by a rising fish.

Nothing moves. The stream's surface, black and secretive, slides silently by. My colleagues opt for downstream beats, climb the stile and stroll off across the meadow.

111

DRY FLY FISHING
The first trout of the season

It's eleven o'clock. I can wait no longer. I put up my rod.

A size 14 Kite's Imperial will serve to represent the large dark olives that should start to appear within the hour. I tie one to the two-pound point of the ten-foot nylon leader, check the knot carefully, dip the fly in a bottle of floatant and blow away the excess liquid.

If the leader sinks, it will drown the fly each time I lift off to recast. Mucilin makes it buoyant, but nylon treated with mucilin looks like a hawser when seen from beneath the water's surface. So I leave the eighteen inches of nylon immediately above the fly untreated, smearing a little mucilin between finger and thumb, running it up the leader from about eighteen inches above the fly to the tip of the fly line, wiping my fingers and then running them up the leader three or four more times to remove the surplus. This done, I take the leader around the back of the reel post, hook the fly to a ring half-way up the rod, and reel up tight. (If you bring the leader straight down from the tip ring and hook the fly to the keeper ring just above the rod's handle, the join between leader and fly line will be inside the rings, and it may prove difficult to get it out through the tip ring when you want to start fishing.)

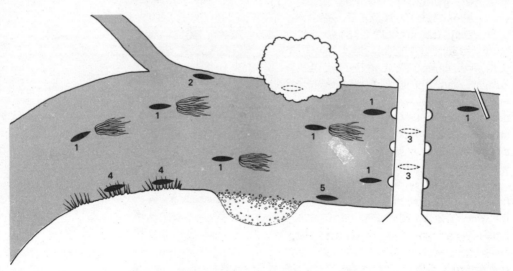

Trout's lies in a chalk stream
1. *In the 'pad' of water immediately upstream of weed beds, bridge supports, groynes and other obstructions*
2. *Immediately downstream from ditch and tributary in-flows*
3. *Under bridges and overhanging trees*
4. *Tucked in beneath tussock grass and other overhanging vegetation*
5. *Downstream from active cattle drinks*

The carrier is deep and narrow here. The autumn and winter have been wet. The water table is as full as it will be this year. The springs are all running. While the level of the river may be no more than six inches or so higher than it was last September, the push of the current is noticeably stronger. I make my way cautiously upstream. The trout are hugging the bottom. A dark shape on the gravel between two trailing, weaving clumps of pale green weed comes to life, lifts a little, curves, and sidles slowly into the darkness beneath one of them.

A little further up, a wild fish, six inches long, is breasting the flow in the shallow, shingly margins, golden bronze, its flanks speckled with vermilion, alert, quivering, darting briefly to right and left to seize tiny unidentifiable morsels of food. It sees me, freezes, drops slowly back for a foot or so, still facing into the stream, then turns and darts away.

The carrier is wider and shallower above the bend, with a dark, narrow, oily glide between a weed bed and the far bank. There is almost always a fish here, tucked in tight beneath the foot-high, black earth bank. I stop, squat down and watch.

A white-rumped moorhen bobs busily in the margin of the stream, pecking aimlessly at bits of floating greenery. A little grebe, bedraggled grey, bulbous head stretched out, paddles urgently downstream beneath the surface. A water vole peers from a hole above the glide, plops into the stream, crosses to a raft of weed, changes its mind, dives and disappears.

Suddenly, the water in the glide humps and an eddying ring thrusts outwards and fades. A little dark grey fly like a tiny sailing boat, a large dark olive, floats for a few seconds, flutters its wings, drifts again, and struggles into the air. Another follows it, and another. The fish rises once more, breaking the surface this time. I am only about ten yards downstream of her but the cast will be a tricky one. If the line is too straight when it lands on the water, the current in midstream will catch it and carry it away, dragging the floating fly across the surface, which will startle the trout.

Drag is the dry fly fisher's most constant enemy. Natural flies floating on the stream do not skid across the surface unless driven by the wind. The slightest sign of drag, often invisible to the angler ten or fifteen yards away, will be enough to warn the trout not to touch our artefact; severe drag may send him scuttling for cover. Drag can be reduced to a minimum by placing oneself as directly downstream from the fish as possible, so that the fly drifts straight back towards you. The further across the current we have to cast, the more of a wiggle we must put into the fly line as it lands, to provide more slack than will be taken up before the fly reaches our quarry. For those who do not achieve it accidentally, a wiggle may be put into a fly line by aiming a little high and then checking the line as it unfurls on the forward-cast.

In approaching this fish there is the wind to contend with too,

113

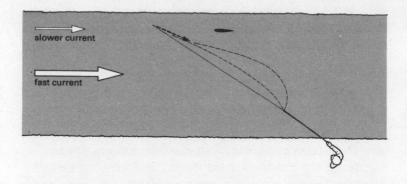

slower current

fast current

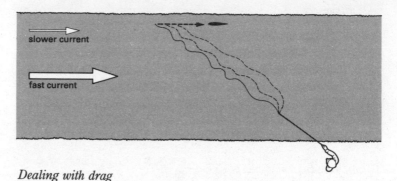

slower current

fast current

Dealing with drag

blustery now and squally, blowing directly towards me.

I kneel on the bank (thank heavens for trousers with waterproof patches on their knees and seat), unhook the fly from the rod ring, pull a yard or so of line from the reel and flick the fly and line out on to the grass in front of me. Then I strip a further eight or ten yards of line from the reel and arrange it so that it will run out freely when I start to cast.

I watch again. The hatch is building up now. A steady stream of flies is being carried towards me on the current. The fish in the glide is rising regularly every thirty seconds or so; further upstream, there are others moving.

I work out line, lifting the rod high and fast into the back-cast, pausing, tapping the line forward into the wind. Three false casts are enough to extend the ten yards I need; one more to check the direction; tap forward.

The fly lands right where the trout has been rising. While it drifts back towards me I pull off an extra yard of line and then lift off. Two more false casts. The fly lands a foot above the fish; a brown neb, a trout's nose, breaks the surface, the fly vanishes, a ring starts to eddy outwards; I lift the rod and feel for the fish before tightening; the water erupts as she thrashes briefly on the surface and then turns and runs downstream, boring deep beneath the bank.

I tip the rod over and apply side strain to ease her head round and bring her into the open water in midstream – not soon enough. She turns and heads doggedly for a weed bed. The rod is hooped over, the fine nylon and the knot joining it to the fly must be stretched almost to breaking point. Slowly, she gives up her quest and turns to face into the current. I move down until I am level with her. She heads back towards the glide in which she was hooked. Again, carefully applied side strain turns her. Eventually, after two or three minutes, she begins to tire. I draw her towards the bank, a deep, golden hen fish of about two pounds, perfectly proportioned and marked.

With one foot in the water, I run my hand down the leader to the hook, caught in the corner of her mouth, and twitch it free. The trout remains still for a few moments, looking bemused. Placing my hand carefully over her back, I ease her head into the current. She is upright, her gills are working steadily, there is no sign of blood. As I stand up, she sidles away across the gravel bed of the stream towards deeper water; then, with a sinuous movement of her body and a flick of her tail, she is gone. The first fish of the season.

Chalk stream rules and conventions

A lot of mystique has been built up around chalk stream fly fishing, some of it having to do with sometimes pompous preoccupation with entomology and with the dry fly, and some of it with rules and conventions – written and unwritten – the reasons for which may seem obscure to the newcomer. Do not be daunted by it. The truth of the matter is that those who developed dry fly fishing did so because it is the easiest and most effective way of catching rising trout, especially on fertile and therefore often heavily weeded waters in which it would be difficult to fish a wet fly upstream, and impossible to fish one across and down, without one's flies becoming snagged repeatedly in the weed.

A basic knowledge of chalk stream entomology is useful and easily acquired. By and large, though, you can fish the season through perfectly adequately with no more than about a dozen patterns, provided you know the time of day and stage in the season to which each is best suited. The table at the beginning of this chapter should help.

Most, if not all chalk stream fisheries lay down quite specific rules about the types and sizes of flies that may be used and the ways in which those flies may be fished. Typically, they will insist that all fishing is 'upstream' – that is, that you may cast only to fish that are upstream of you – and on the use of dry flies and nymphs only, nymph fishing sometimes being allowed only during the latter part of the season – after 1 July, for example. Hook sizes may be limited to 12 or smaller except during the mayfly season, when hooks up to size 10 or 10 long-shank may be permitted to allow for imitations of the outsized natural insects. There is a convention that artificial mayfly nymphs should not be used on chalk streams. And some fisheries forbid the use of weighted nymphs, to discourage people from 'dredging the bottom' with leaded nymph and shrimp patterns.

All of these rules are intended to encourage the use of imitative fly patterns and the art of deception, and to prevent people from 'spinning' for trout with attractor patterns or lures.

The other conventions associated with the chalk streams are quite simple and serve to protect the interests both of the rivers and of those who fish them.

It is generally accepted that you should start at the bottom of a beat and work your way upstream, and that if you have to walk downstream you should keep as far away from the river as possible. Chalk streams are clear and their trout tend to be shy. The fish always lie facing into the current. Therefore, if you approach them from upstream, they will see you and take fright when you are still some distance away – and you will almost certainly spoil the fishing on that stretch of water for some time, both for yourself and for others. But if you approach the fish from downstream, you may reasonably expect to be in their blind spots and to see them before they see you, especially if you move carefully and keep your eyes open.

Starting at the bottom of a beat and working upstream also makes it virtually impossible for one angler to cut in above another who is already fishing. When a stretch of chalk stream is fished, it is inevitable that the trout will be alarmed, seeking cover and returning only gradually to their lies, perhaps over a period of an hour or more. There can be few things more frustrating than to be working your way quietly and cautiously up a stretch of river, only to have some other angler appear on the bank upstream of you and start fishing. For the same reason, it is considered extremely discourteous for one fly fisher to overtake another who is already fishing and then to start fishing above him. And, as a matter of courtesy, you should always leave at least a hundred and fifty yards between yourself and another angler fishing ahead of you. If you approach closer than this, he may feel pressed to move on more quickly than he would wish.

Lastly, it is generally agreed that, on chalk streams, one should cast only to seen, sizable, feeding fish. This is to discourage people from 'fishing the water' – casting here, there and everywhere in the hope that a trout may take the fly, which would almost always be a forlorn hope anyway. It also helps to protect small fish, that they may grow bigger without having been pestered or caught repeatedly. And it discourages people from harassing fish that are resting. It is a rule that is sometimes more readily adhered to in the spirit than in the letter.

Although chalk streams are generally clear, reflections from the water's surface quite often make it easier to see the rings of a rise than the fish that caused them, and big trout can rise remarkably discreetly, making only the tiniest rings.

A year or so ago, I took a friend fishing on the Itchen. We were walking up a wide, placid, smooth stretch of the river when we saw a minute dimple appear on the water close to the reeds that lined the far bank. I knew the stretch well and was reasonably confident that the brief ripple must have been caused by a trout rather than a dace or a small grayling, and that there were few undersized trout in that stretch. My companion took some convincing but eventually dropped a little Lunn's Particular on to the water a foot or so upstream from the spot where the fish lay. Another equally tiny dimple, his rod went up, and he found himself attached to almost three pounds of very angry brown trout.

Rise forms

Rise forms – the ways in which trout rise to different types of insects – provide us with invaluable clues as to what the fish are feeding on and therefore the sorts of artificials we should be using. Essentially, there are five distinct types of rise form.

The bulge or eddy

This is caused by a trout moving quickly between one and three feet beneath the surface, often turning on its side to scoop shrimps or nymphs from the river bed in relatively shallow water. When a fish pushes hard with its tail, it displaces water. If it is upright when it does this, the displacement may be seen as an eddy or whorl at the surface, rather like the whorl you see when bath water drains away. If it is on its side, as trout tend to be when picking food from among the gravel, the water will be displaced upwards and will be seen on the surface as a bulge. Bulging fish are best tackled with weighted nymph or shrimp patterns where these are allowed.

The porpoise rise

This is that wonderful, slow-motion rise which shows the top of the trout's head, its dorsal fin and then its tail in stately procession. It is almost always silent. The deliberateness of this rise form stems from the fact that the trout *knows* that its quarry cannot escape; the silence from the fact that, despite appearances, the fish does not break the surface with its mouth. Its quarry, usually nymphs or pupae rising through the water to hatch, are just beneath the surface, or they may

117

be actually trapped in the surface film. They are *not* floating on the surface. You are most likely to interest porpoising trout either with an unweighted nymph or with a 'damp' fly, like a Gold-Ribbed Hare's Ear, which floats in, rather than on, the surface film.

The glop

The glop is the satisfying sound made by a fish taking an insect that is actually floating on the surface, usually an up-winged dun. Trout rise to such flies quite quickly and positively, because they know they may fly off at any moment. In order to take a fly from the surface, the trout must open its mouth, break the surface with its upper jaw, and engulf a small amount of air along with the insect. It is this action that causes the 'glop' we hear. It is worth noting, also, that having taken the fly, the fish then turns downwards, keeping its mouth open for a second or two, to allow the air to escape through its gills. If you strike before it has completed this action, there is a real possibility that you will simply pull the fly from its open mouth; which is why you must pause before striking when a trout rises to a dry fly.

The Sip

This is the subtle little rise form that foiled my friend on the Itchen. It is caused by a trout taking an insect that is floating but which cannot possibly escape – a spinner, a dead or dying fully adult up-winged fly, often a female who has finished laying her eggs. Feeding trout expend no more energy than they must. They will sidle slowly, almost idly, up to spinners and sip them down. Listen carefully in the evening half-light and you may just hear them, a soft, kissing sound, almost inaudible but sometimes more noticeable than the minute rings that ebb away on the surface. Contrast this with . . .

The slash

Also often seen at sunset, this is the trout's frenzied attack on insects large enough to be worth catching and mobile enough to be elusive – caddis flies. Newly hatched caddis flies often buzz on the surface or scuttle across it, fluttering their wings to dry them and in an effort to get airborne. They move quite quickly and the trout must therefore move quickly too, which they do, hurling themselves after the skittering insects and making a great commotion in the process. A sedge pattern is the answer here, and if the trout will not take it when it is simply drifted down to them on the current, it may well be worth giving it a tweak or a twitch just as it reaches the point at which a feeding trout is lying.

You may also see trout slashing at insects on the surface during the last week in May and the first ten days in June, when the mayfly are up.

The mayfly

Where it occurs – and it does not do so on all chalk streams: much of the Itchen and several tributaries of the Hampshire Avon are almost devoid of mayfly – the mayfly hatch provides a unique and fascinating interlude in the chalk stream fly fisher's year, the so-called 'duffer's fortnight'.

Compared with other up-winged flies, the mayfly is huge, its body being as much as an inch long, and provides plump pickings for protein-hungry trout, which often take it enthusiastically. I say 'often' because it is quite possible to be caught out during the mayfly hatch.

Although the odd mayfly may be seen in mid or even early May, the hatch proper usually starts between the 20th and 25th of the month. Perhaps because of their sheer size, the first mayflies of the season often seem to startle the trout and to make them a little nervous, but the fish become used to them quite quickly, rising confidently and gorging themselves on the duns and spinners, which are often present in enormous numbers. I recall driving across the bridge over the Kennet at Hungerford late one afternoon many years ago, and having to use the windscreen wipers to clear away a veritable snowstorm of mayfly spinners.

So large and so obvious are mayflies that it is easy to presume that rising trout must necessarily be feeding on them and to forget that, at this time of year, several other much smaller insect species will be on the water too – iron blue duns and little claret spinners, medium olive duns and medium olive spinners, small spurwings and little amber spinners, and black gnats.

Once the trout have become accustomed to the mayflies, they will quite often turn their attention to these other flies, taking them very selectively and ignoring the armada of mayfly duns or spinners sailing by. This can be very frustrating but, as always, observation offers the key to success. If a trout will not take your mayfly pattern, watch it closely. If it does not appear to be taking mayflies, or if you cannot see what it is rising to, offer it a Blue Upright, a CDC Olive Dun or a Black Gnat.

It is said that trout feed most voraciously on the fourth day after the beginning of the main mayfly hatch and on the fourth day before the hatch ends, and that they gorge themselves during the mayfly hatch to such an extent that they will fast for weeks or even months after it. I cannot vouch for the truth or otherwise of the former observation, although I suspect it may be based on the subjective experiences of a few individuals. The latter theory is obviously nonsense but raises an interesting question.

No fish can go for more than a few days without food, however gluttonously it may have gorged itself beforehand. So, clearly, chalk stream trout must continue to feed consistently after the end of the mayfly hatch. But this does not alter the undeniable fact that, on rivers that have prolific mayfly hatches, there may be very little surface activity once the mayfly hatch is over – through the second half of June and throughout July and August. The reason, I suspect, has to do with the environmental preferences of ephemerid (up-winged) nymphs.

The mayfly nymph is the only one we have that burrows into and lives among silt on the river bed. Where the bed is sufficiently silted to be attractive to mayfly nymphs, it is unlikely to afford large areas of the sorts of habitats favoured by the smaller summer-hatching nymphs – the stones and moss upon which blue-winged olive and small dark olive nymphs live, and the lace-like fronds of the water crowfoot or *Ranunculus* preferred by pale watery, small dark olive and small spurwing nymphs. The only small nymphs for which it will provide ample grazing are those of the Caenis family, the tiny creatures that will hatch into those infuriating, minuscule, cream-coloured flies known as the angler's curse.

From all this it follows that where the mayfly hatch is prolific, subsequent hatches of smaller flies are likely to be sparse, only the Caenis being abundant, and that where mayflies are scarce there may be substantial hatches of smaller flies throughout the summer. My own experience suggests that this is so, and there may be a sequel to the thesis.

I am privileged to be a member of a club which fishes a particularly lovely and historic stretch of the River Itchen renowned for its wonderful hatches of small summer flies and for the consequent excellence of its dry fly fishing throughout the season. For many years – from the First World War until the late 1980s – our water produced almost no mayflies at all. Sighting of even the odd one caused comment in the club's fishing book.

In 1988 we noticed a small but significant increase in mayfly numbers and one of our members actually took a trout on an artificial mayfly having seen it rise to a real mayfly dun. The mayfly hatch has become successively bigger each year since then, until we now comment only on the abundance of the hatch rather than on its occurrence.

Initially our members greeted the return of the mayfly enthusiastically. Now, some of us are beginning to wonder. It may be too soon to tell but it is our impression that the hatches of small summer flies are declining. Could it be that the nature of the river bed is changing, producing a habitat better suited to mayfly and caenis nymphs than to those of the blue-winged olive, the pale watery, the small dark olive and the small spurwing, which have provided us hitherto with such splendid sport on summer days?

Back to the riverbank.

Waiting and watching

Perhaps the easiest lesson to learn about chalk stream fly fishing, and the most difficult to put into practice, is that the slower you go, the more time you spend waiting and watching, rather than casting, the more successful will you be.

I have a friend who fishes with me on the Itchen from time to time. He is chiefly a stillwater fly fisher and gets too few days on chalk streams. He is also delightfully enthusiastic, always champing at the bit. When I arrive at the water to meet him at some civilized hour, he will always be waiting in the car park, boots on, rod up, pretending he has only just arrived when, clearly, he has been pacing up and down for half an hour or more. Walking the bank with him is like taking an ebullient puppy for a walk on a lead; I can sense the frustration as we move slowly upstream, pausing, watching, peering into dark corners of the river; he seems almost to be straining forward, pawing the ground like a bull about to charge. Left to his own devices, he covers phenomenal amounts of river bank, disappearing at the beginning of one beat and appearing four or eight hundred yards on only minutes later, very rarely with anything to show for the energy expended.

When we fished together in June last year, we stayed on to fish the evening rise, which seldom if ever begins before sunset and which is often preceded by a 'dead' period of two or three hours.

The evening rise

We sat outside the hut, munching our sandwiches and sharing a bottle of wine. By seven-thirty he could stand it no longer. He *had* to go fishing. In an attempt to placate him, I pulled on my fishing waistcoat, slowly, picked up my rod and ambled off with him towards the stretch of main river I had selected for our evening's sport. As we crossed a carrier, he peered anxiously up and downstream, studying the water for any sign of a rise. When we reached the Itchen itself I made him sit on the bank with me, and we nattered about this and that for an hour, despite his evident impatience. As we did so, clouds of delicate, diaphanous sherry spinners danced in the evening air above the meadows, glowing in the golden rays of the descending sun, soon to provide countless bedtime snacks for the waiting trout. Eventually, at about a quarter to nine, with no sign of life on the river, he cantered off, saying he was just going to have a look at the carrier we had fished together in the morning.

The spinners began to fall, and the rise started, just after nine o'clock. By the time my companion returned at a quarter to ten, puffed and sweaty, and having terrified every trout on two eight-hundred-yard beats, I had four fish on the bank and there were two more nursing sore jaws in the river, having made good their escapes. It was almost dark and the rise was petering out. Something rustled in the reeds. Like a white ghost, a barn owl slid silently along the edge of the trees on the far bank.

Oncers and fussy fish

I am often asked what it is that sets the consistently successful chalk stream fly fisher apart from those who appear just as skilful but usually catch only average bags of trout. It is difficult to say, but one thing all really able chalk stream anglers have in common is the ability to catch 'oncers' and 'fussy fish'.

The 'oncer' is the trout that rises once to a natural fly, perhaps on a whim and often when there is no other movement on the river, but then refuses to rise again. The trick to catching him is to identify his position *positively* and then to lock it in your memory.

The rise may be seventy-five or a hundred yards upstream of you. Unless you note exactly where it is – relating it accurately to some feature on the bank, right by the water, and then relating that feature to a landmark at the top of the bank, it is likely that you will be unable to locate the spot when you get within casting range.

Do not gallop up the bank to cast to such a fish. If you do, you may very well frighten half a dozen others on the way. Simply lock his position in your mind; he will wait for you.

When you reach a point ten or fifteen yards downstream of his lie, be prepared to wait and watch for ten minutes or more in the hope that he may rise again and show himself to you. It is extraordinary how difficult it can be to find a particular spot that was orginally identified from fifty or a hundred yards away. If he does not show himself, put up a small (size 14) bushy sedge and cast it to a point just behind the one at which you *think* he rose. If nothing happens, repeat the exercise, lengthening line or moving upstream a foot or so, very cautiously, with each successive cast. Sometimes, of course, the exercise will come to nought, but it is wonderfully satisfying when a great trout, suspected rather than seen, tilts into view and grabs a fly put there specially for him; with practice, it can be made to happen more often than you may imagine.

The same goes for 'fussy fish' – those trout that rise persistently throughout the day, usually taking some minute insect species from the water's surface, often being quite difficult to frighten but refusing resolutely to have anything to do with the angler's fly. Most chalk stream trout fisheries have a few of them and they tend to be referred to as 'Aunt Sallies', because everyone has a chuck at them. They can keep the less thoughtful members of a club or syndicate occupied for hours.

The answer to securing the downfall of such fish is *not* to keep on pestering them, offering them every pattern in your box, which serves only to educate them and to make them increasingly wary of artificial flies, but to leave them alone, returning late in the evening. Most fly species, including the tiny smuts which are so often the cause of an Aunt Sally's infuriating intransigence, hatch for quite specific periods of the day. Only rarely will the species with which a fish was preoccupied during the afternoon still be in evidence at dusk. If she is still rising, as she may well be, you may now be able to tempt her with a sedge or a spinner. But it will be more important than ever to approach her with great stealth and caution, and to make your first cast an accurate one; if she has been bombarded with flies for hours on end, the first suspicion that another angler may be having a go at her may well put her firmly on her guard.

Nymph fishing

Those non-anglers who say they lack the patience necessary for the sport are misinformed. There is no patience required. For those who love the countryside, there is always something to be seen, and the longer you are prepared to wait and watch, the more will you see: orange-tip butterflies among the cuckoo flowers; pale puss moths on willow fronds; sleek damselflies and sturdier, sometimes gaudier, dragonflies; sedge warblers, moorhens and coots, the chicks of the latter as bald as their parents are meant proverbially to be; dabchicks, whose diving 'plop' can so easily fool the unwary angler seeking the first sign of a rising trout; wagtails, reed warblers; teal and mallard; kingfishers painting lines of iridescent azure and orange flame as they dart along the water's margins.

But it is the images within the water itself that develop and mature with time.

Seeing fish

When first we stop, we may see no more than weed waving in the depths, half obscured by reflected light. As we wait and watch, helped by a pair of polarized sunglasses and a broad-brimmed hat, the underwater world will begin to take form. Light patches turn into gravel beds; the weed comes into focus, fronds, pale and dark, undulating on the stream, parting and joining in sinuous dance; deep down, dappled grey shadows become a shoal of dace or grayling, rising on the current, slipping this way and that, forever changing position; there are barred perch among them, fierce little tigers of the depths; a faded log, apparently lying on the river's bed, becomes a jack pike, hovering, unmoving, its cold yellow eyes seeing all around it; an incongruously regular shape at the back of a weed bed is seen to wave and materializes as a trout's tail. Reassured by our stillness, the fish sidles out on to the gravel and hangs there. The smaller fish move away. After a minute or so the trout moves to one side. There is a flash of white as his mouth opens and closes; he slides back on to his lie.

If it is helpful to be able to see trout that are rising, it is essential to be able to see those that are taking nymphs. Rarely will any movement at the water's surface betray their positions. If we are to catch them we must develop the ability to see them, and to see what they are doing.

Fishing the Nymph

Nymph fishing is a little more difficult than dry fly fishing, chiefly because of its three-dimensional nature. You must place a dry fly quite accurately upstream of a rising trout, perhaps eighteen inches to three feet above him and no more than a foot to one side or the other. If you can do this, and if the fly does not drag, there is a reasonable chance that he will take it. A nymph must not only be placed in such a way that it will drift down to within a foot on either side of the trout, it must also be placed so that it will have sunk to the trout's depth by the time it reaches him, and this requires fine judgement. While a trout may move a foot or more sideways in order to take a nymph, very rarely will it be prepared to move up or down more than a few inches.

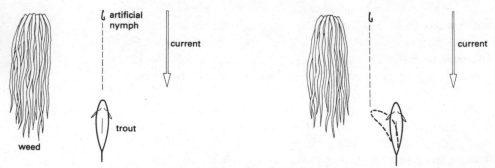

Above left: *It may be very difficult to detect a take to a nymph cast directly upstream of a trout*

Above right: *If the nymph is cast so as to drift down 6 to 8 inches to one side of the trout, the trout must turn in order to take it. Strike as soon as the fish straightens on the current*

It would be nice to be able to produce a table showing how far upstream a nymph must be placed in order to reach a range of specified depths. Sadly, that is impossible; there are too many variables – the weight of the nymph and the speed of the current being chief among them. The only answer is to experiment for yourself. You will find that, quite quickly, you will develop an almost instinctive understanding of the sinking properties of the nymphs you use.

Once you have identified a nymphing fish and found the position from which you can most easily cast to it, you must decide how you will identify the moment at which the trout takes your nymph.

If reflection from the water's surface prevents you from seeing the fish, you will have to rely on the leader floating on the surface and the point at which it cuts down through the surface film. In this case, you can help yourself by greasing the top two-thirds of the leader very lightly, so that it floats and is clearly visible.

If you can see the fish itself, then you should ignore the leader and watch the fish, and there is a trick you can play here. If a nymph is pitched into the water immediately ahead of a trout, the fish – which is almost certain to be facing away from you – may be able to open its mouth, take the nymph, recognize it as a fraud and then spit it out again without you ever suspecting its interest in your offering. And it is remarkable how quickly and emphatically a trout can eject an artificial nymph on discovering the attempted deception. But if you pitch the nymph *just* to one side of the fish's axis, he will *have* to turn in order to take it, and you can strike just as he straightens up having done so. Turned to one side like that, you may even see the white blink as his mouth opens and closes.

George Skues, the father of modern nymph fishing, talked of 'a little brown wink under water' – the flash of bronze the angler may see as a trout turns to take his nymph. I must confess that I have seen it but rarely and would certainly not wish to rely on it. Consistent success in nymph fishing relies on deciding how you intend to spot the take – either by watching the leader or by watching the fish – and then sticking to that method. Nothing will make you miss a take more surely than glancing repeatedly from leader to fish and back again.

If a trout will not take a nymph drifted on the current, without drag, it may be possible to induce him to take it by moving it a little. The aim is to trigger in the fish the response he would make if he saw an insect escaping from him.

Much has been written about the 'induced take'. In truth, the procedure is quite simple. You pitch the nymph into the water well upstream of your quarry, wait while it drifts down towards him, sinking as it does so, and then, just as it reaches him, you raise the rod gently, drawing the line back towards you and causing the nymph to rise abruptly towards the surface. The technique does not always work.

When it does, the result can be dramatic, the trout surging after the fly and very often hooking itself.

The late Oliver Kite, an engaging personality and a fine fly fisher, used to demonstrate that it is possible to take grayling after grayling with a nymph, even when blindfolded. The trick looked difficult but was actually quite simple. 'Olly' would find a sizable shoal of grayling – fish that are markedly less easily frightened than trout – and then cast a weighted nymph to them, lifting it as soon as he guessed it was among the shoal. One fish after another would be tempted by the 'escaping' offering, each hooking itself against Olly's almost tight line.

The season's end

And so to September, a mellow month and sad because it sees the season's end. The days are closing in. The evening rises we saw in summer are mere memories. But temperatures are dropping, and sport can be as spectacular now as at any time since May. The large dark olives, last seen in spring, may be expected to hatch throughout the day; the caperer – one of only two daytime-hatching caddis flies – plays the part of April's grannom; and the trout should be feeding hard in preparation for the rigours of spawning and of the coming winter.

Rules and byelaws on some chalk streams allow fishing to continue until mid October. I am not sure they should. By autumn the mating urge will be upon the trout, they will have begun to move upstream towards their redds and the hen fish will be heavy with spawn. I prefer to close my season at the end of September and to leave them in peace thereafter. But I always do so with a heavy heart, knowing that I have six and a half months to wait before I shall be able to head for the riverside once again.

CHAPTER TEN

Of Lochs and Loughs

After three days of almost continuous rain the soft September sun began to seep through the clouds, bathing the soaked, glistening landscape in a gentle golden glow. In the evening Tony and I crossed the puddled road in front of the hotel in Oughterard, climbed the steps and watched countless salmon and sea trout hurling themselves at the roaring waterfall. Some were great fish of fifteen or twenty pounds, perhaps more; most were much smaller, many no more than twelve inches or so from nose to tail. Time and again, dark, shimmering shapes would propel themselves from the wild water at the foot of the fall and arc upwards. Some made it, gaining fin-holds at the point where the river curved smoothly downwards over the lip of the overhanging rocks, fighting upwards and onwards into the pool above; far more did not, but fell or were pushed back to try again and again.

As we watched, we wondered at the instinct, the compelling urge, that drives these fish so determinedly onwards. There must be many that never make it up the falls and past the rapids, the obstacles that stand between sea and the gravelly spawning redds high up in the hills. Such is the harshness of natural selection.

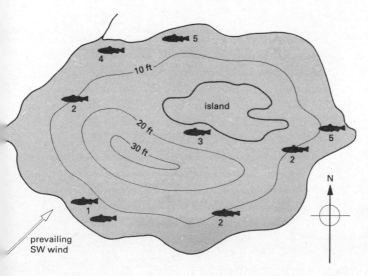

Fish in limestone loughs may be found:

1. Feeding on terrestrial insects blown on to the water
2. Anywhere along the 10 ft contour
3. Around islands
4. Around the inflows from feeder streams
5. Feeding in the shallows at the downwind end of the lough when several days of high winds have stirred up the water

RODS:
Fly rod, for bank or boat fishing: 10–12ft: #4–6: medium to soft action
Dry fly rod: 9ft 6in–10ft 6in: #4–6: medium to stiff tip-actioned
Dapping rod: 15–17ft, telescopic

FLY LINES:
1. Weight forward or double-tapered floating, #4–6
2. Weight forward, slow sinking, #4–6
3. (For dapping) – 10–14lb nylon monofilament and 6–8ft of dapping floss

LEADERS:

Wet fly

Fly line	Braided butt 3ft	4ft	2ft	1ft	1ft	4ft	3ft
		18lb	12lb	8lb	6lb	4lb Dropper	4lb Dropper

Dry fly

Fly line	Braided butt 3ft	6ft	Knotless tapered leader 9ft
		18lb	tapered to 3 – 5lb

IRISH LOUGH FLIES:

Months	Point	Dropper	Bob
March/April	Sooty Olive	Connemara Black	Bibio
	Fiery Brown	Mallard and Claret	Zulu
Mid May to Mid June	Dapped Mayfly Shadow Mayfly (dry – 1/s 10)		
	Peter Ross	Teal and Yellow	Olive Bumble
Mid June to late July	Dunkeld	Fiery Brown	Murrough
	Peter Ross	Teal and Yellow	Invicta
August/ September	Dapped Daddy-Long-Legs or Grasshopper		
	Watson's Fancy	Sooty Olive	Bibio
	Black Pennell	Peter Ross	Daddy

Notes:
1. The flies listed above represent only the most general guidance; take informed local advice whenever possible.
2. All flies on hook sizes 10–14 unless otherwise indicated, 12s and 14s being the preferred sizes in most cases except for Daddy-Long-Legs, which should be tied on 10s or long-shanked (1/s) 10s.

SCOTTISH LOCH FLIES:

Months	Point	Dropper	Bob
March/ April	Peter Ross Black Pennell	Silver March Brown Mallard and Claret	Zulu Blue Zulu
May/June	Peter Ross Black Pennell	Greenwell's Glory Mallard and Claret	Soldier Palmer Zulu
July/ August	Peter Ross Butcher Black Pennell	Teal and Blue Mallard and Claret Greenwell's Glory	Wickham's Fancy Soldier Palmer Invicta
September	Alexandra Peter Ross Black Pennell or dry Daddy-Long-Legs	Teal and Blue Mallard and Claret	Soldier Palmer Zulu

Notes:
1. The flies listed above represent only the most general guidance; take informed local advice whenever possible.
2. With the exception of the Black Pennell, which almost always seems to fish best on the point, the point and middle dropper flies are interchangeable. 'Bright day, bright fly; dull day, dull fly' is a good general rule.
3. All flies on hook sizes 12 to 14 except for Daddy-Long-Legs, which should be tied on 10s or long-shanked 10s.

And do not forget scissors or snippers, artery forceps, silicone floatant, mucilin (red tin), sinkant (Fuller's Earth, washing-up detergent and glycerin), hook-hone, spare leaders or leader material, landing net and priest.

The following morning we made our way down high-banked lanes, between hedges gaudy with pink and purple wild fuchsia, to the lough shore, where we met Michael.

The ghillie

Short and spare, with a fresh, wind-blown complexion and steady, pale blue eyes beneath bushy grey eyebrows and neatly trimmed grey hair, Michael is a man of many talents. With long, even strokes, he can pull a heavy, eighteen-foot, clinker-built boat into wind and wave indefinitely. Without even glancing at the water, he can predict exactly and almost unfailingly where the trout will be rising and what they will be feeding on along the whole of great Lough Corrib's western shore. Even in a stiff breeze, which heaps the grey waves up and breaks their tops into tumbling foam, he can set the boat up precisely the right distance above his chosen mark so that the anglers to whom he is guide and mentor will have settled down to fishing comfortably in an established rhythm just as they reach the rising trout. With only the slightest movements of the trailing oar he can keep the boat steady on the wind, slipping off neither this way nor that, weaving an intricate route along that magical fish-holding ten-foot contour.

He is a fine judge of people, too, knowing exactly when to offer advice and when to remain silent; and the advice he gives is delivered quietly with wit and wisdom, never patronizingly. On a rocky, windswept island, beneath lowering clouds spitting fitful drizzle, he can produce three mugs of strong, steaming hot tea from a volcano kettle and a bundle of twigs in less time than it takes ordinary mortals to pull the boat up, flap their arms against the chill and settle down in the lee of a rock. From his bony, calloused fingers come the prettiest flies you will ever see. And after almost seventy years he has a capacity for fun and for whiskey which would leave most men half his age far behind. In short, he is the perfect ghillie.

I mistrust English fly fishers who say they have no need of ghillies on large Irish loughs. Such waters are difficult to read and can be dangerous. Find a good ghillie, treat him with the respect due to a professional and he will be worth far more than his fee, his tip and the bottle of whiskey that will seal the bond between you. As far as is possible, he will make the difference between a fine day's fishing and one spent groping in the dark. I say 'as far as is possible' because even the greatest ghillie cannot influence the weather or the mood of the fish. Irish as it may be, 'you should have been here tomorrow' is an end-of-drift statement which sums up much of the frustration experienced by ghillies, most of whom are anxious only that their rods should do well.

Boats and boating

While it may be possible to fish large loughs from the bank, most people see lough fishing as being synonymous with boat fishing, and Michael has strong views on boats. Wooden, clinker built and some eighteen feet long, his rides the swell with calm confidence and drifts slow and true instead of bobbing about on the wave tops, scudding along on the wind and veering from side to side on the drift like some more modern fibreglass vessels. Michael uses an outboard motor now, which enables him to take his rods further afield, but he keeps two pairs of good oars in the boat and usually uses them before drifts, believing that the hum of the motor disturbs the fish. The petrol can, a bailer, a Danforth anchor on fifteen feet of chain and a hundred feet of rope, a canvas drogue, four life jackets, a pack of flares, a couple of dapping fly boxes and the famous volcano kettle are all stowed neatly in the bows and beneath the thwarts.

Neatness is essential in a boat. A large, fibreglass coarse angler's tackle box, with a hinged lid and a canvas strap, or even a large plastic or fibreglass tool box bought from a do-it-yourself store, will keep everything accessible and in its place, and is infinitely preferable to the assorted tackle bags, picnic baskets and other containers with which the less well organized so often go afloat. And, of course, tackle boxes should be stowed by the thwarts from which their owners will fish.

The positioning of the occupants of a boat can be important, too. If one of two rods in a boat is a less experienced or less skilful caster than the other, it is sensible to position him so that he will not be casting back and forth above the head of the ghillie, who will sit on the centre thwart. For the same reason, if one of the rods is left handed and the other right handed, they should position themselves so that they will be casting over the bows and stern of the boat rather than across the ghillie in the middle of it.

Tackle and flies

A brisk, south-westerly breeze was rippling the water's surface close inshore and skimming the tops from larger waves further out as we put up our rods. The replacement of cane with much lighter carbon fibre has made it possible to use a ten- to twelve-foot rod all day without tiring. Ours are ten feet long, rated for #5–6 lines, and softish in their actions. Our double-tapered floating lines have three-foot, tapered, braided butts permanently fixed to their tips; to these we added fifteen-foot leaders, tapering from eighteen pounds breaking strain down to four, with two droppers each, one three feet from the point, the other four feet above the first.

On Michael's advice I put a Watson's Fancy on the point, a Sooty Olive on the middle dropper and a Bibio on the top dropper, as a 'bob fly'. Tony followed suit but put on an artificial Daddy-Long-Legs ('Daddy') in place of the Bibio. We laid the rods along the thwarts, stowed our telescopic dapping rods safely, and pushed off. The outboard spluttered to life, Michael knocked it into forward drive and we puttered out of the little bay, accelerating as we turned left a hundred yards or so out from the shoreline.

Clothing

Butting into the grey, rolling waves, pushing sheets of spray out from the bows, it quickly became quite cold. It very often does out on the water, even on sunny days, and it pays to put on several layers of clothing before you set out regardless of the weather – a cellular vest, a warm shirt, a good, warm pullover, a padded waistcoat, a towelling scarf, a windproof, waterproof jacket, warm socks, stout trousers and a pair of waterproof over-trousers. Far better to be able to shed the over-trousers, waistcoat and jacket if you become too warm than to sit, with teeth chattering, wishing you could conjure additional clothing out of thin air. A hat is essential too, and fingerless woollen gloves can maintain the circulation in the hands on particularly cold days.

Fishing the drift

Michael tucked the boat in between a small island and the shore, turned it broadside on to the wind and cut the engine. She wallowed to a halt as he moved easily on to the centre thwart and placed an oar in the upwind rowlock.

As Tony and I wafted eight or ten yards of line out on to the ripple ahead of the drifting boat, Michael explained the geography of the drift; nowhere between the island and the shore was the water more than ten feet deep, although it dropped away quite steeply beyond the end of the island. When we reached that point he would steer a course along the shoreline, fifty to a hundred yards out, until we reached the next island, well over half a mile away.

Simple as it may look, fishing loch-style on the drift requires a delicacy of touch that can be achieved only with practice. You cast your flies ahead of the boat, quartering the water and being careful neither to cast further than your boat partner nor to encroach upon his territory, check the line just before it lands, to straighten out the leader, retrieve at varying speeds until you have three or four yards of line out beyond the rod tip, and then lift the rod slowly, bringing the bob fly to the surface and dibbling it in the ripple for as long as possible before lifting off to re-cast.

It is this dibbling that offers the key to success, but it does not necessarily come easily to the novice. Watch a skilled fly fisher; he will hold the bob fly rippling right in the surface for what seems an age

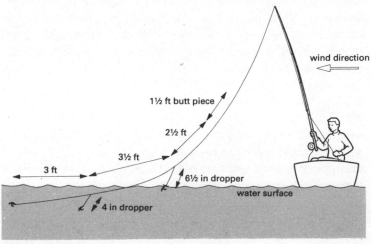

Fishing the drift

before flicking the rod into the up-cast and tapping the flies out over the water again. And this is when most of his takes will come.

There is something intensely attractive to trout about a bushy artificial 'buzzing' at the surface. Perhaps they see it as the efforts of a caddis fly striving to get airborne or as the desperate struggle of a terrestrial insect blown on to the water. Whatever their interpretation, it can be relied upon to catch their attention, bringing them up towards our flies, sometimes to take the bob fly itself, sometimes to be distracted on the way by the point fly or the middle dropper.

As the boat rolled easily on the swell, there was a splash and a grunt of satisfaction. Tony lifted his rod and tightened into a fish. It bored away deep into the dark water, line and leader strumming under the strain, rod hooped over. Eventually it succumbed, wallowed at the surface, rolled on to its side, was drawn over the rim of the waiting net and lifted from the water. At a pound and a half, fin-perfect, deep and firm with myriad black and red spots in pale haloes against a background of glittering, gold-flecked bronze, it was everything an Irish lough trout should be. It had taken the Watson's Fancy on the point.

My turn next.

As I brought the Bibio to the surface and began to ease it back towards the boat, a fish materialized beneath it, a white mouth opened engulfing the fly, and I struck. Three or four minutes later the first fish's identical twin joined it in the boat. By the end of the drift we had netted five trout between us and returned three of them, having imposed upon ourselves an arbitrary size limit of thirteen inches, or about a pound and a quarter – a little over the statutory twelve-inch limit.

We completed four or five more long drifts during the morning, following the white-flecked wind lanes which wound their way north eastwards across the dark grey surface of the lough. Whether on loughs or on reservoirs, you will almost always find fish feeding in and especially along the edges of wind lanes, if they are feeding at all.

At one point, Michael noticed half a dozen gulls stooping low over the water half a mile or so away. We motored across until we were a couple of hundred yards upwind of them, cut the motor and began to drift. As we approached we began to see more rising trout than we had seen all morning – a glop, a swirl, an eddy swamped by a wave, a dorsal fin breaking the surface, a trout's head, a tail waving briefly in the ripple. We netted four more fish in this one drift, but when we tried to repeat it the gulls had flapped away towards the shore and the fish seemed to have gone down.

Eventually we motored carefully into the lee of a gaunt, grey island, skirting great boulders which lurked only inches below the water's surface, devilish traps for the unwary, and pulled the boat up on to the gravelly beach in a little bay. Purple heather nodded among great slabs of stone, and half a dozen skeletal trees rattled, bowed over by the wind, their tops flattened, sparse foliage clothing their limbs like tattered rags on long-dead corpses.

It was warm enough in the shelter of a low cliff – the warmer for a tot or two each of fine Irish whiskey – and we sat munching pork pies, lamb and mint jelly sandwiches, firm, pink tomatoes and crunchy green apples, clutching enamelled mugs of piping hot tea.

Dapping

After lunch, and at Michael's suggestion, we stowed our fly rods and extended the dapping ones – fifteen feet long, their reels loaded with ten-pound monofilament. We tied bare, size 8 hooks to five-foot leaders of six-pound nylon, and fastened four or five feet of dapping floss to the lines, immediately above the leaders, with two slip knots. Some people insert the fluffy, multi-stranded dapping floss between the main line and the leader; I prefer to tie each end of it to the main line, which enables its 'billow' to be adjusted like a spinnaker.

We headed for the upwind shore of the lough, where land-bred insects might be expected to be blown on to the water. Michael had collected twenty or thirty daddy-long-legs by lamplight the night before and a dozen or so grasshoppers while waiting for us in the morning. Tony put a single grasshopper on his hook and I put on two daddies, impaling them through the fattest parts of their thoraces, immediately beneath their wing roots. Not surprisingly, dapped natural insects tempt trout far more consistently than artificial ones, but an imitation Daddy can work well if time or circumstance have prevented the capture of living ones.

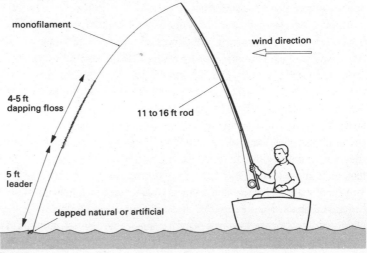

Dapping

Dapping is a pleasant, relaxing way to fish, and a deadly one, too. You drift on the breeze with the rod held up, allowing the dapping floss to be borne ahead of you on the wind. The trick is to keep the insects dibbling on the surface, weaving from side to side, neither drowning them nor allowing them to wave around in the air. A trout's rise to a dapped fly can take you by surprise and calls for a high degree of self-restraint; strike too soon and you will be rewarded with nothing more than a contemptuous swirl as, wholly unperturbed, the fish slides back down into the depths.

It is tempting but unprofitable to allow your mind to wander when you are dapping; if you do so, your response to a rise is likely to be instinctive rather than calculated, and you will almost certainly pull your fly from the fish's mouth. No amount of explanation can really convince newcomers to the sport of the time the trout needs to take a dapped fly, turn down and close his mouth on it. Five seconds from rise to strike is an absolute minimum. No 'God Save the Queen' here; stoke your pipe, pour a cup of tea, re-read that card you wrote last night and meant to post this morning – anything, but *wait*.

Several fish rose to our dapped flies and we caught a few, but the wind dropped away during the afternoon and there is nothing more futile or frustrating than trying to dap in a calm.

Sinking line fishing

By four o'clock the morning's chop had subsided into a long, low, oily swell, with not a fish to be seen. We put away our dapping rods and replaced the floating lines on our fly rods with weight forward slow sinkers, which allow you to fish a little deeper and are less obvious to trout in clear water with a calm surface. I put a Black Pennell on the point, a Sooty Olive on the dropper and a Bibio on the bob.

Apart from allowing the line and the flies to sink for five, ten or fifteen seconds – perhaps even for thirty seconds – before beginning to retrieve, the technique for fishing with a sinking line is exactly the same as that used with a floating one. Takes come quite often during the first few pulls of the retrieve or as you begin to lift the rod to bring the bob fly to the surface. Dibbling the bob fly in the surface film before lifting off to re-cast is just as important as it is with a floating line but – perhaps logically – trout seem to rise to it less often than they do when they are feeding right at the surface, more of their takes being to point flies or droppers.

At last, with dusk closing in and with half a dozen fine fish apiece, we headed homeward along the shoreline. So vast is this lough that we had seen hardly another boat all day. But two or three more were converging on the jetty as we arrived, and small huddles of people were admiring catches, chatting and laughing in the car park. A hot bath, a warm fire, a couple of drams and a decent dinner sent us to bed exhausted but entirely contented to dream of fish caught, fish hooked and lost and fish we had troubled not at all.

Dry fly fishing

The following day, under a clear, pale blue sky, we drove to Boliska Lake, a long, narrow lough – in truth, no more than a major widening of the Owen Boliska River – set among low, rolling, heather-covered hills a few miles inland from the sea. Turning off the main road, and in constant fear for the essential ironmongery beneath the car, we bumped and bounced along a rough track until we came to within a hundred yards or so of a tiny croft nestled in a fold in the landscape, where we parked on the verge.

Along its margins and in the bay beneath us, the smooth surface of the lough was stippled with the interlocking rings of countless rising trout. To the intense irritation of the crofter's turkey, all wattle and gobble, we put up our rods by the car, the same ten-foot, carbon fibre ones we had used the day before. Some might have judged them too soft for dry fly fishing, but their length offered the casting distance we would need and, anyway, they were all we had with us.

Dry fly fishing is an underrated but exciting means of taking trout from Irish loughs. It starts in late May, when a Shadow Mayfly can be deadly, continues with floating black gnat and olive dun imitations on summer days and with bushy sedge patterns on summer evenings, and concludes with similar sedges and dry Daddies in the daytime in late August and through September.

Although there is always the chance of a larger sea trout from July onwards, the brown trout in this lough do not run large; most are around half a pound and a three-quarter-pounder is a monster. So we replaced our wet fly leaders with dropper-less, fifteen-foot ones, tapering to three pounds. I put on a size 14 Fiery Brown dry fly, dipping it in silicone floatant for buoyancy's sake and greasing the leader lightly to within a couple of feet of the point; Tony put up an artificial Daddy.

It pays to be mobile when fishing a lough from the bank, so we reduced our spare tackle and picnics to what could be stored comfortably in our pockets and then waded down the hill, through knee-deep heather, to the waterside. There was almost no breeze. A gentle breath of warm air wafting off the land left the first ten yards or so of the water wholly unruffled; only further out did it crinkle the surface. I made my way round to a miniature headland at the entrance to the bay, whence I could cast across such wind as there was, dropping my fly on the edge of the ripple.

The bushy little offering had not been bobbing on the surface for more than ten seconds when it vanished in an eddying swirl and I tightened into a furious little brown trout which fought doggedly for a fish of eight ounces. Lying on the peaty bank I was able to reach down and twitch the hook free, allowing the fish to rejoin his fellows, a dozen or more of which made similar mistakes during the couple of hours before we broke for lunch.

In the meantime Tony's Daddy was doing similar service, being taken time and again by little brown trout whose diets, in this somewhat acid lough, consisted chiefly of insects blown on to the water from the surrounding land.

We lay back in the sunshine and watched a speck of silver crawling across the sky – an airliner, westward bound, carving a widening white gash across the firmament. Three hundred people or more hunched together in a pressurized, air-conditioned aluminium tube, munching plastic lunches from plastic plates as they hurtled through the stratosphere, utterly oblivious of the tranquillity below, to the green and mauve of the heather, the damp blackness of the peat, the yellow ochre and pastel green lichen clinging to dark-fissured, pale grey rocks lapped about by polished water.

By mid afternoon most of the brown trout had retreated to the depths, but there was still a ring here, a whorl there and the occasional sploosh further out as a sea trout leapt, shuddering, strumming the air with its tail, and crashed back into the water. We rearranged our leaders, each adding a dropper four feet above the point and another five feet above that. I put a Black Pennell on the point, a Sooty Olive on the middle dropper and an artificial Daddy on the top dropper, carefully degreasing all the nylon below the top dropper with the putty-like mixture of Fuller's Earth, washing-up liquid and glycerin.

I wandered along the shoreline until I found a little promontory, covered in tussock grass, leaning out towards a rocky island a hundred yards offshore. Odd swirls and eddies on the edge of the ripple showed fish moving there and I worked out line until I was able to reach them.

I allowed the two wet flies to sink for a few seconds and then began a very slow figure-of-eight retrieve, watching the Daddy and the tiny V-wave it made as it inched its way across the surface. Suddenly it shot under and I lifted the rod as a glittering sea trout arced upwards in a shower of silver spray. It had taken the Black Pennell on the point, and must have tested the knot and the three-pound nylon almost to destruction as it charged off, just beneath the surface, leaving a rocking bow wave behind it. Eventually I managed to slow it and turn it, but it made several more spectacular runs before finally it tired and came to the net. I tapped it sharply on the head and then admired it, a pound and a half of perfection, distinguishable from its smaller brown cousins by its silvery blueness and by the lack of orange-red spots among the slate grey ones on its flanks.

This was the only sea trout we caught that afternoon. Between us we brought another four or five brownies to the net, keeping three half-pounders and releasing the rest; then we trudged back up the hillside. Having edged past the turkey to leave a brace of fish with the crofter's wife, and past him again as we returned to the car, we stowed our tackle and bumped back up the lane to the main road, the hotel, baths, whiskey, a warm fire, warm company and a fine dinner. Served with crispy bacon the next morning, the sea trout and one of the brown trout made a magical breakfast.

Two Scottish lochs

Scotland's lovely lochs fish better from March to June and again in September than they do during the dog days of July and August, but it is in these latter months that those of us with school-aged children must take our holidays, and there is no better way to introduce children to fly fishing than by letting them try for the fit, fierce, greedy little brown trout of the Highlands.

When my son Douglas was born, the late Dick Walker advised me never to try to persuade him to take up fishing. Instead, he said, wait until he is begging to be allowed to go with you; when he does so, hold him at arm's length, only eventually succumbing to his entreaties; *then* he will be hooked for life. I followed Dick's advice and have never regretted it. Douglas, now sixteen, has become a keen and competent fly fisher, and through fishing we have become close friends.

We drove up into the hills above Fort William one scorching summer's day, through rolling grassland and small stands of pines, to

Locating fish in a highland loch. Fish will often be found downwind of deciduous trees, which contain much insect life and through which the wind passes easily. Fewer fish will be found downwind of conifers

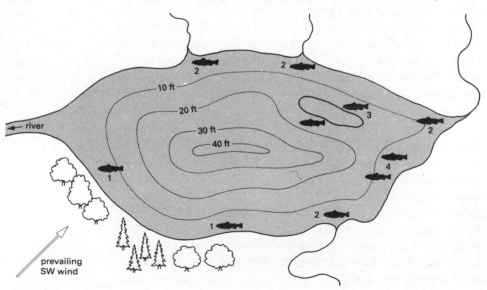

the roof of the world. At the end of the track we came to an immaculately white-painted farmhouse with a slate roof and bright blue window frames. Two dogs dozed in the sunshine. One looked up and gave a token 'woof' before slumping back to sleep; the other, chin on paws, watched disinterestedly and fanned the dust lazily with his tail.

We chatted with the farmer's wife for a few minutes, paid a pittance for permission to fish, gathered our tackle from the car and oars from the house, and strolled down through the meadows to the shore of Loch Lunn Da Bhra.

Perhaps half a mile long and a quarter of a mile wide, it was not a vast expanse of water. There was a bay at the western end fringed with fir trees and guarded by a little island, and reeds waved in the shallows. The banks were green, flecked with hare's tail cotton-grass. Above them, and all around, the hills enclosed us, heather-clad and with fruit ripening darkly on scattered tangles of bilberry.

Two boats were moored alongside the parched-plank jetty that edged one side of a tiny inlet. Stowing the oars, our picnic and the rest of our gear in the larger and drier, we put up our rods – a nine-foot carbon fibre one for Douglas with a floating line and just one dropper four feet above the point of a fourteen-foot leader, tapered to three pounds, and my well-used and much-loved ten footer, with a sixteen-foot leader and two droppers.

In the absence of local advice I put a Black Pennell on the point, a Mallard and Claret on the dropper and a Soldier Palmer on the bob, while Douglas, in the interest of variety, put a Butcher on the point and an Invicta on his dropper. We de-greased the leaders carefully, so that they would not leave tell-tale wakes on the still surface of the water.

There was barely a breath of air as we pulled away from the jetty and slid easily and silently along the shoreline towards the head of the loch a quarter of a mile away, nor was there any sign of a fish, and our first long, slow drift was abortive. Nothing moved. Idly we watched an amorphous flock of sheep on a far hillside come together and ease its way, amoeba-like, towards the valley below, urged on by two busy dogs, the shepherd sauntering along behind. We debated the identity of a great bird soaring in the thermals high above the next valley (golden eagle or buzzard), and failed to reach a conclusion before it sank from view.

The weather can change remarkably rapidly in western Scotland and, whatever its appearance as you set out, it pays to be prepared. As we reached the end of the drift, the breeze freshened from the west. By the time we had rowed back to the loch-head, dark clouds were bowling in low through the valley entrance above us, wrapping themselves around the mountains and spitting fitfully at the now grey and choppy surface of the loch. We pulled on waterproof jackets and trousers before beginning the next drift, along the edge of the rushes and past the mouths of two little feeder streams.

As soon as we had shipped the oars we saw fish rising ahead of us, splashing at something in the surface film, flattening the ripple, leaving stunned patches where wavelets should have been. We cast ahead of the boat, never putting out more than eight or ten yards of line and beginning our retrieves almost immediately. The takes were lightning-fast, quick tugs as we began to retrieve, a slash and a flash of bronze or gold as we dibbled the flies back towards the boat, and we missed far more fish than we caught. But as our reactions speeded up we caught a few, tapping the rod upwards at the first sign of a trout's interest and increasingly often being rewarded with a solid, strumming resistance and then the quicksilver fight of a wild half-pound brown trout.

Lunch forgotten, we fished on into the afternoon until the clouds lifted and cleared as suddenly as they had arrived, the sun broke through and the wind died. Within ten minutes there was not a rise to be seen. The loch looked as lifeless as it had when we first arrived. Had it not been for a couple of brace of better-than-average fish lying in the bottom of the boat, we might have been tempted to believe that the whole interlude had been a dream.

Becalmed in the middle of the loch, I put a dry Daddy on the point of my leader, which I greased lightly to within a couple of feet of the fly. The gangling artefact looked almost absurd sitting on the glass-calm surface. But I left it there while I munched a sandwich.

There are moments in fishing when, for reasons you simply cannot explain, you *know for sure* that your fly is about to be taken by a fish. They have nothing to do with hope or wishful thinking, nor can you conjure them up. They are about *certainty*, and they appear out of the blue. This was one of them.

I put down my sandwich and reached for the rod just as a great brown neb broke the surface, a white mouth opened and the Daddy vanished. I pondered for a moment and then struck, lifting the rod, straightening line and leader and feeling for the fish, which shot off across the loch, stripping line from the reel. My concern grew as he took out more and more line. And then he stopped, turned, and began to move slowly back towards us. I reeled in desperately, trying to keep in touch with him. Then he set off again.

This time he ran for just a few yards before throwing himself into the air and crashing back into the water. The line went slack.

Hooked fish may come free for any of a number of reasons. Perhaps the hook catches through a thin piece of skin on the outside edge of the jaw, or its point catches tenuously on hard bone or gristle, coming free if the line is slackened; holding a fish too hard may enlarge the hole around the hook, allowing the hook to drop out if pressure is eased; a fish leaping and falling back on the leader may break it or tug the hook away. Apart from exercising sensible caution, neither playing a trout too hard nor being too gentle with it, giving line – albeit a little reluctantly – when the fish demands it and dropping the rod point a touch when the fish leaps, there is little to be done to prevent such occasional losses. And there is no point in crying over spilt milk. There are, however, several things we can do to reduce the 'ones that get away' to a minimum.

You should ensure that your flies are tied on sound hooks, testing a couple of hooks or flies from each batch you buy by placing their points in a fly-tying vice and pressing down sharply and firmly on the eye end of the shank. If they break, they are too brittle; if they stay bent when released, they are too soft. You should tie all knots with the greatest care, lubricating them with saliva before pulling them tight and testing them with a couple of good tugs before use. Hooks should be sharpened with a small hook-hone from time to time during use, and tested for sharpness. Drag the point across your thumb nail at an angle of 45 degrees. If it takes hold, it is sharp enough; if it does not, it is too blunt. And check your hooks from time to time while fishing, especially if there are stones, rocks or other hard obstructions in the back-cast area, to ensure that they have not been damaged.

The following day we drove up the Great Glen to take a boat on Loch Arkaig, lurking deep in its valley beneath a leaden grey sky, a stiff, westerly breeze funnelling in across Loch Morar from the Atlantic. The chill in the air was softened by the warmth of the welcome with which we were received.

The boat, eighteen feet long, well made and sound, rowed well. We put out a drogue to slow our drift along the northern shoreline, concentrating on the areas around the mouths of countless little burns tumbling down from the hills and on patches of aspen and silver birch huddled among the stands of Scots pine.

Trout in Highland lochs often depend heavily on terrestrial insects blown from trees and scrubland rather than on aquatic insects, which are scarce in such infertile waters. Conifers sustain few insects and are dense, offering solid resistance to the wind which tends to go over or round them rather than through them. Deciduous trees afford far greater nourishment to bugs, beetles, spiders and so on, and far less resistance to the wind, which passes through them, often carrying resident insects with it – to the delight of the fish.

Four perfect brown trout to three-quarters of a pound came to the Black Pennell on the point of my leader, the wet Greenwell's Glory on the middle dropper and the Wickham's Fancy on the top one apparently going unnoticed. Douglas matched me fish for fish, taking two on a Peter Ross on the point and two on the Soldier Palmer five feet above it. We kept a brace apiece and returned the others, tying the boat up carefully and heading the car towards the orange of the setting sun as the clouds cleared from the west.

CHECK LIST – RESERVOIR TACKLE

RODS:
For bank *and* boat fishing: 9ft 6in–10ft 6in: #6–8: medium to stiff action
For boat fishing, loch-style, only: 10–12ft: #4–6: medium to soft action

FLY LINES:
1. Weight forward or double-tapered, floating, #5–7
2. Weight forward, slow-sinking, #6–8
3. Weight forward (or shooting head), quick-sinking, #6–8
4. Weight forward (or shooting head), high-density, #6–8

LEADER:

Wet fly

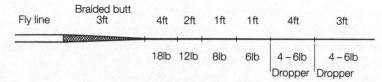

RESERVOIR FLIES AND LURES:

Months	*Point*	*Dropper*	*Bob*
March/April	Alder Larva (1/s 10)	Black Buzzer (10–12)	Suspender Buzzer (10–14)
	Stick Fly (1/s 10)	Blue and Black (10–14)	Soldier Palmer (10–14)
	Black Buzzer (10–12)		
	Viva (1/s 8–10)		
	Appetizer (1/s 8–10)		
	Booby Nymph (10) or		
	Black Buzzer (12–14)	Booby Nymph (10)	
April/May	G-RHE Nymph (10–12)	Black, Green or	Suspender Buzzer (10–14)
	Stick Fly (1/s 10)	Orange Buzzer (10–14)	Emerging Buzzer (10-14)
	Black Buzzer (12–14)		Soldier Palmer (10–14)
	Hawthorn (dry 12)		Wickham's Fancy (12–14)
	Viva (1/s 8–10)		
	Appetizer (1/s 8–10)		
June/July	Damsel Nymph (1/s 10)	Black, Green or	Emerging Buzzer (10–14)
	Stick Fly (1/s 10)	Orange Buzzer (10–14)	Suspender Buzzer (10–14)
	G-RHE Nymph (10–12)	Teal and Blue (10–12)	Soldier Palmer (10–14)
	Sinfoil's Fry (1/s 10)	Butcher (10–12)	Wickham's Fancy (12–14)
	Dry Sedge (10–12)		
	Viva (1/s 10)		
	Appetizer (1/s 10)		
	Whiskey Fly (1/s 10)		

CHAPTER ELEVEN

Reservoir Fly Fishing

Dew shines silver-sharp on grey-green grass in the pale, early-morning, mid-May light. Honey-hued stone walls throw long shadows across cobweb-wrapped bramble thickets. A wooden five-barred gate leans slightly drunkenly ajar. Yellow cowslips nod on the high banks on either side of the road as we pass by. The visor is down against the rising sun. The car radio blurbs banalities and jolly jingles.

Into the village, right at the pub, down the narrow, winding lane. Wheels scrunch on gravel as we swing into the car park and pull up beneath the trees. We might have been the first here, but we are not; people are at the boots of other cars, putting up rods, holding flies up to the sky, threading leaders, tying knots.

July/August	Damsel Nymph (1/s 10)	Green Buzzer (12)	Emerging Buzzer (10–12)
	Corixa (10–12)	Greenwell (12–14)	Soldier Palmer (10–14)
	Caddis Pupa (10–12)		Grenadier (10–14)
	Shipman's Buzzer (10–14)	Shipman's Buzzer (10–14)	Shipman's Buzzer (10–14)
	Plastazote Corixa (10)		
	Buff or Amber	Buff or Amber	
	Hopper (10–14)	Hopper (10–14)	
	Viva (1/s 10)		
	Appetizer (1/s 10)		
	Whiskey Fly (1/s 10)		
September/	Stick Fly (1/s 10)	Shipman's Buzzer (10–12)	Emerging Buzzer (10–12)
October	Caddis Pupa (10–12)		Suspender Buzzer (10–14)
	Corixa (10–12)		Soldier Palmer (10–14)
	Buff or Amber	Buff or Amber	
	Hopper (10–14)	Hopper (10–14)	
	Viva (1/s 10)		
	Appetizer (1/s 6–10)		
	Jack Frost (1/s 6–10)		
	Missionary (1/s 6–10)		
	Muddler Minnow (1/s 8–10)		
	Rasputin (1/s 6–10)		

And do not forget scissors or snippers, artery forceps, silicone floatant, mucilin (red tin), sinkant (Fuller's Earth, washing-up detergent and glycerin), hook-hone, spare leaders or leader material, landing net and priest.

Still sleepy-eyed and with barely a word between us, we fill in the day-ticket forms, post counterfoils and cheques in the box and climb back into the car. Up the lane, along the road; it is only ten or fifteen minutes' drive around the eastern end of the reservoir to North Shore. As we bump along the track towards Orchard Bay, clouds of dancing midges gleam golden in the sunshine. We park the car and gaze out across the lake, flat calm in the still air. A huge splash out in the middle is echoed by the more sedate rings of innumerable rising trout. There really is something magical about Blagdon at the beginning of an early summer day.

Tackle and leaders

Stiffish ten-foot rods, #7, weight forward, floating lines, sixteen- to eighteen-foot leaders tapered to four pounds and with two droppers apiece; with the advent of carbon fibre, tackle for reservoir fly fishing has become almost standardized, whether you fish from the bank or from a boat.

The chief bone of contention is leader point strength. The managements at some reservoirs specify or recommend a minimum point strength in their rules, which is sensible where newcomers are concerned; a fit two- or three-pound rainbow can strip line from a fly reel far faster and with far greater determination than many people imagine, and will snap fine nylon as if it were cotton if it turns sharply or jumps with thirty yards of fly line out. And it is inexcusable to allow oneself to be broken, leaving a fish to swim off with a hook in its mouth, perhaps trailing several feet of nylon behind it.

On the other hand, there can be no doubt that long leaders with fine points take far more fish than short, stout ones do, especially when the water is calm, clear or both. One's choice will always be a compromise between strength and 'invisibility'. If you believe the conditions militate for a fine point and are confident that you can handle any fish you may expect to catch on three- or four-pound nylon, then that is what you should use. But if you have any doubt at all, then go a pound or so heavier, to five or even six pounds at the point.

The 'double-strength' nylon that has become available during the past few years goes some way towards resolving the fineness-versus-strength conundrum but warrants a word of warning. Essentially it is nylon monofilament that has been stretched, its diameter thus having been reduced. As a consequence it has little or no elasticity left in it, which can present problems with particularly fierce takes. It also tends to curl rather disconcertingly and apparently permanently if it tangles or is abraded against anything. And knots tied in it have a tendency to slip and must therefore be tied with the utmost care; the double-grinner knot and the cove or water knot are the only two suitable for joining lengths of double-strength nylon, and only the grinner knot is suitable for tying flies on. (All three knots are illustrated in Appendix A at the end of this book.)

Matching the hatch

Taking our cue from the midges dancing in the summer sunshine and from the way in which the trout are rising – languidly, lazily, in slow motion, heads followed by backs followed by gently waving tails, barely breaking the surface, bow waves turning to rings and then ebbing silently away – we tie Buzzers, artificial midge pupae, to the points and droppers of our leaders: three black ones on mine, size 12s on the point and middle dropper and a size 10 Suspender Buzzer on the top dropper; a size 14 Green Buzzer on the point of Tony's leader, a size 12 orange one on the middle dropper and a size 10 black one on the top dropper. And we grease the leaders lightly from the fly lines to within eighteen inches of the top droppers.

The range of food available to reservoir trout during the course of the year may not be particularly wide but the fish can be very selective, so it is important to understand what they eat, and when. Alder larvae in early spring; hawthorn flies in late April and early May; damselfly nymphs in May, June and July; needle fry in June; caddis larvae and pupae in summer, and adult caddis flies on summer evenings; corixae and daddy-long-legs in August and September; and coarse fish fry in high summer and again in the autumn – all these can distract trout from the midge larvae and pupae that are bread and butter to them throughout the year.

In their search for better and better patterns with which to suggest or represent this range of food forms, many stillwater fly fishers amass huge collections of patterns, carting them to the water in vast containers more like suitcases than fly boxes. Collecting flies is an intriguing and entertaining pastime, and I would not decry it. But it pays to be mobile when bank fishing, and for this reason there is some advantage in limiting the range of patterns you carry with you to those that can be accommodated in a couple of pocket-sized boxes.

Reading the water

However conscientious the stocking of a reservoir, trout will always vote with their fins, showing marked preferences for some areas and avoiding others. Obviously, we should try to concentrate our attentions on areas that are attractive to feeding fish and to avoid those that are not.

The factors affecting the whereabouts and feeding habits of trout are complex. They include temperature, water depth and food availability,

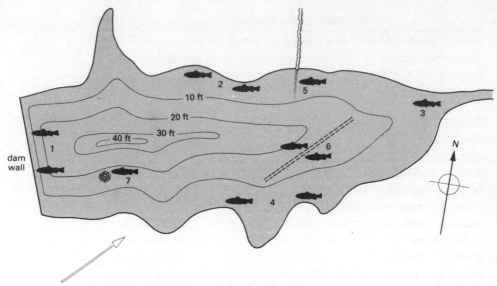

Trout in reservoirs are likely to be found:
1. *Close to the dam wall*
2. *On downwind shores, especially where the wind has been blowing diagonally on to the shore for several days, stirring up the water*
3. *At the mouth of feeder streams, especially in late summer and autumn*
4. *Off promontories*
5. *Around drowned hedgerows and other underwater features*
6. *Along the edges of wind lanes*
7. *Down-wind of acrator 'boils'*

wind strength and direction, the shapes and natures of shorelines, types, locations and densities of weed beds, and, especially in the autumn, the trout's sexual instincts. Were we to try to take them all into account, we would probably end up spinning in circles, wholly unable to decide where to fish. But there are some quite simple principles we can apply in order to stack the odds in our favour.

The better you know a water, the better will you be able to read it. The regular local angler will almost always do better than the occasional visitor. But experience comes only with time. If you do not know a water well, do not be shy to seek expert local advice. Fishery staff, who want you to enjoy your visit and come again, are likely to provide better advice than local anglers, who may prefer to keep the secrets of their success to themselves.

The managements of most major reservoir fisheries publish large-scale maps of their waters. Buy one and use it. It will show you where the deeps and shallows are, where the banks slope down steeply into the water and where the water is shallow for a long way out, where tracks, ditches and hedgerows run down into the water (underwater features such as these always seem attractive to trout), and even, perhaps, the locations of drowned buildings, farmyards and so on.

Generally speaking, the most consistent bank fishing on any reservoir will be found where the prevailing wind blows on to or across a shore sloping down quite steeply into the water to give depths of between six and fifteen feet up to thirty yards out. An onshore wind carries food with it and stirs up the water in the margins, agitating bottom-dwelling insects. A cross-wind has a similar if less pronounced effect and can make casting easy and comfortable, provided that it is blowing on to the angler's non-casting arm – that is, from left to right for right handers and vice versa.

Feeding trout – and particularly feeding rainbow trout, which shoal much more than brown trout – tend to move upwind in fairly straight lines, coming close inshore as they pass promontories but not necessarily following the shoreline into bays. Therefore, having found a 'fishy' stretch of shoreline, it will usually pay to find a small point from which to fish.

Floating line fishing

The remains of a battered hedgerow run down across the meadow to a small promontory pushing out into the lake. Two coots, young in tow, fuss about just offshore, diving to forage for weed and snails, bobbing away as we approach. Beyond the hedge two mute swans are asleep, heads curled on to their bodies, baleful black eyes ever watchful. A great-crested grebe, her brown and black tuft sleeked back, two striped chicks balanced on her back, idles along fifty yards away, apparently going nowhere. Tony heads towards the car park near the entrance to Butcombe Bay.

There is nothing to be gained and much to be lost by wading unnecessarily. Left in peace, trout will feed in very shallow water, close in to the shore. Wading serves only to drive them out into deeper water, and constant wading tramples out of existence the weed and the insect life it sustains, destroying the cover and food that should induce trout to venture inshore.

Crouching quite well back from the water, in the lee of the hedge, I pull no more than ten yards of line from the reel, sweep it into the air behind me, make a couple of false casts and tap the rod forward, checking the line slightly just before it lands in order to straighten out the leader. The two Buzzers on point and dropper cut down through the water's surface; the Suspender Buzzer on the bob remains, hanging in the surface film, visible only as a tiny dot.

'Imitative' fly fishing, whether with Buzzers or with any other sort of nymph, is an intensely visual affair. Do not begin to retrieve at once. Instead, watch the leader floating on the water; watch the tip of the fly line. So many takes come 'on the drop' while the flies are simply

147

sinking through the water having just been cast. If you look away while your flies are sinking, if you use that time to see what your fellow anglers are doing or to watch the world go by, there is every likelihood that you will fail to spot at least half of your takes.

I am fortunate in that I have been blessed with excellent eyesight, although it is less good now than it used to be. Those who cannot see a leader on the water at ten, fifteen or twenty yards' range may like to try one of the several varieties of strike indicators that are now available – small, fluorescent polystyrene beads which, fixed on to the leader, act just like a coarse fisherman's float.

A fish rises ten yards or so away, slightly to my left, moving from left to right. A slow, steady, figure-of-eight retrieve creates the tiniest herring-bone ripple along the edges of the fly line and the floating part of the leader. Nothing. I cast again, trying to put the flies just ahead of the trout, and begin the next retrieve at once. Still nothing.

Another fish rises, a little further out this time but heading in the same direction as the first one. Pull a couple more yards of line from the reel; lift off; two false casts; tap the rod forward; check; the flies plop lightly into the still water; a swirl; the leader slips forward; the rod goes up, almost instinctively, and bends.

The fish charges for the far bank, the leader hissing through the water's surface; slack line is taken up; the reel whines; the rod bucks. Slowly she tires and slows, turning and running parallel with the shore, tugging, boring. Rod and line make a continuous curve, up, across and down to where the trout is turning back towards me.

Rod tip up; reel in; take up slack. She comes to within four or five yards of the bank and then charges off again, going deeper this time and tiring more quickly. At last, exhausted, she rolls on her side to be drawn over the rim of the waiting net and hoisted ashore. Hold her upright in the mesh, tap her on the head, remove the hook – she took the point fly – and admire her: gleaming; perfect; aptly named 'rainbow'; two and a half pounds exactly; a delicate mauve-pink petrol stripe runs the full length of her flanks, pale below, dark olive green above, her lower fins pale, translucent orange-pink, her dorsal and tail fins darker, flecked with tiny black spots.

I invert my marrow scoop and, holding the fish upright, ease it down her gullet, rotate it through 180 degrees and withdraw it. Tapped out into the water in a little plastic box I carry for the purpose, the black mass separates to reveal a dozen or more natural midge pupae, all black and all about size 12, a few strands of weed and a single corixa.

It is always as well to check the stomach contents of the first trout or two of the day. The exercise will often do no more than confirm one's initial choice of fly, especially on reservoirs where midge pupae may make up as much as 90 per cent of the trout's diet through substantial periods of the year. Occasionally, though, it may show that we have misjudged the situation completely, that the fish are, in fact, feeding on something quite different, and that the trout we have spooned must have taken our offering opportunistically and in passing rather than because it resembles what she has been feeding on.

Check the hook and the knots and cast again, fanning round gradually with each successive cast, extending line little by little, putting the flies to rising trout whenever opportunity allows.

The next fish comes to the Suspender Buzzer on the top dropper, a slow, confident, head-back-and-tail, porpoise rise, and the fly, all but invisible suspended in the surface film by its polystyrene bead, disappears. Perhaps I struck too quickly; maybe the trout missed the fly altogether. Whatever the cause, the line simply sags back towards me as I lift the rod. I miss a couple more fish after that and another comes off at the net, but I have three more trout in the bag by the time Tony and I meet up for a late lunch, all taken on Buzzers, making two brace for the morning. Having spooned his first fish, taken on a Green Buzzer, Tony had changed to black and netted four more.

A brisk breeze comes up early in the afternoon, bustling in over the dam and racing across the lake, teasing the water, spreading long wind lanes across its surface, and the fish go down.

Sinking line fishing

I replace the Suspender Buzzer on the top dropper with a conventional one and put a leaded Gold-Ribbed Hare's Ear nymph on the point to take the flies down a little – to no effect. But a change to a slow-sinking line and a stick fly – perhaps the most reliable 'last resort' of all on many reservoirs – produces three more fish.

I have to confess a strong preference for floating line fishing. When I replace a floater with a sinker I tend to do so reluctantly, reverting to the floater at the first excuse. But there is little to be said for flying in the face of reason; when the fish go down it is sensible to go down with them. The hallmark of the truly competent fly fisher is his or her ability to spot changes in the behaviour of the trout and to adjust tackle and tactics to cater for those changes.

The key to consistent success with sinking lines is to be methodical. If you simply cast out, wait a while for the line to sink and then retrieve it, you may well catch a fish or two in due course but, having little or no idea as to how long the line has been sinking, it may be very difficult to repeat the performance precisely and thus to tempt other fish behaving in the same way.

Start by allowing the line to sink for perhaps five seconds before beginning the retrieve, and persist with this for a predetermined period of time, say ten minutes. If you obtain no response, go to ten seconds for ten minutes, and then to fifteen, and so on. Where the water is very deep and you reach the point at which you are having to wait for half a minute or so for the line to get to the required depth, it may well pay to change to a denser line which will sink more quickly.

Lure fishing

While many people find imitative fishing very much more satisfying than lure fishing – because more thought and calculation can go into it – there are times in the year when a lure may prove to be the only answer, especially very early in the season when the water is cold, and in high summer when it is hot.

Although hundreds of lures have been devised, the range needed under most circumstances is really quite small – a black one (perhaps a Viva), a white one (the Appetizer is excellent) and an essentially orange one (say a Whiskey Fly). In addition, though, it may pay to have a few alternatives with which you can ring the changes; any good tackle shop will have a huge array for you to choose from.

When lure fishing from the bank, I generally use a single fly rather than a team, on a leader of between nine feet (with a sinking line) and fifteen to eighteen feet (with a floater).

It is a myth that lures have to be stripped through the water at high speed. Indeed, one of the most effective techniques is to cast across the wind with a floating line and then simply to allow the line to ride round on the wind, towing the lure behind it. Takes tend to be firm and positive, the line checking, its curve straightening, the narrow band of flat water on its downwind side widening.

With sinking lines it pays to vary your retrieve, inching the line in, speeding up with a quick figure-of-eight, trying short, sharp tugs and long, steady pulls. And be prepared for solid, heaving takes, the rod arching over, the sunk line shuddering up through the water, a trout leaping so far away that it can be difficult to believe that it has anything to do with your fly, your line and your rod.

Buoyant lures

Especially when the water is cold early in the year, and in very hot, bright weather in high summer, reservoir trout may do much of their feeding very close to the bottom. This presents problems, both in getting down to them and, having done so, in fishing an artificial without snagging it on the bottom or in the weed. The solution has been available for many years but only quite recently has it been developed as a standard tactic. It is to use a very fast-sinking line and a buoyant lure – a Booby Nymph, which represents nothing on earth, a Plastazote Corixa, a Rasputin, or a Rassler, suggestive of a small fish.

The basic tackle is quite conventional – a reasonably powerful ten-

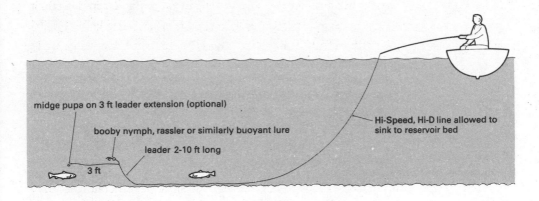

midge pupa on 3 ft leader extension (optional)

booby nymph, rassler or similarly buoyant lure

leader 2-10 ft long

Hi-Speed, Hi-D line allowed to sink to reservoir bed

3 ft

Buoyant lure fishing

foot rod and a weight forward high-density line – but leader length is very variable: from six inches to four or five feet when fishing from the shore (two to three feet being the norm), and from four to ten feet when fishing from a boat. It is essential to find the right length of leader, which will vary from time to time and place to place, and this can be done only by experience and experimentation and by picking the brains of successful fellow anglers.

Cast out, the line is allowed to sink right to the bottom, which may take as long as two minutes or more from a boat over deep water. The lure will float above the end of the fly line and may thus be kept clear of weed and other obstructions. The retrieve should usually be very, very slow, a mere inching back of the line. Takes, when they come, may be felt as anything from slightly increased tension on the line through tweaks and taps to a fearsome, arm-wrenching heave which bows the rod over alarmingly and hauls its tip down towards the water.

Whether this technique can be classified as 'fly fishing' is a debatable point, but it can be both deadly and very exciting, epitomizing the essence of a sport that has so much to do with the element of surprise and the secrets of the deep. And there is a variation of the theme that is unquestionably 'fly fishing'.

Having found that trout frequently tweaked at Booby Nymphs fished close to the bottom, rather than take them properly, I began putting the Booby Nymph on to a single dropper and then mounting a small (size 12 or 14) Buzzer on the point, about three feet behind it. The Booby Nymph keeps the Buzzer clear of the bottom and the Buzzer will often take a bagful of fish when the Booby seems to be of little or no interest to them.

151

Reservoir fly fishing – a dynamic sport

Reservoir fishing in general and boat fishing in particular have changed almost beyond recognition during the past fifteen years or so. When a few British reservoirs were first stocked with trout late in the nineteenth century, fly fishers treated them very much like Scottish lochs, using long, soft cane or greenheart rods and teams of three or four traditional flies. But Ravensthorpe, which opened as a trout fishery in 1893, and Blagdon, where fishing began in 1904, were different. Newly flooded, fertile, lowland valleys provide rich feeding for trout, and browns and rainbows stocked into these waters grew at phenomenal rates. The average weight of the fish caught from Ravensthorpe during its first season was 2lb 6oz, while at Blagdon the average weight of trout taken between 1904 and 1909 was an astonishing 3lb 8oz.

Such large fish with so much food available to them called for different tackle and tactics and encouraged experimentation. Many early Blagdon anglers used spinning and salmon tackle. Others, like Doctors James Mottram and Howard Bell, devised and developed patterns specifically to imitate the creatures trout fed on in the lake. The Irish opera singer Harry Plunket Greene, author of *Where the Bright Waters Meet*, was among the first to recognize the potential offered by floating flies on large stillwaters.

Perhaps surprisingly, very few books about the relatively new sport of reservoir trout fishing were published during the first half of the twentieth century. It was not until Tom Ivens' excellent work *Still Water Fly-Fishing* first appeared in 1952 that reservoir fly fishers had access to sound, comprehensive and authoritative written guidance.

Interestingly, and for all the expertise it contained, Ivens' book did stillwater fly fishing one serious disservice. Tom had a blind spot where dry fly fishing was concerned and effectively wrote it off as a waste of time. Dry fly fishing can be deadly on stillwaters but, because Tom Ivens had dismissed it in the only worthwhile book on the sport, it went almost entirely ignored for many years.

The opening of Blagdon's neighbour, Chew Valley Lake, in 1957 and then of Grafham Water just under ten years later coincided with a period of rapid growth in affluence and mobility, with increasing numbers of people having access to motor cars. As a consequence, the popularity of reservoir trout fishing grew enormously. Many of the newcomers to the sport had never fished before or had been coarse anglers, and were not therefore constrained in their thinking by the traditions and folklore of fly fishing. Some of these people were highly imaginative and inventive, devising and developing new techniques for taking trout from reservoirs and publishing accounts of their findings in a burgeoning game angling press. In particular they evolved a range of lures which, fished intelligently and imaginatively, brought great success with rainbow trout in large reservoirs, trout which often feed at depth and on minute food items.

The problems that followed were caused not by the authors of these ideas but by the way in which the ideas themselves were adopted by the angling public. Drag a lure through a reservoir often enough and you will catch a modest number of trout. So universal had 'lure-stripping' become by the early to mid 1970s that reservoir fly fishing was at risk of being written off by thinking anglers as little more than a mindless pursuit.

The trend was reversed by the publication in 1975 of Brian Clarke's compelling book *The Pursuit of Stillwater Trout*, which demonstrated the benefits to be gained from thinking about the fishes' behaviour, the food they were taking and the selection and presentation of artificials designed to represent that food, and which reintroduced more imitative techniques to the sport. But it was the sudden growth of competitive fly fishing in the late 1970s and early 1980s that led to the extraordinary revolution in boat fishing flies and tactics that continues today.

Organized fly fishing competitions have been held for well over a hundred years; the first took place on Loch Leven in 1880. International matches between England, Ireland, Scotland and Wales have been held since about 1930, and there have been numerous informal matches up and down the country over the years. But it was not until the advent of the Benson & Hedges inter-club competition in 1982 that significant numbers of stillwater fly fishers began to take an interest in this particular facet of the sport.

Whether or not you approve of competitive fly fishing, there can be no doubt that it has been the stimulus of competition that has revived interest in loch-style boat fishing and produced a great deal of radical thinking in terms of both fly patterns and fishing tactics.

Boat fishing
Boat safety

Before we head out on to the water, it is worth saying just a few words about safety. Perhaps because the British are seafarers by tradition, there is a tendency for people to presume that good boat handling is instinctive rather than a skill to be learnt, and to treat boats and water with less respect than is sometimes necessary. In truth, though, and like many Irish loughs and Scottish lochs, our larger reservoirs can be moody places, prone to much fiercer conditions than some may imagine.

All reservoir fisheries provide life jackets, which should be worn or at least, in calm weather, kept close to hand for use in emergencies. Always check that the fuel tank is full before setting out, make sure that there is a serviceable set of oars and rowlocks in the boat, and check the anchor. The anchors provided at some fisheries are less than satisfactory, encouraging many anglers to carry their own; the ideal is a 2kg Danforth with ten feet of chain and sixty to eighty feet of 1.5 cm rope. Anchors and drogues should be fastened to strongpoints in the boat rather than to rowlocks, which they may damage.

Many people stand up when fishing in boats, presumably because they believe that it increases the distance they can cast. In truth the practice is both dangerous and counter-productive – dangerous because an unexpected wave or a false step backwards can tip the angler into the water; counter-productive because the high profile of a standing angler will frighten the fish, more than negating any slight increase in casting distance it may be believed to afford. The answer, of course, is to improve one's casting technique. With practice it becomes quite easy to put out twenty-five or thirty yards from a sitting position.

For the occasional reservoir angler, a vinyl-covered foam cushion may be sufficient to counteract the numbing effect of a hard wooden thwart. But for the regular reservoir fly fisher a proper boat seat can make all the difference. We used to make them ourselves, from simple lengths of planking covered with thick foam rubber encased in heavy-duty polythene. Nowadays, far better ones are available commercially. Built on aluminium frames which lock on to the boat's gunwales, they have padded, sliding seats and trays designed to accommodate fly boxes or loose line. And because they elevate you to the level of the gunwales, there is no doubt that they make casting easier and more comfortable.

Fly lines

Because reservoir trout may feed anywhere between the surface and forty or fifty feet down, perhaps changing their feeding patterns several times during the course of a day, and because versatility is *the* key to catching them consistently, reservoir boat fishing is probably the only branch of the sport that really does require substantial investment in fly lines. If you plan to fish reservoirs often, the least you can hope reasonably to get away with is a floating line, a slow sinker, a quick sinker and a high-density line. And it is sensible to have two rods so that you can change quickly from one type of line to another without having to go through the process of unthreading, changing reels and then rethreading.

Early season

A cold, blustery, mid-April day on Bewl Water. Under low, scudding, slate grey clouds, and huddled against squalls of stinging rain, we butt our way along the shoreline towards the western end of the dam. A hundred yards short of the corner of the reservoir, and with not a sign of a fish on the surface, we cut the engine and put the drogue out over the stern, setting the boat on a slow, stern-to-wind drift along the line of the dam.

Settling down, we begin side-casting with weight forward, high-density lines and single lures on leaders no more than eight or nine feet long – a Viva for Tony and an Appetizer for me.

By putting out long lines and allowing them to sink for twenty seconds or so and to be drawn into a curve by the drifting boat, before beginning quite rapid retrieves, we catch four fish between us in the first couple of hours. Great, heaving, heart-pounding takes that bow our rods over, dragging their tips down almost into the water; rod and line shuddering as the fish surge up towards the surface and leap, scattering showers of silver spray, dragging the heavy lines behind them – heady stuff while it lasts. But this is a tactile exercise rather than a visual one, and a cold one too, a sort of piscatorial 'military campaign', disciplined and relentless, with long periods of near-tedium punctuated by only occasional and quite brief moments of excitement.

There is satisfaction to be had from wrestling with the elements, but after a while the chill and the 'sameness' of it all begins to wear thin and it is with considerable relief that, towards the end of the morning, we notice the wind easing and the cloud lifting a little. There are still no signs of fish coming to the surface but, in order to ring the changes as much as for any other reason, we motor down to the arm of the reservoir leading to the nature reserve and change to a broadside drift.

The 'strip-and-hang' technique is a relatively new development in reservoir angling, devised by competitive anglers to enable them to take deep-feeding trout while drifting 'loch-style', as required by competition rules.

I replace my single lure with a team of three flies on a fourteen- or fifteen-foot leader – a Stick Fly on the point, a large Black Buzzer on the dropper and a bushy Soldier Palmer on the bob. Tony puts up something similar.

With the drogue out over the upwind gunwale to slow our drift, we cast the high-density lines as far ahead of the boat as possible, allowing them to sink for anything from five to twenty seconds before beginning long, steady retrieves, recovering line just faster than the boat is moving in order to keep the flies working through the water as we bear down on them. Takes come most often either on the first two or three pulls of the retrieve as the flies – now quite deep down in the water – begin to turn up towards the boat, or as the bob fly dibbles in the surface just before we lift off to re-cast.

Of all sinking line techniques, 'strip-and-hang' is by far the most

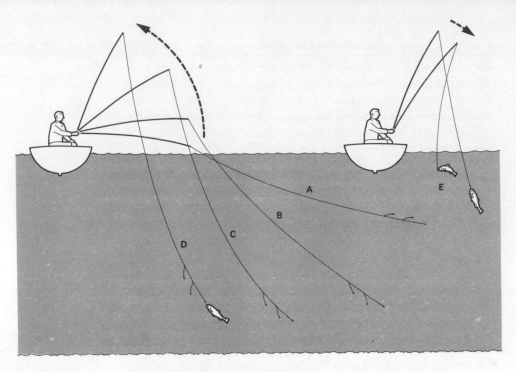

The Strip-and-Hang Method
A. *Cast out line as far as possible and allow to sink*
B. *Take up slack line as boat drifts towards cast*
C. *Retrieve line when desired depth is reached*
D. *Retrieve in long draws. When flies are halfway up, stop, then retrieve more quickly, lifting rod arm simultaneously. Stop when top dropper is on surface*
E. *Lower rod tip and drop fly back again*

interesting and the most difficult to master, chiefly because it allows us to experiment with so many variables – fly patterns (you can try anything from lures and minilures through traditional wet flies to nymphs and buzzers), length of sinking time, and speed and style of retrieve.

Our first take of the drift comes to the Viva Tony has put on the point of his leader. The fish runs rings around the boat for several minutes before coming to the net – a deep, fit, bright rainbow weighing a shade over two pounds. More follow during the course of the day and we stumble ashore in the fading light with a full bag apiece, cold, wet and tired but having had more than our share of fish and a great deal of fun to boot.

Mid-season

Six weeks later a bright, warm, June morning, finds us at Grafham Water. Pushed by a steady southerly breeze, heaped cumulo nimbus roll across a deep blue sky. The boats, bright white and sleek, are bobbing at the jetty, tugging at their mooring ropes, impatient to be off. The outboard motor sputters into life, phutters fitfully, clunks into 'drive', accelerates to a steady hum, and we head out north westwards across the lake towards Savage's Creek, kicking up spray from the bows and leaving a fizzing white wake behind us.

The dividing line between the pale, turbid water inshore, where wave action has stirred up the bottom, and the clear, blue, deeper water beyond it is sharply defined today, and runs northwards almost directly along the wind's path. Trout will often be found feeding near the surface of the cleaner side of such a line, so we throttle down and cut the engine, wallowing to a stop fifteen or twenty yards short of it.

Floating lines, long fifteen- to twenty-foot leaders, each with two droppers, the style of our first few drifts is precisely the same as we would have used had we been on an Irish lough or a Scottish loch – broadside on to the wind, casting a relatively short line ahead of the boat, dibbling the bob fly in the ripple for as long as possible, lifting off and recasting. But because our quarry is primarily the rainbow trout rather than the native brown trout, and because rainbows feed on daphnia and coarse fish fry so consistently, especially in summer, the patterns we use are a little different – brighter, a fraction larger. Tony ties a small Muddler Minnow to the point of his leader, a wet Greenwell's Glory to the middle dropper and an Invicta to the bob; for variety I put a Whiskey Fly (tied on an ordinary-shanked size 10 hook) on the point, Black Buzzer on the middle dropper and a bushy Grenadier on the bob.

A splash fifty yards ahead of us, a swirl off to the right. The boat settles on to its drift and, quite suddenly, we are surrounded by rising trout. One which surges after my Whiskey Fly and hooks itself in the process charges around furiously in front of the boat, very nearly preventing Tony from hooking one that comes, far more sedately, to his Invicta. With a little orchestrated teamwork we manage to keep our respective trout apart and bring them to the net. More follow on this same drift, two to Tony's Muddler and one to my Buzzer. And then it is all over, as suddenly as it started.

Unlike brown trout, which tend to be relatively solitary creatures, rainbow trout have a strong shoaling instinct, and when feeding at the surface they always seem to be on the move, heading into the wind, working their way up the food lanes. The 'joining speed' of a boat drifting downwind and a shoal of rainbows moving upwind can be quite high – one minute they are ahead of you, the next you are among them and a few moments later they are behind you.

We turn and motor back upwind to try to find the shoal again, putting out a drogue behind the boat this time to slow the drift, but they seem to have vanished. Perhaps they have gone down in the water or veered off to one side, or maybe they have turned and are running back towards Sanctuary Bay, twenty feet or so down, before starting another feeding foray. Whatever the reason, we cannot find them and before long we begin to drift into the paler, more coloured water where it curves round along the north shore.

A haze of swifts or swallows – it is impossible to tell which from here – is wheeling and swooping low over the water to the south, towards Valley Creek. Being careful to avoid three or four other boats already fishing in the area, we motor over and tuck in close to the shore, replacing our teams of loch flies and lures with nymphs and buzzers – olive or ginger Shipman's Buzzers on the points and middle droppers, and Emerging Buzzers as the bob flies. The leaders are greased lightly right down to within a couple of inches of each fly, and the flies themselves are treated with a little Gink, the magic potion that seems to keep stillwater flies afloat when all else fails.

The breeze is dropping. Drifting out on to the ripple is like drifting into a dream. Ahead of us, under a now clear blue sky, trout are rising everywhere, rolling, wallowing, humping and swirling. No need to cast long lines. Our leaders float out over the water, check, hover and settle. As we drift towards them, slow figure-of-eight retrieves keep us just in touch with our flies. A fish moves ten yards away to the right, I begin to lift off to cover it, there is a splash and my rod hoops over as an indignant brown trout bores away from the boat and down, deep into the water.

Tony's turn next, then mine again. Fish after fish come to the flies. Some take them as they float in the surface film or hang static just beneath it, some as we twitch them oh-so-slowly back towards us, some chasing and catching them as we lift off to re-cast. Within a couple of hours we have eight trout apiece in the boat, have missed or hooked and lost at least twice as many more, and are confronted with that all-too-occasional bittersweet decision – do we buy another ticket each or pack up and head for home?

Nymph and dry fly fishing

Not for the first time we allow our hearts to rule our heads, pushing off again after a leisurely tea. This time we anchor up in the entrance to Savage's Creek fifty or so yards out from the shore, several hundred yards clear of the nearest bank angler, over perhaps ten or fifteen feet of water.

There are no fish moving at the surface now, so we put on long, long leaders – twenty feet or more – on floating lines and with teams of three nymphs apiece: a Stick Fly on the point for Tony and a leaded Gold-Ribbed Hare's Ear nymph for me, and a couple of size 12 Buzzers each as dropper and bob flies.

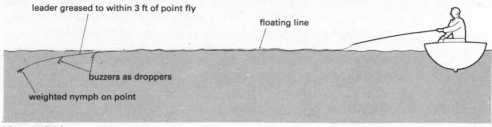

leader greased to within 3 ft of point fly

floating line

buzzers as droppers

weighted nymph on point

Nymph fishing

Cast them out on to the flat, calm water, watch as they sink for thirty seconds or more – so many takes come 'on the drop' – and retrieve with a slow, steady figure-of-eight. It is delightful, relaxing fishing, especially on a soft, warm summer's evening. A murmured conversation between two anglers half a mile away carries quietly across the lake. The tip of the fly line slips forward, the rod goes up, another fine fish comes to the net. Another follows it a few moments later.

Evening creeps on. There is a far-off splash, then another. Soon the surface of the reservoir is covered with the rings of rising trout. They are probably taking hatching midge pupae but I hedge my bets, replacing the Hare's Ear nymph on the point with a bushy Palmered Sedge, shortening the leader to about fifteen feet and greasing it lightly.

Out it goes, checks, straightens and falls. The Sedge looks absurd, like a hedgehog sitting on the surface. Wait; watch. Suddenly, a nose appears beside the Sedge and engulfs it. Wait; tighten. A brown trout this time, fighting deep and strong; the last of the day.

Inexorably the sun, a reddening globe, sidles towards the darkening skyline. A bat whirrs past. Fish are still rising all around, and we cast on into the sunset, fishing increasingly by feel rather than by sight. Eventually we give it best, packing up and motoring slowly back towards the lights of the fishing lodge. A perfect end to a perfect day.

Autumn

Grafham again, in a soft September. A south-westerly breeze fanning the surface, fluffing it into a little ripple, carries us out of Valley Creek across towards Church Hill Farm. Two size 10 Hoppers, one on the point, one on a dropper four feet above it, serve to suggest the daddy-long-legs being blown on to the water from the fields around. The artificials are treated with Gink, the leader is lightly greased, but this is 'surface fishing' rather than 'dry fly' fishing, and the fish seem actually to prefer to have the flies presented to them in the surface film rather

159

than on it.

The rises, while they last, are positive and confident, the trout rolling at the Hoppers and seizing them fiercely, and we net two or three apiece within an hour. But the fish seem easily distracted and vanish as quickly as they appeared. We motor around slowly for a while, searching for clues, and then head over towards the dam.

Suddenly there is a commotion in the water ahead of us, a boiling and churning and a scattering of silver fry. Reservoir trout can become wholly preoccupied with coarse fish fry late in the season, crashing through dense shoals of them, grabbing them as they go and then returning to pick off the stragglers, the injured, the dead and the dying.

Idling the boat to a halt, we change to eight-pound knotless, tapered leaders – a Muddler Minnow on Tony's, a large (size 6 long-shank) Appetizer on mine. The two patterns require very different techniques. Retrieved quickly through the ripple, the Muddler will bring trout chasing and bow-waving after it, grabbing at it, snatching at it and occasionally hanging on. It can provide exciting sport but, in my experience, tends not to be as clinically effective as a white pattern – almost any white pattern – fished 'dead drift'.

There is a great swirl in the water no more than twenty yards ahead of me and a shower of panic-stricken fry bursts across the water's surface. Cast, check. The three-inch lure drops among the rings rocking away from the eruption and begins to sink, slowly. No retrieve – just watch; watch. The tip of the fly line tugs forward sharply. Up goes the rod and a four-pound rainbow trout explodes from the water.

Reservoir trout feed on coarse fish fry throughout the season from the beginning to the end, but particularly in mid-summer when clouds of newly hatched fry drift just below the surface, and again in the autumn when brown and rainbow trout are building up their strength for the winter ahead. It is important to recognize the differences in size between summer and autumn fry. In June and July they may be no more than an inch long and can be represented with similarly small patterns – a Butcher, perhaps, a Teal and Silver or, more specifically, Sinfoil's Fry – fished in teams of two or three. Later, by September or October, those that have survived may be as much as three or four inches long and must be represented with large lures – Bob Church's Appetizer and Jack Frost are both deadly for this purpose, as is Dick Shrive's Missionary, and there are several buoyant fry patterns suggestive of stunned floating fry. Whichever you use, it almost always pays to fish fry-imitating patterns either static or very slowly indeed. And the 'pay-off' can certainly provide a spectacular end to the season.

The author fishing the Arundel Arms water on the little Lyd in Devon

BELOW LEFT: *One of Wales' great rain-fed rivers, the Teivi near Cenarth*

BELOW RIGHT: *The upper reaches of the river Tweed, a river on which excellent trout fishing is often eclipsed by people's passion for salmon*

ABOVE: *The Dove in Dovedale, a lime-stone river fished by Izaak Walton and Charles Cotton*

LEFT: *The river Kennet provides some of the best fishing in England in some of the most beautiful surroundings*

OPPOSITE PAGE ABOVE: *The late Alex Jardine fishing on the Itchen, one of Britain's loveliest and most historic chalk streams*

OPPOSITE PAGE BELOW LEFT: *The river Avon above Salisbury: a classic chalk stream*

OPPOSITE PAGE BELOW RIGHT: *Professor Norman Maclean preparing to net a brown trout from an Itchen carrier*

ABOVE: *Hallowed waters: Andrew Witkowski fishing on the Test*

LEFT: *Dapping for trout on Lough Corrib. A sturdy well designed boat is essential for safe and comfortable lough fishing*

OPPOSITE PAGE ABOVE: *The solitude and beauty of a Scottish loch*

OPPOSITE PAGE BELOW LEFT: *A still summer's day on a Scottish loch*

OPPOSITE PAGE BELOW RIGHT: *The author and his son fishing on the lovely Loch Lunn Da Bhra above Fort William*

ABOVE: *A lone angler fishes Ballinahinch lough in Co. Galway, typical of the lovely waters to be found in the west of Ireland*

LEFT: *Blagdon, the* Alma Mater *of British reservoir fly fishing*

OPPOSITE PAGE ABOVE: *Preparing for a day afloat at Grafham Water, where the boom in reservoir trout fishing began in the 1960s*

OPPOSITE PAGE CENTRE: *Henry Lowe, resident instructor at Grafham Water, drifting alone on a bright, blustery June morning*

OPPOSITE PAGE BELOW: *Bewl Water expert, John Hatherell, boat fishing on a summer morning*

Damerham fishery in Hampshire, one of the prettiest and best-established small still-waters in the south of England

BELOW LEFT: *A fish comes to the net at Langford fishery in Wiltshire*

BELOW RIGHT: *'Two splendid old men were clearly having the time of their lives' (see pages 175–76)*

CHAPTER TWELVE

Small Stillwaters

A sunny, windless, late-April day; golden catkins on the willows; yellow primroses and cowslips on grassy banks and in the meadows; unaccustomed warmth in the air; a sniff of summer. Chatter and cheerful banter in the fishery car park. Bernard, Max and Neil, Ron and John, a brace of Brians, Mike and me; an annual gathering. Friends fishing while wives watch, or join in, or wander together along country lanes. There will be chunks of fresh, warm, crispy-crusted bread for lunch, with cheese, chutney and fine beer, and a barbecue at dusk, chops and chicken legs, steaks and sausages, all sizzling, crisp salad and a glass of wine. There will be a hideous and trivial prize for someone, the rules of the competition to be decided later, and we shall drive home quietly, satisfied and sleepy. For the moment, all that lies ahead of us.

Damerham is a perfect small stillwater fishery for those who would stalk their trout rather than simply fish the water. Spring-fed, the lakes are crystal clear, and in the main they are narrow enough to enable the angler to see deep down into most parts of them. The problem, of course, is that where you can see the fish, the fish can see you.

Concealment

It is wrong to presume that farm-reared fish stocked into man-made lakes are not easily frightened. They are, and a frightened fish will very rarely take a fly, however often and however delicately you may put it to him. It is astonishing how many experienced and intelligent fly fishers, who would creep and crawl up the banks of a chalk stream in order to avoid alarming trout that will almost always be facing upstream, away from them, will stand four-square on the banks of stillwater fisheries flailing away like demented windmills, wondering why the trout are so difficult to tempt.

As an aside, it is a fact that heavily-fished small stillwaters often 'die' in the afternoons, and that those who fish them become accustomed to disappointing or non-existent evening rises. Generally speaking, the reason has far more to do with the way in which anglers fish the water, terrifying the trout, than with any natural reluctance the fish may have to feed in the latter half of the day.

CHECK LIST – SMALL STILLWATER TACKLE

RODS:
For small, clear stillwaters: 9–9ft 6in: #6–7; medium to stiff action
For larger lakes: 9ft 6in–10ft 6in; #6–7; medium to stiff action

FLY LINES:
1. Weight forward or double-tapered, floating; #6–7
2. Weight forward, intermediate or slow-sinking;
#6–7
3. (Possibly, for larger waters very early in the season or in high summer, weight forward, quick-sinking; #6–7)

LEADERS:

For floating line

For sinking line

SMALL STILLWATER FLIES AND LURES:

Leaded nymphs

March/April/May: Alder Larva; Montana Nymph; Mayfly Nymph (all 10 long-shank); Gold-Ribbed Hare's Ear Nymph; Bloodworm; Water Hog Louse; Midge Pupae ('Buzzers') (all size 10 or 12)

June/July/August: Montana Nymph; Damselfly Nymph (both 10 long-shank); Gold-Ribbed Hare's Ear Nymph; Shrimps; Corixae; Midge Pupae ('Buzzers') (all size 10–14)

September/October: Montana Nymph; Damselfly Nymph (both 10 long-shank); Gold-Ribbed Hare's Ear Nymph; Pheasant Tail Nymph; Bloodworms; Shrimps; Corixae; Midge Pupae ('Buzzers') (all size 10–14)

Unleaded nymphs, lures and wet flies

March/April/May: Black and Peacock Spider; Orange Partridge Spider; Black Midge Pupae ('Buzzers') (all size 10–14); Black Chenille; Viva (both 10–12 long-shank)

162

June/July/August: Phantom Larva; Yellow or Green Partridge Spider; Orange or Green Midge Pupae ('Buzzers') (all size 10–14); Black Chenille; Whiskey Fly (both 10–12 long-shank); Damselfly Nymph; Adult Damselfly (both 10 long-shank)

September/October: Black and Peacock Spider; Orange Partridge; Black Midge Pupae ('Buzzers'); Corixae; PVC Nymph (all size 10–14); Black Chenille; White Chenille; Sinfoil's Fry (all 10 long-shank)

Dry flies (May to September)

April/May: Hawthorn Fly (size 10–12)

May/June: Shadow Mayfly; Deerstalker (both 10 long-shank)

June/July/August: G and H Sedge (10 long-shank); Palmered Sedge (size 10)

August/September: Daddy-Long-Legs (10 long-shank)

Buoyant lures (larger lakes only)

March/April: Booby Nymph (size 10 or 12)

July/August: Rasputin; Rassler (both 10 long-shank); Plastazote Corixa (size 10–12)

October: Rasputin; Rassler (size 10 long-shank)

And do not forget scissors or snippers, artery forceps, silicone floatant, mucilin (red tin), sinkant (Fuller's Earth, washing-up detergent and glycerin), hook-hone, spare leaders or leader material, landing net and priest.

Camouflage and concealment are as essential to success on small lakes as they are on any other kind of trout water. Wear clothes that blend with the background; keep your silhouette low; use bankside vegetation and trees and bushes behind you to break up your outline; avoid unnecessary movement; cast as little as possible and keep false casting to a minimum. Do not laugh at those who kneel while fishing, 'saying their prayers'; such prayers are often answered.

Tackle

Back to the beginning.

It is rarely if ever necessary to cast great distances at fisheries like Damerham. Indeed, because it frightens the fish, long casting is counter-productive. Instead, the emphasis is on short, accurate casting – the ability to put your flies to fish you can see, often quite close in.

A fairly stiff nine-foot rod rated for lines in the range #6–7 is ideal. I usually carry two of them: one armed with a weight forward floating line, essential for 'ambushing' cruising fish; the other with a weight

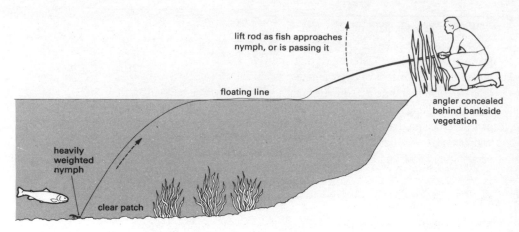

Ambushing trout on small stillwaters

forward intermediate or slow-sinking line, which causes less surface disturbance than the floater and is useful when the trout show a preference for fast-moving artificials.

Fast-sinking lines are unnecessary on waters of this sort which tend to be relatively shallow. Even very early in the season, when the water is cold and the fish tend to feed near the bottom, it should be perfectly possible to reach them with a floating line, a long leader and a weighted fly.

I am absolutely convinced that leader length is crucial on small, clear lakes, especially when fishing with a floating line. I have a three-foot, tapered, braided butt fastened permanently to my fly line. A ten- to fifteen-foot length of twenty-pound monofilament is tied to the tip of the braided butt, and a 4X (about four pounds breaking strain) nine-foot knotless tapered leader is tied to the tip of the twenty-pound nylon. The overall length of the leader – never less than twenty-two feet and rarely more than twenty-seven – is adjusted by shortening and adding to the twenty-pound monofilament.

A four-pound point is the minimum that is sensible on waters where fish of two and a half to three pounds are the norm, four-, six- and eight-pounders are quite common and there is a real chance of a fish of ten pounds or more.

Some people add a two- to three-foot tippet to avoid having to snip away the tip of the knotless tapered leader when they change flies, replacing the tippet each time it becomes too short. I prefer not to do so because it seems foolish to me to introduce a strength-sapping, weed-gathering knot into the leader at what is already its weakest point. Instead, I indulge in a very slight extravagance, carrying a few spare nine-foot leaders with me, replacing the one on the fly line when necessary.

With an intermediate or slow-sinking line it is reasonable to use a shorter leader – perhaps twelve or fifteen feet long overall. I have a six-inch braided loop fastened permanently to the fly line. To this I attach three to six feet of twenty-pound monofilament, using a loop-to-loop join, and then I tie a 3X knotless tapered leader to this butt length.

When stalking fish, either with a floating line or with an intermediate or a slow sinker, I always rub the whole of the leader down thoroughly with sinkant – a home-made, putty-like mixture of Fuller's Earth, washing-up liquid and glycerin.

Flies

Most small stillwater fisheries allow the use of only one fly at a time, which simplifies leader design and choice of pattern.

It is interesting and amusing to seek to 'match the hatch' on small stillwaters, and quite often it will be profitable to do so. But here I think we must be honest with ourselves. The fact of the matter is that most of the trout in most small lakes are farm reared and relatively recently stocked. They are more used to pelleted food than to the insects and other fauna upon which they would feed in the wild, and while they can become quite selective on occasions they are usually prepared to take almost any sensible pattern provided it is presented to them attractively.

When stalking trout with a floating line, it is necessary to be able to get the fly down to the fish quite quickly, and weighted nymphs provide the answer. There are countless patterns and variations to choose from and it pays to have an assortment in your fly box so that you can ring the changes, particularly on hard-fished waters where many of the fish may have seen several patterns countless times. An Alder Larva, a Mayfly Nymph, a Montana Nymph and a Damselfly Nymph, all leaded and all tied on size 10 long-shank hooks, will all take fish consistently, as will a leaded Gold-Ribbed Hare's Ear Nymph and leaded Bloodworms, Shrimps, Corixae, Water Hog Lice and Midge Pupae.

With an intermediate line or a slow sinker, the objective is different. Here, we shall be seeking either to get the line itself down to the fish's feeding depth or to draw the fish up to a pattern being retrieved beneath the water's surface. A leaded pattern may be useful for these purposes, but we are as likely to want to use unweighted patterns – a Phantom Larvae, a Black and Peacock Spider, Orange, Yellow or Green Partridge Spiders, an adult Damselfly pattern, or any one of the unweighted nymphs, midge pupae or minilures that are available.

Stalking Trout

This morning, I pair the floating line with a weighted Alder Larva and the slow sinker with a Black and Peacock Spider – two trusted friends – and wander off down the bank with Neil, past Mayfly Lake and on to Horseshoe, the largest of the five lakes.

With polarized sunglasses and broad-brimmed hats, and with the sun behind us, we can see right down into the deepest, darkest recesses of the lake. Initially the water seems dead but then a fish appears, and then another, and another, shadowy shapes idling along, individually or in pairs, snapping occasionally at unseen morsels. Most of these trout are much of a size, between two and three pounds apiece. It is tempting to have a chuck at them but half the fun of such clear-water fisheries is that they enable us to pick out the bigger fish.

There is a small island towards the lower end of the lake, with a deep channel beyond it. As we peer into the channel, stooping slightly both for concealment and to adjust the reflection from the water's surface, a big rainbow appears heading slowly but purposefully along the bank immediately below us. 'Yours,' says Neil.

The fish swims on towards the island, across two or three light patches among the weed and disappears; no problem. Trout in small lakes, and especially large trout, almost always cruise along on repetitive and predictable paths, following the same routes the whole time. Their circuits may be quite long and they may vanish from view for several minutes at a time, but the patient angler will usually be rewarded, his quarry crossing the same spot time and again.

We watch and wait.

Suddenly Neil points. There she is again, coming towards us, six or eight feet down in the deep water beneath the bank. As she approaches, she pauses and turns off to one side briefly; we see the white gape of her mouth as it opens to engulf some small food item, and then she continues her journey, out across the channel towards the island, across the pale, gravelly patches, melting into the darkness beyond.

This time I unhook the Alder Larva and pull the leader, the braided butt and four or five feet of fly line out beyond the tip ring of the rod. Stripping fifteen or twenty feet of line from the reel, I waft the leader into the air, extending line with a couple of false casts and tapping the rod forward.

As it plops into the water the fly appears to be ten feet or so beyond the largest of the bare patches on the lake bed, but the tension of the fly line and leader will cause it to move back towards me as it sinks, and I guess it will come to rest on the gravel; there is room for crossed fingers even in the most calculated forms of fishing.

Four or five minutes later the fish comes into view again, following exactly the same path, her deep flanks flexing sinuously, her great paddle of a tail powering her along with no apparent effort. Still we watch and wait.

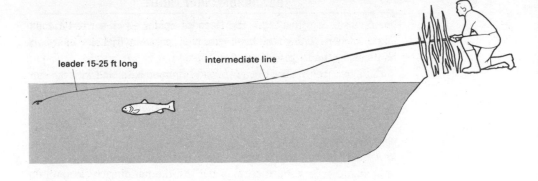

Ambushing fish with an intermediate line. The angler casts to the fish when it is swimming away from him, dropping the point of the fly line behind the fish and the fly in front of it. Once the line has sunk a few inches, a couple of sharp pulls may be expected to induce a take

She swims on towards the island, across the first and smallest of the light patches and towards the next one where the Alder Larva lies in wait. As her head emerges over the gravel, I raise the rod tip quite gently, lifting the fly off the bottom. Crouching behind her as we are, we cannot see her mouth open and close, but she turns sharply to one side and then straightens again, suggesting that she has taken the fly; feel for her and tighten. The rod is hauled over into a tight arc as the fish charges off up the lake; the reel screams.

Gradually she slows, stops and turns, coming up in the water and wallowing at the surface twenty yards away before running along parallel with the far bank. Her fight is dogged and determined and I play her from the reel, anxious not to run the risk of loose line becoming caught up in the bankside vegetation. Eventually she rolls on to her side, comes to the net and we haul her up on to the grass, despatching her with a priest while she is still in the net. Laid out in the late-spring sunshine, she proves to be an immaculate fish – deep and firm, bright silver, with full fins and tail; six pounds exactly.

Two more fish from Horseshoe Lake – one apiece, two-and-a-half-pounders – and we stroll back up to Mayfly Lake, now deserted.

There is a long channel at the bottom end of Mayfly, and as we creep up on it we can see two or three fish moving around, apparently aimlessly. None of them is huge but one, around four pounds, is noticeably bigger than the others. We watch it for a while and then Neil crawls into position and unhooks the Phantom Larva from a rod with a slow-sinking line on it.

Pulling line out through the tip ring, he drops the fly on to the grass in front of him and strips ten or twelve more yards of line from the reel. Many fly fishers try to start casting with the line-to-leader join still

167

inside the tip ring and to pull line from the reel while false casting. Such antics are frustrating and unnecessary and can only frighten the fish. It is much better to get everything sorted out before you start casting and then to use the least number of false casts possible to get the line into the air and the fly out to the fish.

Neil waits until the biggest fish has come to within about ten yards of him, has turned and is sauntering away with its back to him; there is no point in casting to trout that are facing you, and which are therefore more likely to see you. He lifts his rod, the line sails out behind him, he makes a couple of false casts – one to extend line, the second for accuracy – and taps forward. Perfect.

The tip of the fly line lands just behind the fish, the fly twelve feet ahead of it. The line and the carefully de-greased leader start to sink immediately, and after a pause of only a few seconds Neil begins a quick, steady, figure-of-eight retrieve. The fish turns and rises through the water, all its senses focused on the tiny, translucent fly. It speeds up slightly, opens and closes its mouth, points its head down and turns back up the lake – only to be brought up short by Neil's strike and the buffering resistance of his rod. Three or four minutes later, after a fearsome battle, another gleaming rainbow lies on the bank; just over four pounds.

Over lunch back at the hut, we swap stories of the morning's sport, most of them honest or with only the slightest and most forgivable exaggeration. John has taken an eight-pounder from Vicarage Moor, Ron has three pretty fish, all taken from Holyhead on Midge Pupae, and one of the Brians swears he lost a whale in Hawkhill. Everyone has a fish or two with a brace or so in hand for the afternoon. There is very little point in hauling out four fish in the first couple of hours and then having either to buy another ticket, to go home early or to spend the rest of the day as a spectator.

After lunch, we head for the lakes again. It becomes increasingly difficult to see and stalk fish as the sun drops lower in the sky, but we each add another fish or two to those taken in the morning, and the barbecue in the evening provides another opportunity for tall tales of piscatorial derring-do.

Happy days.

Larger lakes

Six weeks later; flaming June.

'Flip-flap, flip-flap, flip-flap,' the wipers spatter their wet, metronomic rhythm on the windscreen for mile after mile. The great aircraft hangar at Boscombe Down is no more than a smudge on the skyline. Stonehenge appears, squat and grey, its square columns and arches dwarfing small knots of tourists, hunched, red and yellow cagouled against the driving rain. On, on; the nearside wheels check in a puddle and slow momentarily; water sprays tinnily against the underside of the car, and then we are free again, or as free as two caravans and a milk lorry will allow, grinding across the Plain at a steady, soggy forty miles an hour.

Through Winterbourne Stoke, on to Deptford and left down the Wylye valley, to the Langfords. Right into Duck Street, aptly named today; across the tantalizing bridge over the river (can there ever have been a true angler able to resist the urge to hang over every bridge and peer into the water below), up the cinder drive and into the car park. The engine dies. Silence, apart from the drumming of raindrops on the roof. Nettles hang bedraggled among white-flowered hogweed beneath the hedge.

We struggle into waterproof jackets, over-trousers and wellingtons before splashing across to the garage that serves as a fishery office. Paul is there, cheerful, welcoming, dry, with news of trout taken and what they were taken on. 'They've been coming well to dry flies right through the day – sedges, mostly, but daddy-long-legs, too. No idea what effect this weather will have on them, though. It looks as if it's settled in for the duration.' We buy our tickets, thank him and head back to the car to put our rods up.

Tackle

With two quite large lakes, Langford is a substantial fishery, by no means as vastly daunting as one of the major reservoirs but no mere pond or puddle either, and the ability to put out twenty-five or thirty yards of line when necessary can be a considerable asset. So the rods we use are those we take to Blagdon, Bewl and Grafham – ten feet long, reasonably stiff, rated #6–7 and loaded with weight forward #7 lines.

On lakes of this size and smaller, where the water is rarely more than ten or twelve feet deep anywhere, the vast majority of my fishing is with floating lines. But an intermediate can be invaluable on windless days when a floater would stand out like a hawser on a smooth surface and cause disturbing ripples the moment you started to move it. And a high-density line with a buoyant corixa pattern or even a Booby Nymph can save the day in high summer, when the water is hot and the fish have gone down deep, unless the weed has become so dense as to render such fishing impossible. Our leaders for larger lakes of this sort are exactly the same as those we use at smaller fisheries like Damerham.

This morning, Douglas and I put up floating lines, leaders of between fifteen and twenty feet and a G and H Sedge apiece, the most buoyant dry flies in our boxes which should stay afloat despite the pouring rain.

Leaving the two or three feet of nylon immediately above the flies ungreased, we grease the rest of our leaders very sparingly and smear the flies thoroughly with Gink to help keep them waterproof.

Dry fly fishing

The walk along between the two lakes is tantalizing. The rain has eased a little, the breeze is just ruffling the water's surface and there are fish rising everywhere. We leave our lunch in the hut and make for the water, Douglas heading for a favourite spot on the eastern shore. I follow more slowly, watching the water carefully.

The rise forms send mixed messages. Some of them shout 'midge pupae' – classic head-and-tail porpoise rolls, the trout's mouths never breaking the surface, leaving double-whorls eddying away in stunned patches in the ripple. Others are fiercer, more splashy, with a distinct 'glop' to them, which suggests that their perpetrators are taking something floating on the surface, but I cannot see what it is.

A gap in the rushes, trampled ground, easy access to the water at the tip of a promontory marking the entrance to a bay. Comfortable casting here today, with the south-westerly breeze blowing from left to right.

A fish rolls fifteen yards out, and then another. Crouching down, I pull out a little line, strip a few yards more from the reel, make two or three false casts and tap the fly out on to the water. It bobs like a white cork, drifting slowly until the wind catches the line and begins to skid the fly across the surface. A fish rises to my right. By pointing the rod at it before I lift off to re-cast, rather than lifting off and then trying to change direction, I can drop the fly in front of it with no more than a couple of false casts.

There is a swirl, the fly vanishes and I strike – far too soon; the G and H Sedge hurtles back towards me, the fly line crumples on to the water.

No matter how often we remind ourselves of the need to pause before striking when a trout has taken a dry fly, the need will always be difficult to translate into practice. When you have hooked a few fish in the day the timing of the strike becomes almost automatic, but it takes a considerable effort of will power to pause long enough to hook those first few fish.

Everything straightened out. Try again.

The fly is quite difficult to see on the ripple in the flat, grey light. Another swirl and a 'glop'. No mistake this time. The leader slips away and the tip of the fly line has begun to follow it before I lift the rod, feeling for the fish, patience being rewarded with a heavy pull and an explosion as a magnificent trout hurls itself into the air and then bores away into the deep water in the middle of the bay. It fights deep, tugging towards the lake bed, and does not show itself until it is almost ready for the net. Then, quite suddenly, it gives up, rolls on to its side and allows itself to be drawn into the bank, landed and despatched. A beautiful two-and-a-half-pound rainbow, streamlined like a salmon or a sea trout, glittering silver with pale pink fins, its great spade of a tail quivering slightly.

The fly has been well and truly munched and drowned and must be changed. Rinsed, squeezed in amadou (the magical fungus that dries floating flies so thoroughly) and re-treated with Gink, it would probably float quite well again. But experience suggests that a damp fly does not float as high as a fresh one and that it is almost always less attractive to the fish. Fortunately there are half a dozen more in the fly box, so I tie one on and smear it with Gink.

Another trout follows the first and I miss two or three more, either through striking too soon or because the fish take only half-heartedly, pushing the fly aside or missing it altogether. Then, for no obvious reason, it all goes quiet.

Grinning all over his face, Douglas comes trotting along the bank clutching a fine three-pounder. He says he changed to a Gold-Ribbed Hare's Ear nymph after missing a couple of rises to the G and H Sedge, and that this is his second fish in twenty minutes.

Nymph fishing

Taking my cue from him, I do what I should have done as soon as it became evident that the fish had moved down in the water, putting away the sedge and replacing it with a leaded nymph, a Damselfly Nymph, just to be different. Fished intelligently on a long leader, a leaded nymph is by far the most consistently deadly way of taking trout on rainbow-stocked stillwaters of any sort. The starting point, the basis for understanding the technique, is to be found in the way in which trout take artificial nymphs.

At one time I was a member of a syndicate which fished a pretty, well-stocked, gin-clear, ten-acre lake in Buckinghamshire. Fifteen feet deep in many places, you could count every single pebble on the bottom, and you could see every mark, every fin, on every fish. It provided marvellous opportunities to study trout and the ways in which they behave; it was as much a laboratory as a fishery.

I used to sit in a boat in the middle of the lake and chuck small weighted nymphs on fifteen- to twenty-foot leaders – mainly Gold-Ribbed Hare's Ear and Pheasant Tail nymphs – to cruising rainbows. At least 80 per cent of all the takes I had came on the drop, while the nymph was simply sinking through the water having just been cast. Of the remaining 20 per cent, at least half (10 per cent of the total) came on the first couple of pulls of the retrieve and almost a quarter (5 per cent of the total) came as I lifted off to re-cast, bringing the fly up through the water. Very few takes indeed came while I was actually retrieving.

Just as important – perhaps even more so – was that takes 'on the drop' were often extraordinarily difficult to spot at the surface. A fish would see the nymph sinking through the water, swim up to it, take it, chew it, spit it out, swim round, have another look at it, take it again and spit it out again, all without causing the slightest movement or with only the minutest twitch at the point at which the leader cut down through the surface film. Two lessons must be obvious from all this.

Firstly, those who believe – consciously or subconsciously – that they are only really fishing when they are actually retrieving their flies, and who therefore fill in the time between casting and starting their retrieves by looking around to see what else is going on on the water, cannot possibly register more than about 20 per cent of all the takes they get – those that come during the retrieve or as they lift off to re-cast.

Secondly, since takes 'on the drop' can be so difficult to see, it makes sense to do everything possible to increase our chances of spotting them.

The thing to remember is that you will be using the leader much as a coarse angler uses a float. If it is to float, it must be greased, but be careful not to get mucilin on the tip of the leader; it acts as a lubricant and can cause slippage in the knot holding the fly.

Unlike those who fish by feel, I love flat calm water and clear blue skies; they make takes easier to see. By the same token, I hate ripples – especially choppy little ripples – and flat grey skies like today's, which produce a form of 'snow blindness', making it almost impossible to see that all-important tiny black dot, the hole caused by the leader cutting down through the surface film.

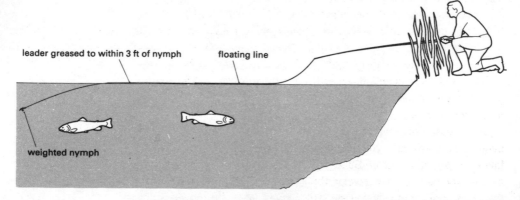

leader greased to within 3 ft of nymph   floating line

weighted nymph

Nymph fishing. The key to success is to watch the leader *for signs of takes 'on the drop', as the nymph is sinking through the water*

From time to time, fellow anglers have said that good eyesight gives me an unfair advantage over many people. Certainly, good eyesight is a great asset. But if you cannot see that magical little dot on calm water at twenty yards' range, it is worth trying one of the 'strike indicators' that are available from most tackle shops nowadays – luminescent polystyrene beads which can be attached to the leader to make takes very much more visible.

Choice of fly for this style of fishing is not critical. On reservoirs, large lakes and lightly-fished smaller stillwaters, a Sawyer's Pheasant Tail or G-RHE nymph, size 10 to 14, is probably all you need. Generally, it is the presentation rather than the fly that matters. But on hard-fished waters, where the fish see countless flies, it pays to ring the changes, offering them patterns they may never have seen before and which may be expected to arouse their curiosity.

Whatever pattern you use, the key to success is to remember that this is a *visual* exercise, not a tactile one – your objective is to *see* the takes, rather than to feel them.

Seek out a quiet corner of the fishery where the surface is glassy calm and, ideally, trees, hills or some other background provide dark reflections against which the leader may easily be seen. Use trees or hedgerows behind you and bankside vegetation to provide cover and cast no more than eight or ten yards to start with. And as the fly begins to sink, watch the leader like a hawk, focusing on that tiny black dot where it enters the surface film. If the leader moves, twitches, tweaks or slithers forward, or if it stops slipping down through that little hole, don't wait to wonder whether you have a take – strike; there will almost certainly be a fish there.

That 'near-certainty' is based on a fact that seems not to have occurred to some people. If a nymph is cast out on to water containing no fish, it will sink at a predictable and entirely steady rate until, eventually, it reaches the bottom or lands on a piece of weed or some other obstruction. As it does so, the leader will slip steadily through that now famous little hole. There is nothing to cause it to do otherwise.

If you know the depth of the water you are fishing over and are satisfied that there is nothing in it to interrupt your nymph's downward progress, then it follows that any change in the leader's behaviour *must* be caused by a fish.

As we saw earlier, that 'change' in the leader's behaviour can be minute. To start with, you may detect only a small percentage of the takes you get on the drop. But practice makes perfect (or almost so!); as time goes on you will develop the ability to spot more and more of the takes until eventually you are striking without really knowing why, simply because 'something changed'.

So consistently deadly is this technique, and so few are the takes we get on the retrieve, that many skilful nymph anglers do not bother to retrieve at all. They just cast out, watch the leader while the fly is sinking, and then, if they don't get a take, lift straight off again to re-cast. This may be counter-productive. Ten, fifteen or twenty yards of fly line being hauled from the water's surface can cause quite a disturbance. It is probably better to retrieve before re-casting, even if you do not expect to get many takes while doing so.

Douglas's G-RHE nymph and my Damselfly nymph stand us in good stead today. When the time comes to head homeward across Salisbury Plain, tired, damp and happy, we have five fish apiece. A great day out.

CHAPTER THIRTEEN

Realities and Responsibilities

From time to time I have seen stories in field sports magazines, written by British fly fishers, about visits to small, 'any method', put-and-take trout waters in France. The authors have usually told of French bait anglers' curiosity as fly rods have been produced from the boots of cars, and of that curiosity turning to amazement – not to say awed admiration – as a niftily presented midge pupa or some such has brought half a dozen trout to the net in no time.

Heading for Provence early one summer, it occurred to me that it might be fun to search out one of these fisheries, to catch a few of its trout, and then to present readers of one of our game fishing publications with a blasé and witty account of it. I have to confess that I also had it in mind to prove *la mouche's* superiority over all forms of bait and the English fly fisher's undoubted superiority over his maggot-dangling French cousins.

Finding the fishery presented no problems. A marvellously lurid sign fixed to the corner of a house in Carcés proclaimed the existence of just such a water at Entrecasteaux, no more than ten kilometres away. As we approached the town a similarly eye-catching board directed us down a long, bumpy, dusty track through a vineyard towards the lake itself.

Perhaps 'lake' is too grand a word for the couple of acres of pale khaki water that lay brooding in the hot sunshine, surrounded by twenty yards of bare, baked clay. But its status as a 'fishery' was confirmed by half a dozen golden orfe circling lazily in a bay and by the *pêcheurs* ranged at ten-yard intervals around the bank. Some were solitary, some had wives with them – either 'ghillying' or fishing themselves – and there were two or three cacophonous family groups. All had stools and most had parasols or straw hats to shield them from the glare.

The tackle in use ranged from cheap spinning rods and reels to long roach poles. The *pêcheurs* sat hunched over them, each gazing intently at a tiny float embedded in the scum that covered the water's surface. Occasionally a float would dip and there would be a localized babble of excitement as a half-pound rainbow trout was heaved unceremoniously from the water, swung ashore and descended upon by its captor and

175

his friends as it flapped about in the dust.

The fishery office was a clapperboard hut with a distinct list to starboard. We ducked into its gloomy interior through the open door to find the *patron*, a jovial soul in his fifties, whiling away the hot afternoon with a pack of cards and two remarkably buxom and sparsely clad young ladies. A couple of days' stubble covered his chin and a Gauloise hung from the corner of his mouth. An unbelievable and somewhat grubby navy and white horizontally striped T-shirt and a similarly unbelievable and similarly grubby black beret completed the picture.

After exchanging niceties, I asked if it would be possible to fish.

'But of course. Sixty francs for the half-day and as many trout as you can catch.'

I reached for my wallet and began to count out the money.

'It will be all right if I use *la mouche*, won't it?' I enquired casually.

Instantly, his whole demeanour changed. A hunted look came into his eyes and he backed away from me, his hands spread in front of him as if to ward off an attack.

'Oh, no,' he said. 'Oh, no! Not on your life. I know all about people like you. Every year some too-clever-by-half damned Englishman comes along, playing the innocent, pulling a fly rod out of the back of his car and cleaning me out. Oh, no. *La mouche* is far too easy. You ruddy well fish with maggots like everyone else, or you don't fish at all.'

It quickly became clear that no amount of argument, no offers of a self-imposed four-fish limit and no amount of bribery would persuade him to change his mind.

Foiled and somewhat chastened, we wandered off around the lake, past a chap using the back step of a battered blue Dormobile as a fishing stool, with two huge buckets full of dead trout beside him, and on to where two splendid old men were clearly having the time of their lives.

They were sharing a monstrous three-piece rod of extraordinarily mixed parentage, heaving trout from the water almost as fast as they could re-bait and re-cast, and giggling like a couple of schoolboys. They told us this was their fourth visit to the fishery but the first on which they had caught anything. They were clearly making up for lost time.

They also explained that not all the bites they had were from trout. Some, they said, came from the golden orfe we had seen basking in the sun as we arrived. And some were from the numerous water terrapins that lived in the lake!

I have seen worse since that day.

At the Fontain de Vaucluse, just east of Avignon, there is a 'fishery' consisting of what looks for all the world like a large children's paddling pool. There is no cover of any sort for the shoals of rainbow trout that scurry around in the clear, concrete-bottomed pond, which is surrounded with tubular-framed plastic chairs. By the kiosk at the entrance gate stands a rack of simple whole-cane rods, each about twelve feet long and each with a small float, a few split shot and a hook attached to the length of nylon tied to its tip. Anglers hire rods and buy bait at the kiosk, and pay for their catch by the kilo.

And we found a similar but simpler 'fishery' near Angles in the Vendée, where carefree campers were hauling small rainbow trout from what was no more than a spring-fed stew pond. Here, there were a few obstacles; making maximum use of the cool water, the proprietor had submerged half a dozen or so crates of beer in the pond, chilling them for the bar he ran nearby.

Sport or entertainment

Amusing as these stories may be, there is a warning hidden within them. The line between such 'pick-your-own' trout farms and small 'put-and-take' trout fisheries – between 'entertainment' and 'sport' – is a fine one. Moot of the countless small stillwater fisheries that have sprung up in this country over the past twenty years or so have been opened in response to a growing interest in the sport of trout fishing. Generally, those who run them seek to ensure that the biomass of trout – the overall numbers and sizes of trout stocked – is realistic, no greater than the natural food supplies in the waters can sustain. The few that have offered 'stew-pond' fishing have been vilified in the angling press and most if not all of them have either closed or changed their management policies. But there are still some unattractive practices which, if continued, could provide ammunition for those opposed to field sports and bring trout fishing as a whole into disrepute.

The big trout syndrome

Fierce competition between small stillwater fisheries has encouraged owners to stock with larger and larger trout. Twenty years ago we were content to fish for trout averaging a pound to a pound-and-a-half in weight; a three- or four-pounder was considered a monster. Today, the average size of the 'run-of-the-mill' fish in such waters is about two to two-and-a-half pounds, and each year sees many fisheries giving up trout of ten, fifteen and twenty pounds or more.

Every single fish we take from a man-made trout fishery has been bought and introduced into it by the owner. Trout are expensive, and the inevitable consequence of the perceived demand for ever bigger fish has been ever higher prices. The more anglers are asked to pay for their fishing, the more they will demand for their money, chiefly in terms of the size and quality of the fish they catch but also in terms of facilities – car parks, fishing huts, manicured banks, lavatories and so on – all of which cost money and push prices up yet further.

There is another 'cost' of increased fish sizes, too. The one- to one-and-a-half-pound trout we used to fish for were eighteen months to two years old and sexually immature. Trout of two pounds or more are older and are sexually mature. Immature trout remain clean, bright and hungry throughout the year; the condition of mature trout varies. Cock rainbows are dreary creatures and do not grow well. Slab-sided and grey through much of the year, they develop ugly kypes on their lower jaws and, from November one year until as late as June the next, spray milt about when caught. During this time, they are almost inedible. Hens maintain their condition better than cocks do but, even so, tend to be grey, flabby and full of spawn from November until April or May.

Solutions to these problems have been found but are difficult and expensive to implement.

Some trout farms are prepared to supply batches of all-female trout, but as it is impossible to tell a cock from a hen until the trout are eighteen months or two years old, they must rear all their fish to that sort of age before selecting the hens, and as the cocks are virtually worthless they must pass on the cost of such selection to the fishery proprietor, who must pass it on to the angler.

Some trout farms will supply 'triploids' – sterile, all-female trout, superb fish which grow quickly and remain clean and bright throughout the year. But this is a two-generation exercise and is therefore no less expensive than selecting females from mixed-sex stew ponds.

The very large trout, weighing ten pounds or more, with which some fishery managers stock their water present further problems. On the whole they are sluggish brutes, dull and drab with tatty tails, and they tend to fight far less well than their two-, four- or six-pound cousins. No doubt those who catch them derive a degree of satisfaction from doing so – although I have to say that my biggest ever trout, a fourteen-pounder, was one of the least memorable I have ever caught. I cannot help wondering, though, to whom the credit for such fish should go – to the mighty hunters who haul them from the water, or to the fish farmers who grow them, like prize leeks or marrows. And I wonder, too, whether fisheries stocked with such fish are not so blatantly artificial as to be damaging to the ethos of our sport which, for me anyway, has chiefly to do with fishing for a natural quarry in natural surroundings. Admittedly, where small stillwaters are concerned that ethos is somewhat illusory, but I wonder whether we should be so eager to destroy even the illusion.

If we may harbour doubts about the upward spiral of stock fish sizes and fishery prices, and about 'jumbo rainbows', how many more doubts should we have about the relatively recent practice of stocking salmon into small lakes?

One or two fishery owners claim their salmon are of a land-locked strain and that the fish are content to live and to feed in lakes and gravel pits. If that is the case, then fine. But it seems to me quite wrong to take farm-reared Atlantic salmon from estuarine cages 'and introduce them into lakes or reservoirs in which they cannot thrive – the more so when the temptation must be to stock with enormous fish which might, technically, break the British salmon record which has stood since Georgina Ballatine took her sixty-four-pound fish from the River Tay in 1922.

If all this sounds a bit 'killjoy' and puritanical, it is not meant to. The vast majority of small stillwaters provide excellent sport for large numbers of anglers, especially in the Midlands and in south-east England, populous areas with few natural trout waters. All I would say is that if we, the anglers, wish them to continue to do so, we must recognize the constraints under which they operate and be restrained in the demands we make of them. It is easy to sneer at put-and-take fisheries if you are fortunate enough to have ready access to natural waters sustaining healthy populations of wild brown trout, but it is arrogant to do so.

Catch-and-release

It is, to some extent, the marked difference between the wild trout fisheries of Scotland, Ireland, Wales, the north of England and the West Country on the one hand, and the stocked (and often man-made) ones in central and southern England on the other, that has led to the continuing debate about 'catch-and-release'. The debate is interesting but those who pursue it should do so from a basis of reason rather than emotion.

People tend to fall into one of two camps. Firstly, there are those who wish to conserve trout stocks. Secondly, there are those who wish to be able to continue fishing regardless of how many trout they may have caught.

Crusading 'conservationists' often quote the American example. The United States has a tradition of making nature's gifts available to all men. As a consequence, most (though not all) angling waters in the United States may be fished by anybody provided they have purchased an inexpensive state rod licence. The result of this is that many of the best waters are heavily fished and lightly funded. Because they are heavily fished, they must be stocked, and because they are lightly funded, that stocking must be economical. Economical stocking means introducing either large numbers of small fish or small numbers of large ones, and protecting those fish by all possible means. It is this game of consequences that has produced an almost fanatical movement for 'catch-and-release' in America.

There are waters in the less populous corners of the British Isles that sustain populations of wild trout, augmented sometimes by introductions of fingerlings or fry. If the objective on such waters is to keep them as natural as possible, then obviously it is sensible to limit the numbers of fish taken from them and to encourage people to return to them trout not wanted for the table.

The fishing pressure on other waters, especially those in central and southern England, is such that they could not possibly sustain wild trout populations. Instead, they have to be managed on a 'put-and-take' basis.

Nobody seems to know how many times a trout may be caught and released before it becomes so wary as to be effectively uncatchable. Evidence from the United States suggests that the answer is probably about half a dozen times; certainly the figure is finite. Anglers go fishing to catch fish, not just to look at them. If a heavily-fished water is to continue to provide catchable fish, both those that have been removed from it and those that have become uncatchable must be replaced with fresh stock. Were this to be done on a water on which most anglers returned most of the fish they caught, you would soon reach a situation in which the water contained more trout than could be sustained by the food available to them, which would be unacceptable. The generally agreed answer is to require anglers to kill the trout they catch and to replace those trout with new ones.

Sound cases can be made for mixing catch-and-release with put-and-take. For example, a fishery manager might insist that anglers kill a certain number of fish (say five), should they be able to catch them, and then allow them to fish on, releasing any further fish caught. Given that only quite a small number of people will catch five fish anyway, it could be argued that the number beyond five that they catch and release will be small, perhaps even insignificant. In other cases it may be arguable that, because newly stocked trout are notoriously gullible, catching-and-releasing limited numbers of fish would produce populations among which would be a number of once- or twice-caught and thus more difficult and interesting fish.

In the final analysis, it is a case of 'horses for courses'. The decision as to whether catch-and-release should be encouraged, allowed or forbidden must depend on the type of water and on the fishing pressure on it, and it is a decision that must be taken by the management in consultation with the anglers, rather than by anglers whose only interest may be in getting as much fishing as possible, regardless of the consequences for the water.

Which brings us to the whole question of 'limits'.

The truth about limits

If I have given anything to this sport of ours, it is the word 'limititis', the sad malaise with which so many fly fishers are afflicted – the feeling that to fail to catch one's 'limit' is, at best, to have been shown to be less competent than one imagines oneself to be, to have had one's status as a mighty hunter called into question and, at worst, to have been cheated by the fishery management. The malaise is fuelled by certain fly fishing magazines which, by filling their pages with stories of huge catches taken by expert anglers and with numerous photographs of those same anglers peering at the camera over heaps of dead fish or across the backs of mammoth trout, lead anglers of average ability to believe that they, too, should be able to emulate the experts. The inevitable consequence of all this is that the average angler's expectations are raised way beyond what he or she may reasonably expect to achieve. When 'limititis' is compounded in this way, disappointment and frustration are likely to displace the fun and pleasure of fishing, and that is a tragedy.

If we are to derive the maximum pleasure from our sport, we must recognize and continue to remind ourselves that when we pay for a day's fishing we pay for nothing more than the right to spend the day fishing. The more we pay, the more we have the right to presume that the water will contain an adequate stock of fish. But the proprietor or manager of that water has no obligation to ensure that we actually catch any fish at all. The limit imposed on us is quite simply the maximum number of fish we are allowed to take if we are skilful enough to do so.

In order to make this essential point clearer, it may be worth saying a few words about why limits are imposed.

They are not there to spoil our fun, to stop us fishing just when everything is going right for us. Less still are they 'targets' to be aimed for. In fact, they are there to reduce the differential between the 'haves' and the 'have nots', between those people who catch many fish and those who catch very few. This point is illustrated most easily with some simple statistics.

The manager of a stocked trout fishery walks a tightrope. On the one hand, he must provide fishing that is easy enough to enable even the beginner to catch a fish or two occasionally. On the other, he must provide fishing that is sufficiently difficult – and therefore sufficiently interesting – to satisfy the skilful angler. Experience shows that a bag average of about two and a half fish per angler (2.5 fish per rod/day) achieves this balance.

When a four-fish limit is imposed on a water with a bag average of 2.5 fish per rod/day, about 30 per cent of anglers will catch four fish, 10 to 15 per cent will catch none, and the remaining 55 to 60 per cent will catch one, two or three fish.

Were the limit to be increased to eight fish and the bag average to be retained at 2.5 fish per rod/day, each angler who caught an eight-fish limit would have to be counter-balanced by two (66 per cent) who caught none – and this calculation takes no account of those anglers who will catch a few fish each and who, if they catch three or more, will increase the number of blank days needed to maintain the bag average.

Value for money . . .

While we are on the subject of fishery management, it would be as well to point out that the profit margins on commercially run trout fisheries are very small indeed and that no fishery owner has the slightest hope of growing rich at the expense of his or her customers. The capital investment in such fisheries is massive and the running costs – the provision of trout, bank maintenance, the provision and repair of benches, fences and gates, repair and replacement of machinery and other equipment, rates, electricity and telephone, insurance, publicity, advertising and accountancy, and a salary for the manager – are high.

Few owners or managers of commercial trout fisheries want their rods to go away empty handed and understock intentionally in order to achieve this; indeed, most of them want them to do well so that they will return, and to this end stock more heavily than perhaps they should. The exceptions are the 'cowboys', self-styled entrepreneurs who know little or nothing about trout or trout fishing but hope to make quick profits from such stretches of water as may come their way, and some (but by no means all) farmers who, having dug Ministry of Agriculture funded irrigation reservoirs on their land, may seek to capitalize on them by turning in a few trout and calling their waters 'fisheries'.

If you want to be sure that you are getting value for money from commercially run trout fisheries, it would be sensible to stick to those waters the owners or managers of which are members of the Association of Stillwater Game Fishery Managers. The Association exists to promote the interests of professionally managed trout fisheries and, thus, to promote the interests of anglers.

. . . and fishing for fun

With all this talk of commercially managed trout waters, it would be easy to lose sight of the fact that fishing is meant to be fun and that there really is much more to it than just catching fish. Of course, the object of the exercise is to catch trout, but it is also about being in nice places with nice people, about having opportunities to relax and unwind, about being able to watch the wildlife around us – the animals and birds of the waterside, the fish themselves, the creatures they prey upon and the creatures that prey upon them. We are privileged to have a sport that offers us so much, and we should recognize that that privilege places certain obligations upon us.

The first of these is respect for our quarry.

We should always seek to ensure that we use tackle and knots that are strong enough for the task in hand – that we never allow the fish to swim off with a hook in its mouth and, perhaps, a length of nylon trailing behind it.

If we mean to return fish, we should use barbless hooks; we should subdue our trout as quickly as possible, so as not to exhaust them; we should handle them as little as possible – or not at all; we should ensure that they are fully recovered before allowing them to swim off; and we should not release them if we believe them to have been injured to the extent that they may not survive.

If a trout is to be killed, we should kill it as quickly and humanely as possible, while it is still in the net and the hook is still in its mouth, using a proper priest carried for the purpose.

The second obligation is respect for the countryside and its wildlife.

We should park considerately. Gates should be left open or shut, as we find them. We should avoid walking through growing crops or alarming livestock. We should not light fires, and we should take all our litter home with us – especially monofilament, in which birds and small animals can so easily become entangled.

The third is respect for our fellow anglers.

When bank fishing on a lake or reservoir, we should leave at least fifty yards between ourselves and other anglers; we should wade only when absolutely necessary; and we should not allow ourselves to be drawn into that most irritating of habits, planting a landing net in the bank or in the shallows while we are not fishing in order to reserve a fishing spot for later.

When boat fishing we should leave at least a hundred yards between ourselves and bank anglers or other boats, and we should avoid cutting in in front of another boat that may be drifting or motoring across its line of drift.

On rivers we should be careful never to cut in above another angler who is moving upstream or below one who is moving downstream.

The fourth is respect for the fishery rules.

Most people who run fisheries – and most anglers – would choose to have as few rules as possible, but there is no escaping the fact that, when a number of people fish the same water, it is necessary to have some rules to protect their interests as a whole. Some rules on some fisheries may seem unnecessary, but they are almost certainly there for perfectly good reasons.

Some years ago, when I was running a fishery of my own, I became increasingly concerned about the annoyance caused to anglers by the dogs that some of our rods brought with them when they came fishing. One particular small hound yapped almost continuously from the moment it arrived at the fishery until the moment it left, the racket rising in a crescendo every time its owner hooked a fish. Another, whose master supervised it less than closely, had a disconcerting taste for other anglers' ankles. A third, whose owner refused to keep it on a lead, had a taste for picnics and spent much of its time rummaging in unattended fishing bags searching for sandwiches.

Eventually I banned dogs altogether. Most of the rods thanked me warmly (if discreetly); the only complaints I had were from the owners of the three main offenders, all of whom swore that their dogs caused no trouble at all.

On a more practical note, a small party of people used to come down from London to fish with us almost every weekend throughout the season. They were pleasant and friendly and we were always pleased to see them. One day, a couple of them asked if they could come with me when I went to feed the fish in the stew ponds. I agreed and we chatted casually about the fishery and its management as we walked around the enclosure. In the course of this conversation one of the rods asked, apparently quite innocently, whether I really minded if people 'took an extra fish or two once they had caught their limits'. I hope my silence conveyed my answer adequately.

At that time, in the early 1980s, every average two-and-a-half-pound fish in those lakes had cost me £2.50; an 'extra couple' taken was exactly the same as having a £5 note stolen from my pocket. What was worse was that our stocking policy was based chiefly on replacing fish we knew to have been caught. People who took an 'extra couple' of trout could not declare them on their return cards – to have done so would have been to admit to theft. If they did not declare them, I could not know they had been taken and could not therefore reasonably be expected to replace them, which meant that, in theory, there would be a couple less fish for the next day's anglers to fish for. Multiply this 'couple of fish' by an unknown number of anglers repeating the performance, week in and week out, and you begin to get a picture of the scale of theft and of the damage done to other people's sport.

Of course, we had a formula for compensating for losses through theft and other causes, but the story does illustrate the realities that can lie behind a little almost innocent 'rule-bending'.

The Fly Fisher's Knots

The reel knot – for attaching backing to reel

Attaching the fly line backing or nylon mainline to the reel spool

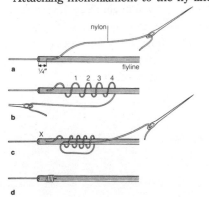

The glued splice

Attaching braided monofilament to the fly line

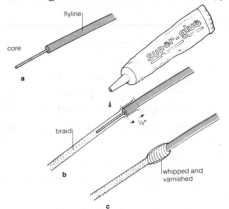

The needle knot

Attaching monofilament to the fly line

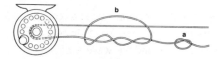

The double-grinner knot

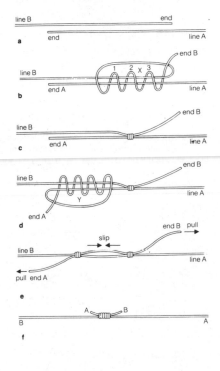

The nail knot

Attaching the backing line to the fly line

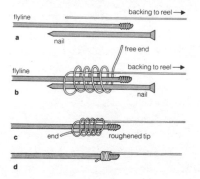

The blood knot

Joining two lengths of monofilament

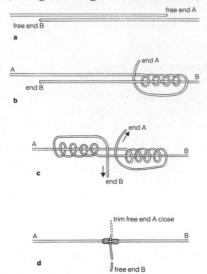

The turle knot

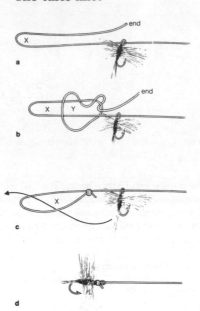

The water (or cove knot)

Making droppers in leaders

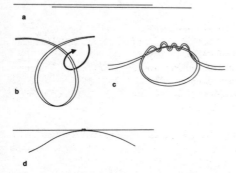

The grinner knot (or duncan loop knot or uni-knot)

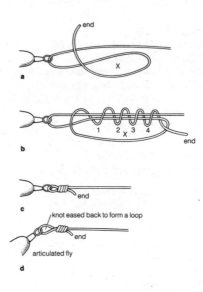

The tucked half-blood knot (or clinch knot)

Attaching a fly to a leader

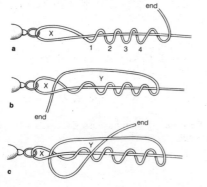

Bibliography

The world is full of fishing books. The following have been selected as the best available to help the reader to delve deeper into particular subject areas. Books that are out of print may be obtained from John and Judith Head, 88 Crane Street, Salisbury, Wilts.

The fly fisher's quarry
The Trout, by W. E. Frost and M. E. Brown, Collins, 1967.

Entomology
Trout Flies of Britain and Europe, by John Goddard, A & C Black, 1991.
John Goddard's Waterside Guide, Unwin Hyman, 1988.

Where to fish
Where to Fish, published biennially by Thomas Harmsworth Publishing.
The Haig Guide to Trout Fishing in Britain, edited by David Barr, Collins Willow, 1983.
Trout Lochs of Scotland, by Bruce Sandison, Unwin Hyman, 1987.
Trout and Salmon Loughs of Ireland, by Peter O'Reilly, Unwin Hyman, 1987.

Flies and fly dressing
(It is much more fun if you tie your own!)

The Pocket Guide to Trout and Salmon Flies, by John Buckland, Mitchell Beazley, 1986.
The Fly Tier's Manual, by Mike Dawes, Collins, 1985.
The Fly Tier's Companion, by Mike Dawes, Swan Hill, 1989.
Fly Tying Techniques, by Jacqueline Wakeford, Benn, 1980.

Fishing (General)
Freshwater Fishing, by Hugh Falkus and Fred Buller, Stanley Paul, 1988.
The Complete Fly Fisher, edited by Peter Lapsley, Stanley Paul, 1990.
A History of Fly Fishing, by Conrad Voss Bark, Merlin Unwin Books, 1992.

Spate river fishing
The Pursuit of Wild Trout, by Mike Weaver, Merlin Unwin Books, 1991.
West Country Fly Fishing, edited by Anne Voss Bark, Batsford, 1983.
The Art of the Wet Fly, by W. S. Roger Fogg, A & C Black, 1979.
River Trout Flyfishing, by Peter Lapsley, Collins Willow, 1991.

Chalk stream fishing
The Trout and the Fly, by Brian Clarke and John Goddard, Benn, 1980.
River Trout Flyfishing, by Peter Lapsley, Collins Willow, 1991.

Loch-style fishing
The Art and Craft of Loch Fishing, by H. P. Henzell, Phillip Allan, 1937.
Lake, Loch and Reservoir Trout Fishing, by Malcolm Greenhalgh, A & C Black, 1987.
Trout from Stillwaters, by Peter Lapsley, Unwin Hyman, 1988.

Reservoir fishing and fishing small lakes
Reservoir Fishing with Tom Saville, by Tom Saville, H.F. & G. Witherby, 1991.
The Pursuit of Stillwater Trout, by Brian Clarke, A & C Black, 1975.
Trout from Stillwaters, by Peter Lapsley, Unwin Hyman, 1988.
Fishing with Bill Sibbons, by Clive Graham-Ranger, Crowood Press, 1990.

For the sheer pleasure they give
Fly Fishing by J. R. Hartley, Stanley Paul, 1991.
Fishing in Wild Places, by David Street, Golden Grove, 1989.
Fishing Personally, by W. M. Hill, A & C Black, 1986.
A Fly on the Water, by Conrad Voss Bark, Allen & Unwin, 1986.

Useful Addresses

Instruction

The Association of Professional Game Angling Instructors (APGAI), Hon. Secretary: Donald Downs, The Mead, Hosey, Westerham, Kent TN16 1TA.

Societies and Associations

Every angler has a duty to join The Anglers Co-operative Association (23 Castlegate, Grantham, Lincs NG31 6SW), which is wholly dedicated to prosecuting those who pollute angling waters.

The Fly Dressers Guild (Hon. Secretary J.G. Hickson, 41 Hercies Road, Hillingdon, Middlesex UB10 9LS) is a friendly association with branches throughout the country for those interested in fly fishing and fly tying.

The Grayling Society (Membership Secretary Mrs Claire Pickover, 20 Somersall Lane, Chesterfield S40 3LA) brings together those interested in grayling and grayling fishing and promotes appreciation of the grayling as a game fish in its own right.

The British Field Sports Society (59 Kennington Road, London SE1 7PZ) seeks to represent the interests of all field sportsmen and women in the United Kingdom.

The Salmon and Trout Association (Fishmongers' Hall, London EC4R 9EL) seeks to represent game fishing interests throughout the United Kingdom.

Out-of-print fishing books

John and Judith Head, The Barn Book Supply, 88 Crane Street, Salisbury, Wilts.

General Index

Index to Artificial Flies and Lures

Index to Natural Flies and Insects